PAN-AFRICANISM
FROM WITHIN

RAS MAKONNEN

PAN-AFRICANISM
FROM WITHIN

*as recorded
and edited by*
KENNETH KING

1973
OXFORD UNIVERSITY PRESS
NAIROBI LONDON NEW YORK

Oxford University Press, Ely House, London W. 1

GLASGOW NEW YORK TORONTO MELBOURNE WELLINGTON
CAPE TOWN IBADAN NAIROBI DAR ES SALAAM LUSAKA ADDIS ABABA
DELHI BOMBAY CALCUTTA MADRAS KARACHI LAHORE DACCA
KUALA LUMPUR SINGAPORE HONG KONG TOKYO

Oxford University Press, P.O. Box 72532, Nairobi, Kenya

© OXFORD UNIVERSITY PRESS 1973

ISBN 0 19 572018 0 (limp)
ISBN 0 19 572312 0

MADE IN EAST AFRICA

LIST OF CONTENTS

LIST OF PLATES

ACKNOWLEDGEMENTS

I owe a special debt of gratitude to Fenola Jarek, Lucy Griffiths, Ann Creager, and Pravina for their aid in detaping, and to the following friends for their suggestions upon reading the typescript: Richard Pankhurst, Colin Leys, Ian Duffield and Christopher Fyfe.

K. J. K.

RAS MAKONNEN:
A BRIEF BIOGRAPHICAL SKETCH

R AS Makonnen was born under the name George Thomas
Nathaniel Griffith, in the small Guyana* village of Buxton
at the beginning of this century. After completing his primary
school there, time was spent in associating with his father's
mining ventures before he went on to secondary education in
the Collegiate School and later Queen's College in Georgetown.
After the First World War, Makonnen and his cousin, David
Talbot, were drawn beyond their interests in local politics by
the impact of Garveyism and other North American influences.
They were soon enough anxious to go to America for further
studies. Makonnen himself left on a student visa, intending to
continue his interest in mineralogy through college in Texas.
He arrived in New Orleans in late 1927, just a few days before
the final deportation of Marcus Garvey back to his native
Jamaica.

En route for college, Makonnen was persuaded by fellow
West Indian clerics in Beaumont, Texas, that he should join
the YMCA and help to build up a coloured branch of the
organization in the town. During the three and a half years
he was engaged in local YMCA activities in Beaumont and in
the surrounding black colleges; he was kept in touch with the
wider work of the YMCA through its summer schools in Chicago
and King's Mountain, Virginia. These schools afforded him his
first significant contacts with African students in the United
States, while intellectually he steeped himself in the philosophy
of the international YMCA. During one international conference

*The modern spelling of Guyana has as often as possible been preferred in this narrative,
although in fact Makonnen is talking of the former colony, British Guiana.

ix

of the YMCA in Toronto, Makonnen was offered a scholarship to study in the university there, and in 1932 he had left Texas for New York State, to proceed to Canada. Immigration authorities, however seem to have obstructed this aim, and after a short stay in Buffalo, he used a number of his YMCA contacts to gain a place in Cornell University.

His course of study there lasted from spring 1932 until late 1934, and was mainly in the fields of agriculture and animal husbandry. But because of Cornell's proximity to New York, Makonnen was able to develop a close knowledge of the politics of Harlem, and equally gain an intimate understanding of the politics and thinkers of the white Left. The Cornell period was further important for introducing him to a number of Ethiopian students at the college at a time when the crisis was building up between Italy and Ethiopia. When, therefore, he left to continue his agricultural and veterinary studies in Denmark in the spring of 1935, he already had a close commitment to the Ethiopian side, and had letters of introduction to Ethiopians in Europe.

After a stay of perhaps two years in Copenhagen, interrupted by frequent visits to England and other European countries, he came to settle in London by early 1937. For a time he shared a flat with George Padmore, and clearly played a part in the founding and organization of the International African Service Bureau. From then till the outbreak of war in Europe, his activities were the same as Padmore's—continual propaganda through weekly and sometimes daily meetings on Ethiopia, Africa and the world. By 1939 he had his own flat near Paddington Station, but proceeded soon to move up to Manchester. He stayed there for a time with a Guyanan doctor, Peter Milliard, but then branched out on his own. He lectured briefly at the Co-operative College, took courses in Manchester University, but gradually became more and more involved in establishing a chain of restaurants. The proceeds of his enterprise were used in a wide variety of pan-African activity, the best known being the organization of the Fifth Manchester Pan-African Congress, and the Pan-African Federation press.

Close contacts were maintained not only with black organizations in Britain after 1945 but increasingly with those African leaders returning to prepare their own countries for independence. Like Padmore, he was close to Nkrumah, and after a preliminary visit to Ghana in 1956 went to settle there just before independence the next year. He worked first with Padmore in an advisory committee on African affairs, then moved to direct the African Affairs Centre, where refugees from both independent and non-independent countries were stationed and looked after. While still doing this he became involved with the Hotels and Tourist Corporation, but after leaving the Centre, the Tourist Corporation and later, from August 1965, the State Bakery became his main duties.

Although critical of much in Ghana he remained loyal to Nkrumah until the overthrow, and was consequently imprisoned for several months after February 1966. It seems that his release was in part brought about by an encounter between General Ankrah of Ghana and Kenyatta, and he left for Kenya shortly after. Once there he became an adviser in the Ministry of Tourism (a position he still holds) and a citizen of Kenya in 1969.

MAKONNEN AND PAN-AFRICANISM

M AKONNEN'S account of pan-Africanism that emerges from the following chapters is refreshingly different from the traditional approach. Instead of the chronological treatment of each of the pan-African conferences with careful listing of delegates and resolutions (Padmore's own approach), Makonnen has focused his attention on the cluster of attitudes essential to his own brand of pan-Africanism. Firstly, for him the pan-African movement should be entirely African directed, and avoid the sort of entangling alliances that had so often hampered black objectives. Blacks should be able to finance and run their own movement. While there was no harm in accepting the help of whites for short-term requirements, the movement could be greatly compromised through becoming the wing of a larger and more powerful white body. This was the root of Makonnen's suspicion of those pan-Africans who were also members of the Communist Party. The 1920s and 1930s had shown only too clearly that Moscow could change its attitude on anti-colonialism to suit its European priorities, abandoning one month the blacks it had encouraged in their anti-imperialism the previous month. Those speaking on African grievances should instead be seen to be motivated by their own concepts of African unity or freedom. There were too many people who still doubted African initiative, and it simply confirmed their notions of the continent's dependence if its people could be portrayed as agents rather than as their own spokesmen. Naturally this attitude helps to explain Makonnen's attack on Nkrumah at a time when he too seemed to be more interested in the British Communist Party than in expanding the pan-African organization that Makonnen and others had built up. It also sets Makonnen somewhat apart from Padmore and Wallace-Johnson, both of

xiii

INTRODUCTION

whom at certain stages were giving a lot of their time to working and writing for Britain's Independent Labour Party (ILP). To Makonnen, Africans who worked too closely with Brockway's ILP or his later Movement for Colonial Freedom simply continued the tradition of relying on whites to dictate the terms of African freedom. And if their white guide or tactician such as Brockway decided for instance that Mau Mau in Kenya was a reversion to savagery, it became difficult to take an independent line.

An extension of this feeling for the primacy of Africans in any consideration of Africa can be seen in Makonnen's attitude to Somalis, Egyptians, Northern Nigerians and certain groups of Indians in East and South Africa. Just as he felt African students could not serve both pan-Africanism and Russian communism, so people living in Africa must decide whether their loyalty was primarily to Africa. Islam and degrees of Arab solidarity had made it possible for certain countries to straddle the Middle East and Africa, but to Makonnen's mind the possibility for conflict in loyalties was too great to allow this. Arab-African relations had been too much scarred historically by slavery and racial discrimination to let such countries continue to look over their shoulders to the politics of the Middle East. This was the reason why Makonnen spent time during his Manchester period in getting people like the Somalis to see that their future lay in looking boldly into Africa. Equally with the Indian Congress leaders in England, it was possible to work for a policy whereby an independent India would give no protection or encouragement to those expatriate Indians who did not want to identify with Africa. This is not meant to suggest that Makonnen was hostile to either Islam or communism, but only to people who belonged to these faiths in ways which allowed them to be manipulated from outside the African continent.

A further critical undercurrent in his view of pan-Africanism is that there should be a basic solidarity amongst the Africans of the three continents—North America, Africa and South America. Slavery in the Americas, and the corresponding ravages of the slave trade followed by colonialism in Africa should have given an awareness of a common heritage, and of the need to fight the colonial mentality adopted by New and Old World blacks alike. Sometimes indeed such a solidarity could be found

xiv

in England, America or Panama, when blacks were reduced to a common level in the face of discrimination, but too often, as Makonnen shows, the peoples from the different black regions have carried with them their little prejudices against their fellow blacks: British Guyanans against the island blacks of the West Indies; West Indians against black Americans; West Africans against West Indians; and Africans generally against the 'slave pickins' or blacks of the diaspora.

One of Makonnen's main purposes during his twenty-odd years in London and Manchester was precisely to combat this divisiveness through an organization that would act as a clearing house for affairs of the black world as a whole. The International African Service Bureau and the Pan-African Federation which followed it have been presented too often as bodies principally responsible for floating the Fifth Manchester Conference in 1945. This particular conference was clearly very significant, and, as Padmore admitted, was as much Makonnen's doing as anyone else's; however, pan-Africanism is not a history of conferences, and it is therefore equally important to see the Manchester Conference as a high point in a vast variety of pan-African activity with which Makonnen and the Federation were concerned. Much of this can be called practical pan-Africanism—holding a watching brief over the African world, and being ready to move whenever some case of colonial or police brutality came to light.

In as far as there was a division of labour in this activity, Padmore was more able with his literary talents to bring pressure to bear when the cause was international, and Makonnen was responsible for the home constituency in England. Being always more of a speaker than a writer, he was most formidable when people had to be lobbied face to face, or when a local committee had to be formed to fight a particular grievance. Thus British immigration authorities could be browbeaten personally over their treatment of West African stowaways; if Somali restaurant keepers were running into trouble with the police in Tyneside, pressure could be brought to bear on the local MPs and the mayor; and in the many incidents of race hostility between West Indians and local whites after the war Makonnen had the contacts and the finance necessary to arrange bail, legal defence or whatever was necessary. Again, the dramatic defence by Norman Manley of a West Indian accused of murder in

Manchester was only one peak in a large number of less spectacular cases that came Makonnen's way.

Finance was critical in this work, and undoubtedly the commercial success of the Manchester restaurants allowed black independent action in their own defence. If blacks were discriminated against, he felt they should break as far as possible with the habit of expecting philanthropic whites to defend them. Let them defend themselves with their own money and their own black lawyers, and let them stop being the wards of others. Most important, whatever local grouping they might have, let them also affiliate to the Pan-African Federation, so that they could see that they were not just a little group of Kru seamen, or Jamaican technicians in England, but part of a much bigger thing. However, pan-Africanism was not only leading local black communities into an awareness of a larger black potential; for Makonnen, it was also a question of dealing with individuals. He was keenly aware at a time when there were still relatively few blacks in Britain that the individual black was on trial, and his failing was too easily taken as the failure of the race. This situation inspired Makonnen's concern that blacks should rigorously avoid giving the white racist any opportunity to point the finger. So Makonnen waged a long (and personally expensive) campaign to convince his fellow blacks that a destitute Trinidadian seaman in Cardiff, or the neglected offspring of black American servicemen and white women, were a communal black responsibility. At the grassroots, pan-Africanism meant that, whatever their country, blacks should be able to look after each other.

None of this is meant to suggest that Makonnen's sphere of activity was restricted to the home-front during these twenty years. Indeed, there were few delegations from the West Indies or Africa to England that did not hold discussions with Padmore, Makonnen or both in these years. After all, the rationale of the Pan-African Federation was partly that joint activity and understanding amongst expatriate West Indian or African groups in Britain would facilitate relations later in the wider arena of Africa and the Caribbean. As many of the black students resident in Britain then were shortly to assume positions of importance in their own countries, there was much to be said for anticipating in Britain the obstacles of the future. Thus if Makonnen, his Sudanese and Ethiopian friends, Kenyatta and certain of the

Young Somali leaders could reach accord in their various informal meetings in England, it was at least to be hoped that this most sensitive area of Eastern Africa could be substantially defused once independence came.

Another role of this small group of British-based pan-Africans in the international sphere was related to the colonial blacks' conviction that there were really two Englands—the England of the colonies and that of the metropolis. Most delegations therefore from the West Indies or Africa came to London in the belief that pressure for constitutional change could be more effectively exerted at the centre than at the colonial periphery. And it was consequently the task of people like Padmore and Makonnen to exploit their intimate knowledge of British politics so that a delegation could meet the most influential figures and get the most powerful publicity. In this way, they came close to constituting what could be called a black lobby with their ability to brief the right MPs whenever a critical debate was imminent. Transcripts of crucial debates were then circulated back to the African and Afro-American newspapers, and thus sections of the black world were continually kept in touch with developments elsewhere. Here again Padmore was primarily responsible for composing these colonial bulletins, while Makonnen was more at home in lobbying by telegram, or paying for a special delegate to attend New York, London or Paris.

A very potent influence in Makonnen's drive for black solidarity came from his perception of the Jewish parallel. In fact, almost every chapter of the book highlights the feeling that blacks have much to learn from Jewish group solidarity and the sacrificial element in Zionism. The black diaspora, by contrast, had too often held confused notions of its relations to the African home-land. On the one hand, there had been the stark lesson of the Americo-Liberians with their manifest destiny to rule and civilize the natives of Africa. On the other, the blacks of the diaspora had sometimes been used by the colonial powers in ways that made future New World-African relations very brittle; for instance, the West Indian Regiment had too often been used against West African countries and peoples for a legacy of resentment against West Indians not to be left behind. Black Zionism was also infinitely more remote than the Jewish brand since the blacks of the New World lacked the financial base to implement their obligations to Africa, and on those occasions when an obligation consisted simply of setting sail from New York or London to help Ethiopia against the Italians, black volunteers could be effectively blocked by the word of the passport office. Granted these obstacles, Makonnen continued to be haunted by the example of the Jews; in his Ghana period he was one of the architects of involving the Israelis in African development, and was continually struck by the relevance of the kibbutz agricultural model to the African scene. The bitterest pill, however, for some exiles who did actually return to Africa, was the absence of institutions designed like those in Israel to introduce the new arrivals into the language, life and customs of the African state. This African indifference, or at worst hostility to the returned black American or West Indian, flames out from time to time in Makonnen's text, and is the more bitter because it contradicts the very principles lived by in the London and Manchester days.

Makonnen's statement is finally pan-African in that his commentaries on the four sections of the black world he has lived in are each informed by parallels with other parts, and by a continuing concern with what is happening today amongst the Africans at home and abroad. Thus the growth of the Guyanan freedmen villages and the native bourgeoisie is contrasted with the similar developments in Sierra Leone. Equally the golden age of Guyana's black technical class is related to the loss of those skills to the West Indies once Britain required black technicians during and after the Second World War. Nor is the interest in Guyana dropped once Makonnen leaves it for North America; rather, the struggle between its Indian and African elements in the 1950s is linked to his discussion of the plight of Indians and blacks of South Africa, and even in the 1970s he is exploring the possibility that South African exiles may be able to go and settle in his native Guyana.

Similarly for the spell of almost ten years in the United States, he is able to draw together a great deal of new material on pan-Africanism, and in particular to examine thoroughly the effects upon North America of the West Indian migrations there. This leads him to consider how the black American looked at the other areas of the black world in the 1920s and 1930s: what was his image of Africa? Did he really feel that 'I ain't lost nothing in Africa'? And how much was there in the old allegation that black American-West Indian relations were strained to breaking point at this period? Here he is able to put the tensions within the black communities into much better perspective by contrasting inter-black relations with the much greater violence of certain inter-white relations, as each new wave of European immigrants fought their way into America. Again, when looking at the controversial subject of black business in the United States, he does not limit his analysis to the Afro-American, but sheds fascinating light on the various West Indian and African business entrepreneurs of the time. And even when he turns to black religion in the States the pan-African perspective is maintained; the style of Southern States Christianity is set against the more sober denominations of the West Indies, and both these are contrasted with the urge to independency of cult in the Americas—whether to become black Jews and follow that connection, like Rabbi Ford of Barbados, back to Ethiopia, or to notice that the few Somali and other African Muslims in the States could beat the Jim Crow laws with their little turbans and long robes; perhaps black Americans could do the same. The last critical aspect of pan-Africanism in North America was the contact with Ethiopia. Already in the early 1930s the pageantry of Ethiopia had given a new religion to Jamaican Rastafarians; and now Makonnen in his Cornell days was one of many thousands of North American blacks to identify with Ethiopia as the political menace of Italy came nearer. Certainly the Ethiopian crisis, and the relative remoteness of America from African affairs, were the deciding factors in drawing Makonnen into the European theatre just a few months after Italy had begun her advance into the Ethiopian heartland.

His nearly twenty years in Britain provide some of the least-known material on the dimensions of pan-Africanism, and equally is one of the first commentaries by a participant about blacks in Britain of the 1930s and 1940s. Work has been done by Banton, Little, Patterson, Drake, and others more recently on the growth of particular black communities in England, but Makonnen's chapters are crucial for understanding the position of blacks in Britain from within, for that period before it was decided that she too had a 'black problem'. The quality of black life is presented in its diversity. The formative years of many present African leaders is juxtaposed with the plodding and often middle-aged African 'students' in the courts of law, and in a series of cameos, Makonnen presents the Kru community, Nigerians, Ghanaians (usually toasting the King), the Bevin Boys from the West Indies, black playboys and black revolutionaries. Throughout all this is sketched the growth of a pan-African ferment; initially stimulated most powerfully by the Ethiopian crisis, but its subsequent energy is not the result of isolated black forces of anti-imperialism alone, but of being a part of a much wider European ferment of the Left, against fascism and against empire.

And then to Ghana in 1957. Ghana of course has been more researched than any other area that Makonnen is dealing with in this book. Even so there is much here that breaks new ground in interpretation, especially in revealing the powerful constraints against socialism in Ghana, and the equally strong suspicions towards non-Ghanaian blacks in the country's politics. It is particularly interesting (as Padmore died without making a mature assessment of Nkrumah's Ghana) to have Makonnen describe not only his own work in the African Affairs Centre, but something of the political style of Nkrumah and his closest associates. Makonnen, however, was much further from the centre of power in his last years in Ghana. This was not only because like Padmore he was deliberately excluded by those to whom the word Manchester meant nothing, but also because it was perhaps difficult to mask a disenchantment with the 'power-sweet' philosophy of the day.

His recent four years in Kenya have in no sense been a retirement from pan-Africanism. Events in every corner of the black world are scrutinized as closely as ever, and South African exiles, Caribbeans and Afro-Americans continually call at his office and home to listen and give information. Now in 1971 one of his prime concerns is to provide on a piece of land granted him by Kenyatta that sort of institution Africa has too frequently failed to provide for visiting Africans and blacks of the New World: a reception and instruction centre for the many blacks who cannot get to grips with Africa from the confines of its tourist hotels. It is intended at the same time to be a repository for pioneer work by blacks and whites on the African past, and to offer an on-going forum of criticism and discussion of the African present.

As to the genesis and form of the present study, my attention was first drawn to Makonnen's most recent history by Dr. St. Clair Drake during a discussion with him about Ghana in 1967. I made contact with Makonnen shortly after arriving in Nairobi in 1968, and although we met from time to time during the next year, and he gave occasional lectures in one of my university courses, it was not until the summer of 1970 that we decided a book could be usefully done. My original purpose was to provide an essential text for the University of Nairobi course on 'Africa and the Black Diaspora', for which there was still almost no suitable material, but as we proceeded it became clear that it would have a much wider application.

The present book is the result of some thirty two-hour sessions of taped interviews spaced over a nine-month period. In each case the framework of the proposed interview was discussed in advance, and the session taped as a single conversation piece. It was not possible to reproduce verbatim the transcripts of these pieces,[1] but generally my method was to transcribe two or three tapes at a time, and with some fifty pages of type before me I re-ordered and connected the subjects discussed into the most logical and readable sequence. Annotation has been provided by me, particularly for those areas, such as Blacks in Britain, where scholarship has so far been sketchy, but much less for the heavily researched areas like Ghana.

Although a biographical line does run through the text, Makonnen's purpose has been to provide a study in attitudes, and not, as has been mentioned, a close chronological account of meetings and events. Indeed, although Makonnen has a near-perfect recall of the substance of a conversation or a speech, he can frequently be some distance out on the dating of the particular occasion. As far as possible we have tried to tie down a memorable speech or meeting, but it must be remembered that people like Padmore and Makonnen were speaking two or three times a week at a variety of London meeting houses and in the open air during the 1930s, and it is not surprising that recall of dates is sometimes vague.

Because of the historian's bias towards the written rather than the oral, it is understandable that Makonnen's place in the written record of pan-Africanism has so far been slight. A number of his speeches on Ethiopia were carried in Sylvia Pankhurst's paper, *New Times and Ethiopia News*, and in the *Keys* of the League of Coloured People, while in his own journal, *Pan-Africa*, there are a few editorials by him and at least one article. Scholars of the pan-African movement have naturally tended to give greater coverage therefore to men like Wallace-Johnson, Padmore and C. L. R. James who were very much more prolific on paper: but it does seem that a concentration on the written word, whether that of DuBois or of Padmore, results in the omission of a whole layer of pan-Africanism that can only be captured in conversation. Along with the deep concern about the pan-African movement, Makonnen includes the comic and ridiculous side of some of the people he discusses, where it can be assumed that Padmore might have hesitated to commit this to print. But the difference is perhaps that Makonnen has a humour in his analysis of blacks that Padmore lacked. This comes out particularly when he puts words into some of his character's mouths and, again, it must be stressed that the historical accuracy of the words used is not so important as the emotion or attitude conveyed.

However, this combination of informality with a searing concern for black intellectual stature and integrity does give Makonnen a claim to have been one of the first to portray pan-Africanism from within, and to have portrayed his pan-Africanism as simply a necessary stage towards a wider humanity amongst mankind. This conviction of the link between pan-Africanism and humanism has been with him for several decades, and his formulation of 1947 remains relevant today:

> It is certainly not possible to draw up a programme of immediate action in which the Kingdom of the Ethiopia, the coloured people of the Cape and the restaurant keepers of Tyneside would feel their interests equally at stake. And yet, we know that all their wrongs arise from the world's neglect of certain fundamental truths and that all their hope of redress depends on the building of a world community in which those truths will be accepted in practice.[2]

Kenneth King
Nairobi, 1971.

NOTES TO INTRODUCTION

1 However, the original pages will be available for consultation and comparison from mid-1973 in Nairobi, Edinburgh and Syracuse Universities.

2 T. R. Makonnen, editorial, *Pan-Africa*, i, 2, 1947, p. 2.

CHAPTER 1

SLAVERY AND SELF-RELIANCE
IN GUYANA

I'VE always wondered why it took the blacks of the West Indies almost a hundred years from their emancipation in 1834 to work up feelings of militance about their past and present conditions. It may be that they were just too busy preparing to enter the new categories of jobs which opened up with the end of slavery. Suddenly it became possible to leave the slave sheds, and move into independent activity as a farmer, teacher, doctor or clergyman within a single generation; and this required one to concentrate upon the present and the future, and neglect all the misery one had been through. It was a tragedy, because it meant that the spirit of revolt that had been quite largely responsible for bringing their slavery to an end faded out.

In so many of the West Indian colonies there had been a formidable record of revolts and risings in the period before freedom. This is now fortunately well documented, and it is no longer possible to depict emancipation as the merciful act of some far-off abolitionists. The generality of slaves was by no means so docile as scholars used to assert. In fact any careful reading of the missionaries' letters of the 1820s would have shown how widespread the feeling of unrest was. We had had the famous 'Bush Negroes' or Jukas in the Guyanas, who had begun to revolt against their Dutch masters as early as the seventeenth century. They had been so successful that they had been conceded rights to independence, in the same way as the rebellious Maroon slaves of Jamaica forced the British to agree to regional autonomy.[1] Then again in Guyana, just ten years before emancipation, there had been another large-scale revolt; it was one of

1

many, but it caught the public eye because a white missionary, John Smith, appeared to have been implicated in it, and later died in prison at the hands of the Guyana plantocrats.[2] However, the prime example of slave militancy was in Haiti, associated with the name of this cab-driver, Toussaint L'Ouverture[3]. What was interesting about it was that it was part of a wider revolutionary movement in Europe; the black slaves of Haiti were simply claiming the same rights of equality, liberty and fraternity that had brought a new dawn to the people of France. Nor would it be the last time black protest would be linked to white; our own later pan-African movement in England was inseparable from the wider ferment in Europe in the 1930s.

But as a child in Guyana in the early twentieth century, these patterns of slave resistance had to be pieced together. Communication was bad enough in the first two decades; the steamers came irregularly, and we children, for instance, took a long time to work out that there was a war on in Europe. As relatives went missing, we simply heard that they had gone off somewhere to fight for king and country. But communication was much worse in the era of the three-masted barquentine, and it is perhaps no wonder that individual West Indian colonies did not understand the extent of the slave system that had been imposed on them. Only later with the aid of the researches of Eric Williams or Ragatz could you begin to appreciate the dimensions of slavery.[4] One could see the way in which the successful black revolutionists in Haiti tried to spread their gospel of freedom in the neighbouring islands, and even down to places like Bolivia in South America. You could also begin to piece together the strategy of the white plantocrats; when slavery was destroyed in Haiti, you could see them doing a quick-one over to parts of the Southern States, or going off to Cuba or Puerto Rico. Then when the British islands became free in the 1830s, again there were movements, especially down south to Brazil where slavery was going to continue for another half century.[5] It was all a bit like the tactics of certain white settlers in Africa over the last twenty years. When for instance it became clear that Kenya was not really going to be a white man's country, you could see the settlers who had been entrenched packing up and moving south to Rhodesia or South Africa. Similarly, in both Kenya and the West Indian colonies, other whites were

2

prepared to adjust their style, so as to continue living in those countries. So the planters who did not sell up their estates at emancipation, got rid of some of their old bullying overseers, and replaced them with more tactful creatures. It was a time, too, at which European companies were actually able to increase their hold on the West Indian economy, because they were able to buy up cheap the huge estates that the plantocrats were abandoning. And there are obvious parallels in white adjustment to independent black Africa.

But you couldn't pick up much about Guyana's experiences of slavery in the past if you asked people in the 1910s. They still knew about some of the slave names. There was the Congo man who was always meant to be a bloodthirsty fellow. Another dangerous type was the Coromante slave. The owners were always dubious about taking on Coromantes. By reputation he was always ready to revolt, and soon you'd find him organizing a revolution on your doorstep. You wouldn't mind taking a few Coromante slaves mixed up with a lot of more peaceful fellows. But if they were all Coromante together, then God help you! The Coromante were actually part of the Akan peoples of West Africa, who were found throughout Southern Ghana, but they got a terrible name for themselves in parts of the New World, especially in the slave revolts of Jamaica.[6]

Apart from these few slave names, the only other significant survival was the obeah man. He was the man who could cure you or put a spell on you, and his influence throughout the New World black colonies probably stemmed from this almost universal African belief in the fetish. But it was still there when I was growing up in Guyana; you knew that each obeah man had his own peculiar fetish, and he would resort to all sorts of devices to make his face appear something out of this world—to create a certain degree of respect in his clients. If children had fits or other illnesses, people would say, 'Don't mind about this new doctor; take him to Aunty Fifi, and she'll settle it in a few minutes'. This woman would then boil up her bark and other herbs, and try to cure you. But there were good obeah men and bad. Some could liberate you from the ju-ju that somebody else had put on you, and others were real sorcerers.

But this was about all there was left in Guyana from the early period of slavery. And there was no concern to find out any more.

Take the blacks who were our models as we left school—people like Patrick Doggan, the brilliant lawyer, or Orgle, MacMillan and Fredericks. They had all done well in their studies at the Inns in London, but when they returned to Guyana, there was never any attempt to generate any spirit of revolt against the whites in the government or in business. They certainly never made anything of the heritage of slavery. In fact you would think from observing them that they really had no notion that their ancestors had been the products of the greatest sell-out in history. They had been to the metropolis, and, as I said earlier, these fellows were trying to find themselves in the new dawn. It was not a question of slavery and its stigma, but the professions were opening up, and advantage had to be taken of every opening.

They and their fathers before them had concentrated on self-improvement and self-reliance. Not just as individuals, but whole groups had had to pool their resources to enable one chap to go abroad for higher education. It was like the development one noticed in Nigeria and Ghana in the 1930s and 1940s, where voluntary clubs and associations would band together to send a man of their tribe to the metropolis for medicine or law. It was the only way if one had no resources of one's own.

Equally these men, and with them many of the older members of my own family, had been conditioned by the self-reliant villages that sprang up after the end of slavery.[7] You had a whole series of these between the seashore and the end of the old slave estates; they ran from ones like Kitty on the Demerara River side of the country down past Beterverwagting, Clonbrook, Canegrove and Belfield, to the Surinam River at the borders with Dutch Guiana. As you can see from the name Buxton, they were modelled consciously on the English village, and probably the missionary and anti-slavery elements in England had a lot to do with their original character. They were well laid out, with their little streets criss-crossing regularly, and they produced a fierce village pride in their inhabitants.

But this was also due, I think, to the manner in which they had been acquired. There was admittedly plenty of land in Guyana by comparison with other areas of the West Indies, but it would be a fallacy to believe this meant that the ex-slaves got hold of it cheaply. On the contrary, as a man like Eric Williams of Trinidad has shown in his *Capitalism and Slavery*,

4

land prices were very high. Sometimes they were higher than before emancipation, and this I think was simply an attempt to keep the freedmen working on the old plantations longer. They had to be paid now, but if you kept the price of land high, the freedmen would have to go on working for you until they had collected the full price they required. There's no question, therefore, that the slaves had to pay fabulous sums for their land, and this has been shown pretty clearly in the work of the missionary Knibb in Jamaica.[8] In fact it was general throughout the New World. The only difference between the British slave colonies and the American slave South was that the Americans at one time actually talked about giving their slaves forty acres and a mule each, but didn't give it, while the British didn't give an inch of anything away to their slaves. Instead they presented the planters with some £20 million in hard cash, to compensate them for losing their slaves. Once one had heard the injustice of this deal, one couldn't forget it. Indeed it was precisely this crime against the slaves that made me, much later on, protest in Geneva at the idea of colonizing Guyana with 10,000 Syrians. I said on that occasion, 'What are you going to give all these Syrians free land to develop for, when you didn't concede any to the freedmen who had worked for four hundred years through slavery?'

But land prices were not so hard on the large firms which began to come into the country just after emancipation. Companies like Booker Brothers were attracted to buy up the land of those planters who had decided to go home or to move south to Brazil, and they were much more able to do so than the blacks who had no capital.[9] For the moment, they were content to buy up the individual estates where before each planter had crystallized his own sugar with his two hundred slaves; but it wasn't until after the First World War—when I was almost twenty[10]—that you had the phenomenon of full-scale monopoly capital in Guyana, with the merger of twenty or thirty relatively small units into one highly productive mechanized operation.

In this situation, what were the blacks to do? They had come out of slavery with almost no savings, so they had to pool their few resources co-operatively in order to buy land at all. Each village was therefore created through the operation of the

5

osusu principle—the same word for co-operation being used in Guyana as on the West Coast of Africa. Each person in the group put his little contribution weekly into the 'box', as it was called. One person would be made the custodian; so that if there were two hundred joining and putting a shilling in each week, it meant that each in turn could have the use of sh. 200/- to buy his own plot of land in the village they were planning.

Even though land purchase was not easy it did not mean that the blacks were going to remain in their slave sheds, working for their old masters a moment longer than they needed to. This naturally produced a tremendous labour shortage, and soon the planters and the new companies were desperately importing Chinese and later Indian coolie labour to fill the gap left by the blacks. It wasn't that they were against agriculture *per se;* but freedom did mean that you weren't going to work for somebody else if you could help it.

Now the only land that was obtainable was beyond the great estates going towards the sea, and often it was only marginally arable. Unlike the estates which were criss-crossed with drainage canals and other channels for punting the sugar cane to the factories, the village settlements had usually only one large canal of sweet water coming from the hinterland. It ran through the village and the people would live on either bank. We young boys had to fetch the water for our homes from there, and carry it back to the houses in those large kerosene gallon tins. Then, if you wanted to swim or to wash yourself before going to school, you went to the punt-trench at the back of the village—the dividing line between the free settlements and the old estates.

The village had its various patches of land, and these were put into fallow from time to time, just as in European husbandry. Only in Guyana you do not put land into meadow; you swamp it with this sweet water from the canal. You use certain large pumps (usually made in Scotland) with a large hose, and you pump night and day until this water covers the fields protected by their dykes. Under this rich water, the land is allowed to rest for perhaps eighteen months. Then it was finally drained off.

We boys always remembered this because it was the time you could collect stranded fish like the *patois* and the *huri*. The whole system obviously owed something to the early Dutch influence

6

on the colony, especially around the mouth of the Berbice River. But once I had later gone north to America, I would see similar systems operating in the Mississippi area.

The people owned their little pieces of land, but an element of co-partnership operated—not very different from the African set-up. The neighbours helped each other if it was a question of planting cassava or yams; both of these crops took almost nine months to mature, so it meant keeping your plot weeded throughout. It was easier therefore to call upon your neighbours. They would all come to your plot one day, and finish it that same day, and then you'd move on to finish all fifteen family plots within a week or two. There would still then be plenty of time left for other business before the grass again reached such a height. I remember the scene very vividly over at my grandmother's place; you would find certain of the women cooking there for the fifteen helpers and others would be weeding.

This particular grandmother on my mother's side was born in Guyana, but I never knew the grandmother on my father's side. I did, however, know quite well other members of my father's family. They were quite an unusual-looking brood; a bit like aliens, like some of the people I have since seen from Ethiopia and Somalia. One should note, however, that when one of the blacks married one of the indigenous Amerindians, you got the same sort of Somali features coming out in the children. Also on my father's side was a Mr. Brenner, who was actually a relation of my grandfather. He used to be in public works, and built roads. But as there were no stone quarries in the area, one had to burn the earth to make burnt bricks for the job. It was a skilled job burning this red earth right, and he had men with him who also knew the business. A development of this same skill led to another small industry which was called burning 'goblets'—a kind of clay pot used for water carrying. He was also involved in producing clay cooking-pots, which I later saw were remarkably like some you can find in West Africa. Personally I did not meet this man; however, he was eventually given quite a lot of land by the government for his road work. But this land was quite far from our own family abode in Buxton and Plaisance; it was up the Demerara River some forty miles.

7

My grandmother was one of those who was directly connected with the foundation of one of these villages; she was part of the proud element which had come into its own after slavery. They were the ones who had made the village laws. They would ring the village bell to summon people to come out and cut the common grass, so as not to have snakes, or to dig the drains. She was a Buxton woman, a Buxtonian, and it had the strongest traditions of any. On occasions if the women wanted to make some point to government they would actually lie down on the train track. In their view, nobody was going to be allowed to by-pass Buxton.

A man called Baird was married to this grandmother. Actually he had two or three other wives, because the end of slavery did not end this custom. But nobody was bothered much about this sort of thing. Still, this grandmother was quite an important figure in Buxton; especially in an area called East Dam, just over the railway line. She had another relative whom we called Aunty Peggy, an interesting woman who worked as a trader from her stall in the Buxton market. Peggy was the mother of my great boyhood friend, David Talbot, who was also going to find his way like me, via America to Africa.[11] Yet a further family in the clan was the Roberts group, and they too lived tenaciously near to the others. But what was interesting to me once I had become interested in the history of blacks in Guyana was how little they knew about the past. If you asked any of them about the traditions of their family history, all they could ever answer was, 'I'm a Buxtonian'. One could not get any further back, as you could in the United States. There you found many blacks who could tell you the whole story: how their grandmother was a slave in such an such a plantation; then one year the crops were bad; so the master had gone to Georgia to buy another farm and so on. But I could never get into any discussion of slavery with Lady Scott (as my grandmother was called),[12] or Aunty Peggy, Mrs. Valentine or Mrs. Roberts—any of these people that I looked upon as my mother. One didn't even find out how Lady Scott got her name, because people didn't want to talk about the past; but I assumed it was because of her lady-like qualities.

She also had an important role in the church which at that time was another basis for group solidarity. I remember she was herself in charge of a 'box'. Aunt McKenzie too was something of a leader, though she was not a real aunt. They were both able subsequently to get a number of youths during certain months after school to go to the plantation to work. Some of these women (not so much my grandmother but Mrs. Nurse and Mrs. McKenzie) were noted for having these gangs working under them; they would set out in the early morning, about fifty or sixty children over the age of fourteen with them, and would not get back till the evening. The money that the cropping of this entail brought to the woman leader would then be distributed to each child's mother. So their status was very important, and just like in all African communities, the woman was not a scrounger. She worked. I can see now, looking back, that they were doing a kind of task-work. Aunty Peggy, Mrs. Valentine and the others had a link with one of the overseers, for each of the overseers was given a certain section of, say, the 20,000 acre plantation for which he would be responsible. Under him there would be foremen, entomologists, ecologists; all doing their various jobs. Therefore, to avoid any entanglement with price rises, I can see this now, it was useful to have your own people who had long been accustomed to come and work under overseer X.

These old girls, then, had their gangs, and there was really no difficulty in getting people to work—such was the desire by many to enter the money economy. You could not of course get anyone to go during school time. This was taboo. Education was too precious. But by any standard these women labour recruiters were important personalities in their village communities. For one thing they always had money, and were often responsible for the 'box'. And beyond that, they tended to have sons who were also successful in different ways. They were able to get niches for them. Some of the sons, for instance, became engineers and surveyors, for it had not been difficult for such prominent women to get a letter from someone recommending their sons. You tended therefore to get almost a new class emerging by virtue of the function of the family. The apprenticeship system had caught on quite widely for the period after high school or seventh standard as it was called. So a fellow might well go on to the Botanical Gardens in Georgetown in order to learn something about agriculture, or equally he could

9

attach himself to a plantation in order to learn about the crystal-lization of sugar, or rye-making. Such technicians we called chemists. However, their initial recommendation came from their families.

How my father met my mother—these things were never told; but I knew. There was an uncle Joe on my mother's side who went to apprentice himself as a boiler-maker in the town of Kitty not far from Georgetown. His master was a certain Pilgrim, the owner of a big factory, who dealt in the repair of boilers in the big railway yard there. Now, most of these sorts of undertakings had their own football or cricket club, and apparently my father was able to meet my uncle Joe at one of these affairs. He was then invited to come to Buxton which was having a tournament at the time, playing games and touring with bands of music to help work up the spirit. And from there the relationship developed.

My father had also a number of aunts, many of whom, it was said, I resembled much more than those on my mother's side. Especially one called Margaret. She was a terror and a very bad woman. She did not think twice about fighting a man. And even my father at a certain period was afraid of her coming because her mouth had no licence. Unlike many of us she was not a town woman, but had gone through many metamorphoses. For instance, she was never honourably married. On the credit side, though, if anybody was owing my father money and would not pay it, or if anybody was trying to do anything against my father's side of the family, Margaret would come from hell to the family's defence; it made life very difficult at times.

For instance, there was the incident with 'uncle' Sharples.[13] He was one of the renowned educators in Georgetown—feared and loved because there were so many thousands of people who had had the honour of attending Sharples' School. This was originally a private school and was only one of the going concerns of this large, originally Buxtonian, family. They also had sawmills and were very powerful. Well, one day Margaret overheard that uncle Sharples had whipped me at school—in fact she had it quite wrong, for it was uncle Weekes, the mathematics teacher, who had done this because I had not toed the line over punctua-lity. At any rate, this woman tied her coat like a typical West African in a fighting mood, and went down to abuse uncle

10

Sharples after school. Of course she had the wrong information but nobody was going to touch her brother's child and get away with it.

Another aunt was the image of my father. Long hair flowing down, she smoked a pipe even as a young woman. And this aunt Rosa was rather beautiful—another outstanding character. But I don't know where she got this pipe business from. Maybe from the Indians. Now I come to think of it, in fact she looked like an Amerindian even!

My father at this time was engaged in the mining industry with this man, Evan Wong, a Chinese. Then mining meant chasing after outcrops and deposits here and there. Only quite recently have miners in that part of the world become reconciled to stationary mining. A man might well travel all the six hundred miles from the Mazaruni River to the Essequibo, because he had heard that someone there had got so many thousand carats, giving up everything on his original site. Father was in gold or diamonds, depending which was in greater supply at any time.

It was my grandfather who got us this mining streak.[14] He was actually an Ethiopian who had been brought to Guyana in the company of a Scottish miner who had met him in Eritrea. Now this was back in the 1880s at the time when you got these miners going all over the world, and some of them ending up in Ethiopia. They were attracted by the reputation of that ancient kingdom, in rather the way that Sir Walter Raleigh was lured to Guyana in search of Eldorado. You had therefore a number of these freebooters turning up in Ethiopia, and there are still in Tigre province of Ethiopia today a number of white families whose roots stretch back to the Klondyke. Mining made for a tremendous movement of peoples.

Now from what little I have gathered about the Tigre people at that time, there seems to have been considerable Christian influence working its way into Ethiopia, in addition to the native form of the Coptic Church which had been there for centuries. There had been the famous expedition of Samuel Gobat in the 1830s,[15] and after that you had Swedish and Italian missions all trying to find a place in the sun. My grandfather must have been involved in some of this, because people remembered that he could play the piano and could render a number

11

of these European Christian hymns. He was one of the many who were leaving Ethiopia at this period: some had made their way to Egypt and were working for Englishmen there as 'houseboys'. Others I found later in West Africa and particularly in Sierra Leone and the Gambia. This diaspora may have been connected with that famous expedition of Napier against Emperor Teodros, because some of the native troops used for that may have gone to serve with the British in other parts of the empire. The same thing happened with the Second World War, and you can meet in many parts of Africa families where the husband served with the British in Ethiopia against the Italians and where the wife is an Ethiopian. I even know a family here in Kenya like that; the man is quite a professional landscape gardener from Ghana, but his English colonel kept him on in Kenya after the Ethiopian war, and he's got an Ethiopian wife from Asmara. He still speaks Twi to his children!

So my grandfather was one of the Ethiopian dispersals, and the reason he ended up in Guyana with this Scotsman was that suddenly the Guyana-Venezuela region was projected as the next mining boom area. It was a very troubled period and there were frequent skirmishes between the various competing interests. But what has always puzzled me is what role the freed blacks played in the take-off of the gold and diamond industry. We know of course that the fierce Jukas, or bush Negroes of Dutch Guiana, possessed a lot of gold; but they just picked up the nuggets, they didn't mine them systematically. Admittedly there had been West Africans in the Gold Coast region who knew the whole process, but at the moment it seems as if the blacks in Guyana had to be taught the industry by the big foreign entrepreneurs or by people like this Scotsman.

Now by virtue of this early heritage, the family had acquired certain lands up in the hinterland. Concessionaires like my father in due course used to send boats up the various rivers and in his case it was mostly up to areas of the Mazaruni River. This is a very long river going right on to Brazil, and there are a number of tributaries joining it, like Eping and Crampazo. In one of these Evan Wong and my father had a number of shops to serve the porknockers (prospectors) and those who pulled the boats. In fact the arrangement with Evan Wong had started just about the beginning of the First World War; at that

12

time my father had been hoarding a number of diamonds waiting for the price to rise with the war needs. He did a deal with a Syrian on the understanding that he would get this higher price for my father, but the man simply pushed off with the diamonds and wasn't seen again. In this situation, my father got credit from Evan Wong, and from there the arrangement prospered. My father got to know Chinese, being a meticulous businessman and good at languages; and in return he got a good outlet for his diamonds. You see, Evan Wong had become a tremendous dealer in diamonds, with the outbreak of war, and I think he was using one of his sons, Robert, to find the best market. At this time Robert was over in Scotland studying engineering, but he used to go over to the Hague in the vacations and along with his father's other contacts try to arrange a good sale.

While my father was in the diamond and gold business he had many good friends and was well liked. This was not very usual in the game because the competition was fierce, and you could hear many blacks letting off about the 'bloody Portugee' or the 'bloody Chinee'. But nobody was antagonistic to my father, or 'Ganje', as he was called. This was one of his many nicknames and I've always wanted to know where he got it from. I thought it might have been connected with this pipe, *ganja*, the Amerindians used to smoke, because, as I said, my father had these particular features, but I'm not sure. At any rate, this new partnership with Wong was obviously more stable than father's earlier liaisons with the Portuguese, the Syrians and the Amerindians, because by this time the Chinese had acquired some of the bigger businesses in town. They had been the earliest of the indentured labourers, and as soon as their indenture periods were up, they had moved off smartly to the towns, and opened up their little laundries and other businesses.

During their partnership, David Talbot and I began to frequent the rivers to try out the mining. It was quite a romantic affair, the draw of these great rivers with their exciting names: Demerara, Potaro, Rupuruni, Berbice, Barima and Mazaruni. There was an element of pride too in trying to apply one's knowledge from school to the finding of diamonds. I wasn't interested either in working under someone else; I wanted to dig and make finds personally. In this, Dave and I employed the open mining method, using the pan (or battle as it was called)

13

for gold. But we also used the square. One would start first by the hillside, digging into it about four feet to see what way the gravels ran. Samples of gravel could then be worked using a combination of a sieve, troughs and a 'tom-iron' to separate the smaller and large particles of gold and diamonds. It was especially satisfying to work with the 18-inch diameter sieve, which, if you used it skilfully, could leave you with a little cluster of stones in the centre, once you had jigged the lighter sands out over the top into the water. Generally, however, my practice was to dig a number of such pits and look for indications of diamond through the presence of other stones like jasper, felsite, etc. They were usually part of the diamondiferous complex.

Once when Talbot and I were up on the Kurupung tributary, I made a find of diamonds. Immediately I began the process of charting out my concessions which I would then get registered in Georgetown. But just at that point, old man Evan Wong came past in his little boat with its outboard motor: 'Oh, you're at this too,' he said. 'I thought you were not going to follow your father's footsteps, but that you would go like my son abroad to study law or something. And now you've turned out a gold-digger. What is happening?' Well, he was more impressed when he saw the stones; I told him I would chart it out under my present prospecting licence and then transfer the thing to my father. It wasn't eventually going to prove my life work, but until I found what that was, there was no harm in increasing our family empire if I could.

One picked up a lot of business acumen in this way actually, especially on these long trips with my father. We people who owned concessions could sublet them to porknockers; then you had a double game of provisioning them with the various foodstuffs of rice, salt-fish, sugar and liquor; but you had also to keep an eye on the porknockers. Otherwise they could keep back all the good diamonds and pass off only the small stuff to you. In this case, you would hire an Amerindian ranger to spy on the sorts of finds they were making. If he reported finds in plenty, then you waited for the porknockers to come and you would settle up with them: 'I'm not my father, you know. I am a small boy, but I am a bad boy and I know your game.' Immediately you would take your own group of men up the river and work the plot just next to the people you suspected, and once you had proved that they had been bluffing you all this time, you could actually drive them off.

There was a real atmosphere of adventure about the mining business though, and on the rivers plenty of folk singing about men and the chances they always take. There were axioms for every eventuality. For instance, if a man went overboard in the rapids and began to shout, 'Save me! Save me!' the men in the other boat would laugh back: 'If God wants to save you, he'll put you on a rock. If not, pass on to eternity, my friend!'

Other porknockers had extravagant names and gestures, and would almost make a burlesque of their whole life. On one occasion Dave and I were checking our various concessions when a group called us across. A man, Sultan, cried out, 'Ganje pickin (child), glorious things of thee are spoken. I'll have a bottle of Black and White.' Well, we gave it over, and they drank it off. 'Repeat!' Sultan yelled. I checked with Dave and we discussed whether he might be able to pay. Then we handed him another. 'All right, do you have a scale big enough to weigh the stone I've just found?' I told him if we hadn't we could always improvise, and he brought out a beautiful diamond, perhaps 32 carats. Even though Sultan owed the family several hundred dollars there would be plenty to spare with this; so he cabled people in Georgetown, and when the party got back to town, they rented a hearse and drove solemnly through town with it. Everyone asked them, 'What's the matter? Who's dead?' 'Canadian Bank is dead,' Sultan shouted back. 'They won't have money enough in their vaults for this diamond!'

Many a time after I had left Guyana, I used to think back on these episodes, and reflect that we blacks had been our own executioners. Look at that fertile land we had had there, and yet we never attempted to clear areas in the hinterland where we could grow our own foodstuffs. There was this terrible tradition of not being sedentary, never settling down to really work at a place. Of course, it's typical of all mining communities; you regard the thing as a lark, a great adventure. You don't save; you just hope that one day you can be translated from poverty to wealth by a single find. So what was the point of growing vegetables up there? You would just continue to be indebted until you made your big break. And having made it, you would

15

spend it all in a few days.[16] Thinking back, one can see how much wiser it would have been to go up there with one's family and bring them up there, using the saw and cultivating as well as mining. Then, when you did eventually strike it rich, you wouldn't immediately have to sell off your diamonds to buy your liquor and provisions. Live by all means the free and unfettered life, but be in a position to really damn the world.

NOTES TO CHAPTER 1

1 For the bush Negroes of Dutch Guiana and their militancy, see J. G. Stedman, *Narrative of a Five Year Expedition against the Revolted Negroes of Surinam in Guiana, 1772-77* (2 vols, London, 1796); for the Jamaican Maroons, H. O. Patterson, *The Sociology of Slavery* (London, 1967).

2 cf. *The Missionary Smith: Substance of the Debate in the House of Commons on Tuesday 1st and on Friday 11th of June 1824 on a Motion of Henry Brougham respecting the Trial and Condemnation to death by a court martial of Rev. John Smith* (London, 1824).

3 C. L. R. James, *The Black Jacobins: Toussaint L'Ouverture and the San Domingo Revolution* (London, 1938).

4 cf. Eric Williams, *Capitalism and Slavery* (Chapel Hill, N. C., 1944) which is itself dedicated to L. J. Ragatz and his pioneer work, *The Fall of the Planter Class in the British Caribbean* (Washington, 1928).

5 For a valuable introduction to this new historiography of slavery, see L. Foner and E. D. Genovese, *Slavery in the New World* (Englewood Cliffs, N. J., 1969), and bibliography therein.

6 On the Coromante slave in the New World, Patterson, op. cit.

7 The genesis of village self-reliance is sketched in R. T. Smith, *The Negro Family in British Guiana* (London, 1956); also, R. Farley, 'The Rise of the Peasantry in British Guiana', in *Social and Economic Studies*, ii, 1 (1953), pp. 87-103.

8 For Knibb's role in Jamaica, see C. P. Groves, *Planting of Christianity in Africa* (London, 1954), ii, pp. 33-40.

9 See Michael Swan, *British Guiana* (London, 1959), p. 85, for the role of Booker Bros. in Guiana.

10 The year of Makonnen's birth is a little uncertain. His cousin, David Talbot, has mentioned the year 1899 (interview of 25 July 1970, Addis Ababa). On the other hand one of Makonnen's university textbooks from the early 1930s has inscribed in the first page: 'Born 1903 in Plaisance, British Guiana.'

11 Talbot, after a long period of interest in Africa, eventually emigrated to Ethiopia in 1943.

12 Talbot has mentioned however that this particular grandmother, who lived to a great age, frequently talked of Africa, and in particular of a place called Coromante in the Gold Coast: 'Especially my grandmother told us of this place she came from and what they had done with the cassava and plantain there. As for my coming to Africa, that was the thing that sparked me; it grew in me—a thirst to see the place that the old lady was talking of.' (Interview, op. cit.)

13 The use of the affectionate 'aunt' and 'uncle' to address adults was common in Makonnen's childhood, and is continued with his children.

14 There are a number of points about the naming of the male side of the family. Makonnen's father was called George Thomas Nathaniel Griffith, and Makonnen used the same names as his father right up to the middle thirties. Indeed his Cornell textbooks, dating from 1932 to 1934, either have these four names written in full or the initials stamped 'G. T. G.' Those who knew him in London first remember him as 'Griffith', but as he became more and more deeply involved in the Ethiopian cause he took the name Ras Tefari Makonnen. By the time of his first mention in the *New Times and Ethiopia News* (in the spring of 1937), he is already known as Ato (Mr) Makonnen. Like his grandfather who is described as coming from Tigre Province, Makonnen used to use the expression 'We of the Tigre' in certain public meetings on the Ethiopia question. Later the order of the initials was changed to T. R., often expanded to 'T. Ras', and more recently still to 'Tomatsio Rwaki'.

15 See further, S. Gobat, *Journal of a Three Years' Residence in Ethiopia* (London, 1834).

16 This was clearly the attitude of Makonnen and Talbot at a certain stage: 'We made a lot of money as young men in the diamond fields; but we squandered most of it on the best entertainment—girls of the highest social rung. We spent our money flamboyantly, even hiring cars quite frequently. We had quite a fling and we took pictures of every important aspect of our life' (Talbot, Addis Ababa, 1970).

CHAPTER 2

THE EMERGENCE OF THE BLACK BOURGEOISIE IN GUYANA

MOST people had felt that this business of emancipating the slaves would be a failure; they were sure that the anti-slavery element in England like Buxton and Wilberforce would be proved wrong, and in fact they used to mercilessly caricature such people as sentimentalists. 'They don't understand human nature and conduct, and don't realize that these lazy niggers after a life of duress will simply return back to the coconut tree and lie down there; and when the tree gets too tall, he'll probably train a monkey to climb up the tree and throw down the nuts.' This was the prevailing attitude, and the anti-slavery set were naturally anxious that the freedmen should show themselves to be hard-working and self-reliant.

They were greatly encouraged therefore by the activity in the freedmen villages, but, as we have seen, the blacks could not be stopped from leaving the cane plantations in large numbers. The Chinese substitute did not prove particularly successful; perhaps the strenuous work was too much for him; but Indian coolie labour was so adaptive that it was used for upwards of fifty years. It wasn't only on the plantations that the Indian made a significant contribution to the Guyanan economy; they also set a new style in food crops. Up to the time they arrived in large numbers, the blacks had been dependent upon these root crops, plantain, cassava and yam, which were abundant in Guyana as they had been in West Africa. These took nine months to mature, and if you were working the ground individually with that slavish instrument, the four-toothed fork, it meant a lot of work. You had to put it into the ground with a tremendous *elan*, really rape the ground, for it was tough clay, and then lift the clod and break it into pieces.

This is where the Indians had the advantage; their crop, rice, took only three months to mature, like other grain crops; and in cultivating the soil, the Indians employed their traditional method of the bullock and the plough. He used the same bullocks as were needed for pulling the sugar-punts up the canals, and was a very careful guardian of them. The African by contrast was not a very eager animal husbandman. Traditionally in many parts of Africa it had not been his cup of tea. So gradually as batches of these Indians finished their indenture period, you could see a gap becoming established between the African and the Indian economies. You see, what the single Indian family could do with a working bullock in one day, even ten African families with their four-teeth forks could not match in the space of a day. Automatically the Indian was placed in a better position also because his commodity rice had an international market, whereas the African's banana, plantain and cassava were the objects of barter.[1] Remember, it would be almost a century before bananas would begin to go to Europe.

And yet, despite this increasing economic gap, the African continued to despise these Indian coolies and often deserted his agriculture for the lure of the mining industry, or if he stayed in his village, his husbandry was very cramped; everything was jammed into his half acre of land—ginger, manioc, corn, sweet potato and the other root crops. By contrast, Indian methods quickly made a primitive accumulation of capital possible, and this in turn was used to establish a position of material superiority over the blacks. The latter were so keen on sending their children to school and then into the professions that they were prepared to mortgage their land and even their homes in the village community to many of the Indians. Relations, therefore, worsened, because in a subtle form of usury, the Indians never asked for their loans back, but just continued to accept the interest.

This meant hardship temporarily for some of the black families, but don't forget that they were doing all this to try to supersede the whites. They had been conditioned to this from slavery days, and now they were free they were determined to wear the hat and coat correctly in emulation of the English. There was a great striving for this sort of thing—not only English manners but

19

the whole English way of life. It made yet another difference with the Indians, who clung doggedly to their own styles, and may help to explain why the Africans were frequently closer to the Chinese. These, too, in their public life had adopted the English norms, although they retained their own manners and customs in their homes. Here I know what I am talking about, for many of my playmates when I was about eleven or twelve were people like the Mansa Hings, the Wongs and the Lees. We had so much in common at school, but when we went to their homes, it was a different cultural world. Anyone who has eaten Chinese food in a palatial Chinese home can never forget this impression of variety and difference.

Now, of the blacks who went into the mining industry, some were quite successful. And when they returned, they built two-storey houses and fine bungalows, then helped to educate their children. These in turn went abroad and entered three professions —law, medicine and the ministry of the church. A number of blacks, it is true, had been handicraftsmen at housebuilding during the slavery years, and had maintained the plantation housing. This was rather reminiscent of the manorial period of English history, for the manor had to create its own skilled men to maintain the society around it. Similarly, in the sugar plantations many skills derived from the changeover from windmills to the steam engine. Then later the coming of the railway produced plate-layers, engine drivers and others. But sugar processing itself was almost a black industry. Once sugar had been cut and put into the punts, it was black crane drivers who lifted out the chained bundles. The cane then goes down a shaft to the mill where it is crushed, and in these operations in the mill, the engineers are blacks. The white man had previously had the supervisory powers, but this, too, was subsequently done by blacks. The juice is then removed into great tanks, for clarifying; it is boiled, and reduced, and during these operations the key men are the chemists—all of them black. They work out the amount of acid in the juice, and from certain equations, how much sulphur must be added to neutralize this. From there you get the black sugar, clarified to brown, and then the off-product of molasses. An almost all black industry, with the exception of certain whites in the branches of morphology and pest control.

Furthermore these skilled and semi-skilled blacks were not town blacks, but members of the village community. But just as in slavery days you had a division between house Negroes and plantation slaves, so you had the same strata apparent in the village community. It was not a fundamental separation. But one's job merited a certain position, and one was respected for it. I would know Mr. Orgle and Mr. McLennan, who were not only important personalities on the estate as pot-boilers or chemists, but also in the First Methodist Church or the Anglican. All of these villages, as I have mentioned, had at their head men who stood out, who were literate and understood things. They were the debaters and the members of the village council.[2] And if there were any disputes in the period before the professional lawyer class came to divide the community, they would settle them. Certainly we can see in this the gradual evolution of classes, but we did not have any demarked line, for after all we had the same common origin. When therefore Mr. Orgle's son returned from England or Scotland as a lawyer, the whole community turned out, just as today in Kenya the Kikuyu will go to the airport to meet this boy from their village. His success is the village's success.

This flowed, of course, from the communal nature of village enterprise. So that when Mr. Marcus was building his house, a neighbour would not hesitate to help, with the expectation that when the neighbour's turn came, Mr. Marcus would be able to return the help. Literally hundreds of people went in for this combined work, and even the estate workers like Mr. Marcus would go back to this community for the three months that work was slack in the sugar mill. Even if you were a professional and went to Georgetown or Berbice to practise, there was always the rigid link with your community. Some of this may have been fostered by the British ideas of communal spirit, but whatever its source, a man was proud of his village and would tell you, 'I'm a Buxtonian', or whatever the name of his village.

But continuing the theme of the skilled black class emerging, one might examine the period when with the emergence of charcoal as an important industry, you got the parallel development of boat-building. There was Sprostons, an English firm with a long history, and also McKenzie and Co. Now most of

21

the skilled craftsmen with these firms were Africans, and in all probability they had in the early period been taught by Scotsmen who had come from the Clyde. When the time came they went away, but things were in capable hands—blacks like my friend Massey who became a famous boat-builder. Smith, also, had his own yard. They made these barquentines, and were also able to construct the punts for the waterways and the ships that could sail between Barbados and Trinidad.

In addition to these boat-builders, there were boiler-makers, who could also make ship's anchors and other things. Thus a group of black technicians evolved. There were no Indians competing on the scene at that period. In particular there were people like Barnwell, and R. D. Nurse, a famous contractor. Taken together you could call them the journeymen of the society—the master craftsmen. The government, too, recognized the existence of this class and instituted a system of apprentice-ships for lads to be taken on at the shipyards, the railways or Booker Bros., McConnell and Co. and the sugar plantations.

This, of course, was the class that laid the foundation for the emergence of men like Patrick Doggan, the lawyer, or Wood, the solicitor. Both were before my time, back in the eighties, and I only saw their photographs. But they and their generation were almost the third after slavery. Their importance was in laying down a standard for the black community, and showing the capability of the black man—that he could in fact rule the roost. Often the sons of these men went even further. They would be articled clerks in Guyana for a number of years; then after nine months in England, they would return as full-fledged barristers. Subsequently they would take silk, become K.Cs., and be equal to their counterpart in any part of the world. All this looks a little like the development of a similar class in Freetown, Sierra Leone, but in reality those West African Creoles were small boys compared to these men. Furthermore, Guyanan society was much healthier economically than Sierra Leone's. Remember, there was no sugar or rum industry in Freetown, nor indeed the famous mahogany wood that was marketed for use in railway carriages. Whereas Guyana and Honduras were two of the chief sources for this, and even in the building of the Panama Canal the greenheart wood used for driving piles was a product of Guyana. So, unlike Trinidad and Barbados also, there was a degree of prosperity in Guyana, and the whole thing was helped by the large amount of land (98,000 square miles) and the relatively small population. Therefore, although you had sugar plantations in European hands, you did not get that wholesale ownership of land by a plantocrat class that obtained in St. Kitts, Grenada, and St. Vincent. Coffee could be grown by the locals in Guyana, and not just on some white-owned plantation. And in the process of expanding your coffee land on the west bank of the Demerara, you could get further profit by felling and selling off the giant timber resources. You really had then a class of people much more formidable than that little island of Creoles in West Africa.

To look more closely at the pattern of this class, it was easy to see in each case a loyalty to a particular village, be it Belfield, Ansgrove, or Mahica; then there would be a lucrative place of work in one of the towns like Berbice. One would return during the holidays to the ancient village scene. But one would have one's palatial home in the city, living if possible around Queen's Street in Georgetown where the governor lived. There they would be with their fabulous homes—made of wood like the Anglican cathedral and not of stone or brick. They stood out in the various residential districts of Georgetown with their carriages, and when the automobile made its impact, they also got their automobiles. Some of them brought back English wives from abroad, and these along with their children became part of the whole set-up. They maintained a certain tone of life, with their regular concerts, and in their church life too, there was rich activity. You even had celebrities coming from Europe to perform in the local town hall, touring round the various islands, and by the time they reached Guyana, they had made a packet. There was, then, a cultural atmosphere with people discussing the range of voice of this particular *prima donna* and how she compared with the others. Among them there were blacks who also came, like the Jubilee singers from Fisk University in Nashville, visiting especially churches of the same denomination as themselves.

Each family was proud of its own denomination, of course, or rather of having a better preacher than the others. 'My man went to Switzerland—the man know book . . . He can knock book (meaning he's well-learned) and the example he give!

23

He know the thing.' So they would say, there was no need to put on rosaries and those other things to cloak your ignorance; their man really knew his Bible. This was the pattern, therefore; yet I can't say one observed any real degree of snobbishness, because if one tried anything, they would say, 'Who are you? Your father was a carpenter and simply because you have turned a lawyer, you think you can parade on people?' As I have said before, there was always this feeling that one was not far removed from a common origin. Perhaps the most respected of all was the local schoolmaster, holding the fort in the village community. And in front of him even a lunatic given to abusive language would hold his filthy tongue, or indulge in some burlesque . . . . 'If the schoolmaster was not coming here now, I'd finish you off, boy . . . but good morning, Mr. Schoolmaster, sir.'

Now generally at this period of the late nineteenth century, people were still going to Europe for higher training. America was only going to project itself on the population after the First World War. Of course some did go to America before that time, but usually they did not return. They got lucrative jobs as teachers and in other professions. Especially as dispensers, because this was another by-product of sugar processing. Such people— you could call them pharmacists of a sort—played a very important part in Guyana as well, and in these various villages, they would be known as doctor. In Buxton, for instance, there were about ten doctor families. They built palatial homes with the shop or the dispensary downstairs. Sometimes their daughters would be renowned as musicians as the fathers wished to maintain a certain standard and cultural level. And their relations might enter commerce with a grocer's or butcher's shop in the community.

Interestingly enough, this cultural activity was transferred to Africa by West Indians to some extent. Creole elements came to the Gold Coast through Sierra Leone, Maroon remnants from Jamaica, and West Indians in the Ashanti wars who never returned with the West Indian Regiment. Instead they would settle down, some becoming sergeants in the constabulary and holding important posts. Then there were others who came across when the railways were being built in West Africa and helped to manage them. In fact, you wouldn't have one of these places like the Gold Coast and Sierra Leone where there would not be a West Indian dominating the scene, whose name and family have been a continuum. Occasionally they would even become chiefs like Otunfu Moore, the man who led the delegation from the Aborigines Protection Society to London, or its famous lawyer secretary, Wood.[3] And often the link with the West Indies was maintained, with the children going back for education, entering the professions and then perhaps returning to West Africa. Take Abbensetts who was the attorney-general in Ghana; his father was a celebrated lawyer in Guyana who migrated to West Africa. His son in turn was born there and subsequently succeeded to his practice.

These are only a few among the many. Down in the Fanti areas around Sekondi, for instance, you can also find a very mixed set-up with the West Indian and other remnants all present. Nor is this only true of Ghana. In Nigeria there are some very notable examples of the same influence from the West Indies. Firstly in the period after 1838, the Welshman Knibb had been playing a very important part in making the blacks of the New World aware of their obligations to Africa.[4] Through collection of money they were able eventually to establish in Calabar a branch of the Myco College of Jamaica. This Hope Waddell High School, as it was called, was at times actually maintained by these ex-slaves as teachers, men originally from St. Kitts, St. Vincent, and Trinidad. And if they could not get enough from the New World, they would draw on teachers from the Sierra Leone Creoles, or even from Liberia. So there was this continual cross-fertilization. Then at Lagos it was a different situation, because most of the immigrants were from Brazil, the Fernandezes, de Souzas and other Portuguese names. Slavery had of course continued in Brazil up to the 1880s and so you had a number of communities in places like Sao Paulo setting off for Lagos to escape it. This partly explains why in the early period Lagos had formidable technical skill coming with the Creole element—quite apart from the indigenous skill of Benin and other places.

This migration continued into my time also. I well remember Van Sertima. I wasn't his age, of course, but my father had a garage for Buick cars which he would rent to the chief justice of Guyana and others; this brought about contact with Van

25

Sertima, who was one of our leading lawyers, a K.C. with a very good record at the Inns. He, too, had served in the First World War. But then he subsequently went to Gold Coast and became attorney-general there. And it wasn't only blacks who moved like this. You got someone like Donald Cameron coming from an old white Guyanese family and entering the colonial service to work in Nigeria at the time of the Aba Riots and then later in Tanganyika Territory.

Even today in Kenya there are a number of these black fellows from the New World, some of them working for international organizations. But they all congregate at the house of the Guyanan justice, Miller, who now lives here. Recently he went back to Guyana to represent Kenya at some function, and was given high honour by Kenyatta himself. So here he is, a member of this diaspora, with his home a Mecca for the other people like himself. And now a number of others are coming from Trinidad. Since Eric Williams, the Prime Minister, seems to have faltered in his politics somewhat, there's a brain-drain out of that island too.

Now let us fill in some of the detail of this black group in Guyana in the period just after the First World War. You had some very noted thinkers involved. Edmund Fitzgerald Fredericks, another of these Buxtonians, had played a part in the early Pan-African Conference of 1900, and had followed this with an important role in America before returning to Guyana.[5] Then there was Bruyning, whose ancestors were from Trinidad but he identified with the local community. These men, along with Dr. Nichols and a number of others, created a group reminiscent of Garvey's Universal Negro Improvement Association.[6] It was primarily a cultural group they created in Guyana, but it nevertheless had an impact once it had been fanned into a flame. They began, for instance, to talk about creating scholarships, because the single scholarship offered by the British government was not enough. And so they set out to find schools and colleges abroad, exploiting their own old connections with places like Durham University. In this they were very effective.

As a counterpart to this class there was a group formed round Hubert Critchlow, a Barbados man who had come to Guyana.[7] Men such as he had no roots on the land as they did not have one of these villages to which they owed loyalty. They therefore engaged in jobs like stevedoring. Much later, I met Critchlow myself when I invited him and paid for his passage to attend our Manchester Conference of 1945.[8] But we shouldn't underestimate the leadership of people like him. In fact, the first strike I heard about was due to him and his followers. They knew their power and made the government recognize it too—just after the First World War. I was of course a little boy, but I knew this thing; it affected me. Especially when the government invoked martial law, and these fellows retaliated by tearing the whole place to pieces in the Georgetown riots.

In order to set the Fredericks group, however, within its true perspective, let us look at the wider distribution of power in Georgetown at the period they emerged. After the great George-town fire (that was in the 1910s), the Chinese who had been holding commercial power began for one reason and another to move away to Cuba. The Indians meanwhile were beginning to enter trade, backed up by their barristers and their high priests (many of these coming direct from India). Also important here is the emergence of Gandhi in India with his celebrated newspaper, *Indian Opinion*, which gave a new *elan* to the Indians abroad. Now, to be fair to Gandhi, he reflected somewhat on the impotence of the Negro or African in South Africa when he was evolving his *Swaraj* idea, and had rather expected that the Africans would also develop something similar by this discipline.[9] Well, this did not in fact happen, and he recognized the difference of culture and background. But for the Indians of the New World, this sort of thing gave them a new set of values, and made them more militant in a number of situations. It was this spirit that brought Indian immigration as contracted labour to Guyana to a standstill towards the end of the first war.

So here you had them entering commerce at a time when the 'Portuguee' and the near-white were losing their importance. Indians like Thomas J. Flood were beginning to carve out their empires (he was a Christianized Indian). This was associated with the fading of power in the sugar industry and the boom in rice. And as Indians were mostly in the rice business, they were able to go to the remote sections of the country to develop it further. Gradually whole areas came under their control, and remained so until the last five years of the 1960s with the Jagan-Burnham business.[10] But prior to that they had had no

27

competitor as so many of the talented blacks had simply left the country for Cuba and further afield.

Back now to this black group with its strong cultural influence and American bias—or rather an American-cum-African bias, because you had people like 'cousin' Eleazor and 'uncle' Brown who had served during the first war in the Gold Coast and South Africa. There were men like these in every village and they returned to tell the story about our 'relatives' over there in Africa. On the American side, many of the blacks were becoming aware of Negro progress in the USA; they had their pictures of Booker T. Washington. And this was why Fredericks, Bruyning and another Eleazor called for the formation of that group I have mentioned: the Negro Progress Convention. When they wanted celebrities, they were able to call people like Madame Patty Brown, the great soprano from America. And on the scholarship side, they organized to send students not only to Europe but to places like McGill in Canada. Manitoba and other cities were quite an attraction, not just because of the wood or bauxite connection but because you had there almost the same English training, and the advantage of being able to make enough money in summer work to continue your studies for the rest of the year. These Canadian visitors were equally aware of Negro progress in America. And all of this American interest encouraged West Indians to make use of the quota system which allowed so many British citizens from the New World to enter the USA.

It was not, however, the Negro Convention that first stimulated interest in going northwards from Guyana, for prior to that period the building of the Panama Canal had had a tremendous impact. You could almost in fact say that it ruined the great development that had taken place in Guyana from 1880s. The Canal needed labour so badly that they were prepared to offer stupendous sums to attract people. Many of our boys therefore—even those who stood out—went over there. Take Dr. Milliard who went there after his long doctor's training in Edinburgh, and established himself there temporarily.[11] Too many of our kinsmen, however, were completely lost. So while it was easy enough to find such fellows retaining their self-respect when they went to Africa, once they entered the Christobole zone in Panama, they were submerged in a terrible

28

conflict between the various types of Africans or Negroes there. It was a hellish affair, what with the bunch of whores, and the Trinidad man emerging as a professional 'sweet man', living off immoral earnings. Yet taken altogether the people going off to Panama had a certain vogue, with their flannel trousers, slick jackets, their silk shirts and handkerchiefs at the neck. The only two groups that really succeeded there were the Jamaicans and the men from Barbados, because they were very hard with money. But the thing had a tremendous effect. The belief got around that by going to Panama in this American zone you could qualify after a few years to go to America itself. So many fellows left our place, some of whom, I was told, were clever or quite brilliant boys—only to be lost in this melting pot. Some took to women or drink; a few of these from fine families had been accomplished pianists and performers in Georgetown. You could see the same thing happening at the time the West Indian 'Bevin Boys' went to England after the outbreak of the Second World War. That, too, wreaked havoc upon the development and economy of Guyana, because you got highly skilled men going off to England, giving up their technology to become factory hands or workers on the Underground. On both occasions it was the Guyana community that suffered through the loss of some of its best talent. And perhaps the blame here lies with Britain for turning a blind eye to this Panama emigration. It was a tempting policy since starvation was widespread in some of the islands that contracted for canal labour. Jamaica, for instance, was bursting at the seams, because the property factor was still in the hands of vested interests, living in Europe and drawing in the rents.

What was interesting in this situation in Panama, however, was that you got a certain triumph of the masses over the middle class that we have seen emerging. 'Oh ho, you used to be schoolmaster. Now you're digging shovel like me!' The situation almost suffocated that educated element and levelled them out. 'While I may ask this man to write a letter for me, I remember at the same time making no money at home I couldn't talk to him; yet today he's in the rum shop talkin' big King George English.' There, too, you got the calypsos and these other things that now mirrored the social status of these people and their problems. At the end of their contract work, this educated element seldom returned; but the masses who had been nobodies did sometimes return. You could tell by the way they flaunted this Panama suit. It was the graduates of Queen's College who fell by the wayside.

Now within the context of Guyana, it was precisely this sort of failure that the Negro Convention was trying to combat. And even in my time there, before I left the country for America, I used to attend the meetings.[12] Cousin Talbot was a famous baritone singer; he sang and won prizes at some of these Convention occasions, while his sister Emmice was a notable poet. But this movement was all over the country, moving from one section to another in Convention, and telling the people of their lost heritage. How our forefathers had built up this country, and that we had better get together. One reason, of course, why it is now called the Co-operative Republic of Guyana was that Fredericks and others had been preaching this doctrine, plus the need for a new economy and a new outlook. They appealed to the gold miners who were living by fortuitous circumstances, advising them that the good days would not always be there: you are taking something from the earth that you cannot replace. I remember this advice exactly from these orators.

Of course the cultural side of this, as I suggested, was quite European, for nobody at that time would try to resurrect the folklore of the community. One might sing the odd Negro spiritual, but the stories of 'Nancy' (*Ananse*, the spider) and such things that remained from the African heritage, were not encouraged by the English.[13] Not like in America where it was thought better to let these niggers alone and let their culture take on an institutional form. Here, rather, the task was to make Englishmen out of you; so naturally you knew more about Shelley, Byron and reciting the sonnets than local songs. This is why it was always challenging to hear these people like the Fisk Jubilee Singers coming from America demonstrating their own folk music. Even with the calypso, I don't think Guyana is an ideal place to study this, because there it got so overlaid with the cultural setting of the eighteenth and nineteenth centuries. In Trinidad you had your celebrated calypso men, but the doggerels you found in Guyana were most likely borrowings and not new approaches.

There was a tiny hard core of the old music, but it was not really vital. Country people when they were having their weddings would knock the drum for twenty-one days. There would be other times when you would go to see these Congomen making their dance in the village—the wind-dance, fisherman-dance and so on. But nobody sought to exploit these things; one was just aware of them. Perhaps the best parallel is with the Zongo areas in Ghana, which have separate aliens; there outside the Ghanaian village communities you would get groups of Yoruba-men or some other musicians, with their different folk ways and habits. They had not surrendered to the central culture. So, too, in Guyana you'd get people saying 'Don't confuse me with those educated people; I'm a true African man.' They would talk like that, just as the man in Jamaica would mention, 'I'm a Nimba man' (one of the Gold Coast remnants), or 'I'm a Fanti man' or, 'My people belong to the Maroons that never paid taxes.' So you got these pockets in Jamaica, and if you went into some village there and people would tell you: 'That woman is one hundred years old: she's part of the Maroon affair,' then the whole village would lapse into the lingo of the Maroons. But none of this survival in the West Indies was as virile as the cults in Brazil where the people come out in their tens of thousands to celebrate the *mardi gras* festival.[14] That's where you see the old heathen cults and people with effigies on their faces.

Generally, however, these things have not been replenished, and the Negro Progress Convention which you would have expected to, did not take a strictly black revival line; it took rather the Negro-in-the-New-World line: the Booker T. Washington ideas about our being part of western society and our taking the best from it. That did not prevent us from sending some of our sons to share with our less fortunate African brothers, or collecting money to send for this or that missionary venture in Africa. Similarly, if one day news came of a ship in Georgetown with some African crew, people would take them round, invite them, and let them feel there is a link of brotherhood that way too.

We must differentiate, however, this respectable Negro Convention from the North American Garvey affair which was designed to incite you into blackness.[15] When you were a black man in Guyana and had attained the heights, there was nothing to bother you about being a black man; you knew it, but it made no difference. 'I'm a barrister at law; I sit with the governor. I go in my carriage and with my horses to the sea wall, and listen to the band playing Beethoven. If the other blacks in Africa and America are like me, then it's all right. So you don't have to talk to me about my blackness.' Garvey, on the other hand, was out to agitate you, making the masses know that the Indian man had a different culture. It was a racist doctrine, which fed on evidence of discrimination. But my social stratum was not kicked about in the community; it was able to go into the best store and buy what it wanted or try on the best boots; and if they didn't fit, one could say take them back, without any European daring to say that he did not want to try on those boots because some nigger had put his dirty feet into them.

But Garveyism did appeal to some sections despite this.[16] You have perhaps a young intellectual with his limited life, confined to the British Museum Reading Room in London. He may want to get away from this limitation, and being aware of modern trends, he reads about this fellow Marcus Garvey, this black man who had made the white Americans jitter. A man who has been able to mobilize 60,000 black people in Madison Square Gardens, and get them to realize that Africa is their homeland. Well, to the inquisitive young man this might seem worth investigating. So you had the *Negro World*, Garvey's paper, coming even to Guyana, and also some of our chaps—the Codrington and Queen's College graduates going to America and becoming part of Garvey's literary act. Someone like Louis Walrond (his father was a doctor) went there and was one of Garvey's staunch editorial fellows.[17] Anyone with any literary verve could play a valuable role in publicity.

Equally the average Negro dentist or doctor who was not a success at the time became very important props to the Garvey movement, because Garvey would say, 'Now, you have a black doctor; so go to him and show your loyalty. Prove you are free from racial inferiority.' In this way, therefore, in many of these colonies, the black people went over to Garvey because doing so brought about race consciousness and the awareness of spending your money where you can work. 'If the white man won't give you a job, then put your pennies together, establish a store and that coloured girl can work there.' People would suddenly see this. 'Look, that Indian man is taking his family to that Indian store; so what Garvey is saying is right.' The masses then who were unable to read for themselves but who had the *Negro World* read to them, would begin to say, 'Well, God give us a Garvey too!'

I saw and read the *Negro World* myself in Guyana. This man A. A. Thorne, a great scholar, had a bookshop not very far from the King George Hotel which was owned by my father in Georgetown. And I, along with Talbot who was much more racially conscious, used to go there and buy it,[18] sometimes with another friend of mine, Gorin, whose father was a successful miner. Thorne carried all these black magazines from America like the *Crisis*;[19] so we were not cut off from trends in America. It was quite simple, for American boats began to come to the port once a fortnight after the first war. Anyway, Garvey was such an important factor that even when a cynic like the editor of the *Standard* used an opportunity to attack Garvey, people would want to know why this 'mad' man in America was being castigated. There was a lot of information therefore, and people were expecting things to happen at any time.

But this interest in Garvey was not simply because he was a West Indian. Don't underestimate the divisions within the West Indies. The man from Guyana is such a tribalist that he says: 'Don't mix me up with this small little island people; I'm from a continent, while this island man has no place to move other than the sea. But when you see me you know you're seeing a South American.' Well, this is a dubious way of giving yourself some satisfaction. But there is the crucial factor of land involved. The Guyana man has land, plenty of land, and he's not Mr. Codrington's slave or the King of England's serf, for some of the King's relations still actually controlled these island estates in Barbados and elsewhere. You get the same contrast from the ditties: 'Twenty Barbadians live in a room, and not one of them will buy a broom; they're so stingy.' All right then, 'I'm a Guyanese; I'm a big man' shows you the tug-of-war between these places.

Again, all the islands have their different dialects to set them further apart. And general characteristics too. Guyanese would point out that they were not Barbadians who would always be ready to take Betsy out of their pockets and cut you long, wide and deep until the doctor couldn't stitch you. They got the same reputation for cutting as the Southern boys in the United States. The Jamaican, too, is meant to be cruel and rough, and not respectable; he'll break through anything. The Guyanese meanwhile was proud of being tarred with a little of the English brush and taking the gentlemanly air. Unfortunately, this was all the prevailing norm, and did cause a lot of trouble within the groups.

For all this, there was something in Garvey's opinion and philosophy to make most of us stop and reflect why the black man was making no headway. He made you think of the golden age of Guyana with boatbuilders like Massey I mentioned, and made you wonder what had happened. I felt this myself when I went back to Guyana much later, and saw this deluge myself—Indians all over the place, in the celebrated family houses of Georgetown. They'd bought and occupied them. And although this was later on, it was already a situation that the Fredericks group was beginning to attack.[20] They did not really get down to the basic factors as I would have liked to tackle them. Many of these folk going up to the diamondiferous areas did not lack the pioneering spirit, but did not know how to consolidate their gains. They rushed off to Georgetown or their village to build a great house with their money, but when they returned to the hinterland they did not take any black-eyed peas or crops to develop.

Similarly after the First World War, with growing unemployment among the returned soldiers, and their being offered a gratuity and twenty acres each, the Fredericks group did not attempt to analyse the economics of this settlement scheme. In fact from a Marxian point of view you can see Fredericks and others with their legalism as turning the edge of the class struggle and preventing it from deepening. No one tried to analyse why that particular scheme failed. This was tragic for it is necessary in this whole question of Negro settlement schemes to look at the Israeli example and even that of Lloyd George breaking up the large estates into ten acres to create a new yeoman class in England. The blacks have yet to study or borrow the techniques of the whites in this settlement business; they have never set up institutes where the future settlers are made to realize that they are going to succeed and not to fail. But if you look at black settlement ventures from Liberia in the 1820s, you can see that it was only fate that kept those people going; while in Sierra Leone, the parallel scheme, it was more the European doggedness and the friends of the blacks that perpetuated the venture at the crucial times. Too often, also, the really talented blacks did not go at all, or if they did, they were driven out of the scheme like the celebrated Edward Blyden.[21]

NOTES TO CHAPTER 2

1 See further, R. T. Smith, 'Economic Aspects of Rice Production in the East Indian Community in British Guiana' in *Social and Economic Studies*, vi, 4 (December 1957), pp. 502-22.

2 For an example of these village council constitutions, see R. T. Smith, *The Negro Family in British Guiana*, op. cit., p. 17.

3 For Moore and Wood, see G. Padmore, *Pan-Africanism or Communism?* (London, 1956) p. 195. For the Aborigines Rights Protection Society in the Gold Coast, see David Kimble, *A Political History of Ghana* (Oxford, 1963), chs. 10 and 11. References to West Indians in West Africa in the nineteenth century may be followed up in C. Fyfe, *A History of Sierra Leone* (Oxford, 1962), in index under Afro-West Indians.

4 On the various West Indian missions which established themselves in West Africa after emancipation, see C. P. Groves, op. cit., ch. 2, 'Contribution from the Caribbean'.

5 The most recent account of the first Pan-African Conference is contained in J. Langley, 'West African Aspects of the Pan-African Movements: 1900-1945' (University of Edinburgh Ph.D. thesis, 1968). Fredericks was certainly at the First Pan-African Congress of 1919 in Paris, see also ch. 9, p. 148.

6 In 1924 the officers of the Negro Progress Convention were E. F. Fredericks (president); T. T. Nichols (vice-president); J. A. Dingwall (treasurer); and E. P. Bruyning (secretary); see enclosures in Sir Graeme Thomson to J. H. Thomas (Secretary of State for the Colonies), 9 April 1924, C.O. 111/652, Public Record Office (P.R.O.), London. Unlike the mass base of the U.N.I.A. the government considered the Convention to have 'been organized by a small group of educated negroes, lawyers, doctors and ministers of religion'.

7 Critchlow's part in the Georgetown riots is documented in Thomson to the Secretary of State for the Colonies, 13 April 1924, C.O. 111/652, P.R.O.

8 For the Manchester Conference, see ch. 10, pp. 163-8.

9 Gandhi's attitude to Africans in South Africa is usefully explored in P. F. Power, 'Gandhi in South Africa', in *Journal of Modern African Studies*, vii (October 1969), no. 3, pp. 441-55.

10 For the Jagan-Burnham dispute, see below ch. 11, p. 193.

11 See further ch. 9, p. 133 for Milliard in England. Garvey's attitude to the conditions of workers in Panama can be gathered in E. D. Cronon, *Black Moses* (Madison, 1966 edn.), pp. 14-15.

12 In addition to singing, Talbot and Makonnen were both much in demand as after-dinner speakers: 'I would tell him about his delivery and he about mine. We both patterned ourselves after a brother of mine, Joe Talbot, who was a spell binder.' (Talbot, interview, Addis Ababa, 1970.)

13 An account of the use these originally Akan folktales were put to in Jamaica is contained in H. O. Patterson, op. cit., p. 249.

14 Writing on Afro-Brazilian cults is extensive; see, however, M. J. Herskovits, *The New World Negro* (Minerva Press, 1969 edn.), pp. 226-65. Also D. Pierson, *Negroes in Brazil* (Chicago, 1942).

15 See, for instance, A. Jacques Garvey (compiler), *Philosophy and Opinions of Marcus Garvey;* also Cronon, op. cit.

16 The earliest mention of the impact of Garveyism in British Guiana is contained in Governor Collet to Milner, 10 May 1919, C.O. 111/623, P.R.O., where it is noted that the *Negro World* is one of a number of Afro-American papers being sold in increasing numbers. By 1921, one of Garvey's representatives, Rev. Richard Hilton Tobitt, an Antiguan, had been holding meetings in Guiana under U.N.I.A. auspices, and had been supported by the British Guiana Labour Union in selling subscriptions to the *Black Star* line. Collet to Churchill, 7 June 1921, C.O. 318/364, P.R.O.

17 For Walrond's role in the *Negro World*, see Cronon, op. cit., p. 46. An example of Walrond's prose style can be found in A. Locke, (ed.), *The New Negro* (Atheneum reprint, New York, 1969), pp. 115-26.

18 Talbot's reaction to the *Negro World* is interesting: 'What did stimulate us was the *Negro World*—it gave us a stronger idea of sometime joining in the atmosphere that was greater than the local one. We used to sit down and read that paper together. The fellow Garvey was fiery. We were thinking we might be part and parcel of this thing, but didn't know how.' (Addis Ababa, 1970.)

19 The *Crisis*, the publication of the National Association for the Advancement of Coloured People (edited by DuBois), generally had less international news than the *Negro World*, but at this particular post-war period it gave wide coverage to the series of Pan-African Congresses in Europe.

20 It should be noted that a major reason for the formation of the Convention was to combat the growing power of the East Indian population. One of its main programmes was to encourage greater African immigration to the colony from West and South Africa. See, for instance, 'Memorandum of "Reasoned Statement" submitted by the Negro Progress Convention on behalf of the Negro population of British Guiana to His Excellency the Governor, Sir Graeme Thomson, K.C.B.' (Georgetown, 1924), enclosure in Thomson to Thomas, 9 April 1924, C.O. 111/652, P.R.O.

21 The most useful treatment of Blyden's involvement in settlement schemes in Sierra Leone and Liberia is H. Lynch, *Edward Wilmot Blyden: Pan-Negro Patriot* (London, 1967).

CHAPTER 3

THE BLACK YMCA:
FROM GEORGETOWN TO TEXAS

COMING from an environment in the capital of my country dominated largely by middle-class values, it was natural for me and members of my circle to be influenced by the visible expressions of those values; I mean particularly the Anglican church, the Roman Catholic cathedral, the Methodist Wesleyan church, the Monrovian Brethren, also by the Society for the Propagation of the Gospel (SPG) which we called Spug. Of course other religious groups also operated throughout the country, but the prevailing culture was Christian, and the main customary festivals we observed were those linked to the Christian Church, such as the Passion Plays at Easter.

At other times, Chinatown would be resplendent with its myriad of lights and beautiful balloons, lanterns and explosives; and the Indian group had their *puja* (prayers), a colourful sight in those pyramidal temples. There was then an abundance of coloured paper beautifully designed, and the accompaniment of drums, cymbals and flutes. While therefore the Chinese and Indians were able to embrace with pride their own national festivals, the Negro or African community in the country had a hybrid festival. During August, for instance, there were thanksgiving services—thanks to God for their emancipation from four hundred years of slavery. These and other occasions brought out the fife and drum, the brass bands along with masquerades, men-on-stilt turns. A carnival. And needless to say, I found it very difficult to restrain my emotions. I could always be found with the dancers, outdancing them, but there was usually a price to pay for my hilarity; condemnation from my father who

37

took the opportunity to point out that I would never amount to anything more than a ruffian if I mixed with that side of things. There was this emphasis on middle-class values; you must suppress your emotions, and sit at proper concerts listening to cantatas.

But there was always the temptation to be with a bunch of troubadours, chanterers; singing the latest candles about 'woman who don't know a good man, then your puckanpanamy will make you run'—partly in patois. You get the same sort of division in Ghana and other parts of Africa today. It's not necessarily the 'cultured' element that is creating the culture — I mean the boys from the university. In fact, most of the calypso boys are ordinary chaps, ruffians, nondescript fellows in the community with no status. In this sense I'm talking about a mass-culture in the West Indies, because the masses were setting the pace. Not a particularly high pace either, for if you really knew your high-life songs and transcribed the patois into English, you would find it frustrating; they all boil down to sex and woman talk. Now there may be higher forms in some of the islands, but generally when you take these famous calypsonians like Lord Kitchener,[1] and strip down their material, there's nothing else.

Some had naturally been to college, and had learnt a little bit of poetry to hide it, but on the whole it was a very low type of culture which we now call West Indian—as if all our problems are sociological, and deal merely with man and woman relationships. You know the songs—all about the girl being born out of wedlock, or the father who was not the father. They gave the impression that our main concern was the loose marital ties, whereas the Negro spirituals in America had a more divine form. They had a type of rebellious attitude towards the *status quo*; they suggested that the 'massah' was not altogether what he should be, and even if the forms did not allow you to sing of the master being a terrible tyrant openly, you could mould the spirituals to make the same point in a deceptive way.

But let's look more closely at the Georgetown culture. On these festive occasions you had the choral groups of the churches—whatever the status of the particular churches—gathering with the congregations to perform cantatas in the town hall. It was a big competitive event drawing choral groups from all over the country, and prizes being given out for the performance and the perpetuation of a culture that was not natural to the community. And it was not natural because in the plantation days the lords and nobles in the big house had dictated the forms, and then in turn the missionaries, when they came, became the watchdogs of the same culture. They were successful, too, in making the people afraid of nonconformity with their own norms. Thus when once or twice a year you had a murder trial, everybody throughout the country talked about it as something beyond the pale. And even with much lesser crimes, there was none of the tendency to examine the larger sociological factors behind the crime. Instead the clergy and others did not hesitate to show that the chap who was out of step with the norms of the community was really the devil.

Perhaps in time this created a sort of character that was afraid of nonconformity. A great reverence for 'standards'. So you got the same attitude to the policeman as you had in Britain. You respected the cop, but if he married your sister or your daughter, then you were afraid. Because you were told this man had taken a pledge even to arrest his own mother if it was warranted! The people who adopted these values were of course the doctors, lawyers, engineers—the men who mattered. A middle class but not quite like their opposites in Britain. For in Britain you would not get these people dressing up their butlers and maids in uniform and headdress, and then sending them round to the neighbour to borrow the paper! Yet this was done in Georgetown without any loss of face.

In music, then, you had this division between the middle-class element with their quadrilles and waltzes, while the lower-class element indulged in its masquerades, singing these terrible songs, but neither of these styles derived from Africa; that strain had already departed. If you examined the masquerade with its grotesque figures, you would see the features of the Portugee, his nose and his beard—the Vasco da Gama appearance. Always the cult of the top-hat, and the bat-wing or opera collar; and even when the devil was being whipped in effigy, he was still wearing that top-hat. Really, then, these were survivals from seventeenth and eighteenth century Europe rather than 'African survivals'. However, in the much larger and elaborate carnivals of Brazil and Trinidad there may well be an element of African form even if the content has been completely lost. I'm thinking of these months of preparation that each of the carnival groups takes to make up its songs and dresses, the competitive element. This system of competing guilds resembles some of the groupings among the Akan, or from Nigeria; there, too, you get, during the artistic festivals and the thanksgiving festivals to the gods at harvest time, groups of sculptors and designers preoccupied in preparing their guilds for the great occasion. But you can't trace much of this in the Santa P boys of Guyana with their flannel trousers, silk shirts and neckcloths; these seem closer to the English barrow boys than to West Africa.

I've already mentioned the obeah man, the devil incarnate, in the Guyanan context; there were still traces of the practice in my time, but the Christian church had played an important role in crushing all these symbols of the devil. The Guyanans had adopted the attitudes of their white missionaries, and even where you had the blacks going to Africa as missionaries, you would hear the same theme sung about the people of darkness who had embraced the devil. That is why they tried to isolate the fetish of the African community by drawing young boys into a Christian community that condemned the fetish. And in fact it was not until our own time, in the 1930s and 1940s, that the missionaries (black and white) came under attack for this cultural imperialism. Look back to the New World blacks who went to Liberia and Freetown, and you will see that they did not separate themselves from the missionary stance, but joined with them in full condemnation of fetishism and African practices that might creep into worship. With this analysis one can appreciate at this moment why there is a certain amount of anti-West Indian feeling in some parts of Africa. They appeared to have lost completely their own culture, they were different and de-classed; most important, they had joined with missionaries in trying to destool us Africans, and root out our polygamous beliefs.[2]

There were a number of institutions in Guyana which rein-forced the middle class element in these foreign values. The British administration set the tone; so when the governor and his wife got up and led the way in functions, there were plenty who wanted to follow. You had to accept the governor's values— seeing you had none of your own. Similarly as you did not have any amenities at home, you aspired to go to England for universities or qualifications. At dances or balls you would bring out your daughters in the governor's presence.

But an institution which was influential in confirming these middle-class values was the YMCA. Through the tennis, swimming and Bible classes were projected some of the central philosophical insights of the founder George Williams. We were pointed back to the early YMCA days in England after 1844, the drudgery of the drapery shops, and were told how Williams, this fellow from a nonconformist home, saw the dissipation of his colleagues in their work. He founded therefore a small Bible study group, so they could meet and pray. Then they set about examining themselves away from dissipation, gambling and the other temptations, and gradually the YMCA movement began to emphasize the whole man—body, mind and spirit— they tried to portray Christ, the Galilean, as a man who resisted whores, and who built up a sterling character against evil by hard work.

I learnt a great deal more about the philosophy later on, when I became connected with the YMCA in America. But there, too, the philosophy quickly found its way amongst young working men. Large sums of money were given to build up hostels so that the men, after long hours of work, would not go to the nearest joint to get drunk, but would instead return to the YMCA hostel for comfortable accommodation, and next morning, fresh as a fiddle, these men would be back at their jobs. You can therefore look at this arrangement as a tool of the industrialists, as well as a medium of middle-class values. These capitalists did not therefore hesitate to give large sums of money to build up YMCA hostels all over the USA. It is interesting to note that in America it somewhat changed from the 'Y' we had known in Guyana; there it had been a strait-laced affair of Bible classes; but in America you got an emphasis on physical culture. The 'Y' helped to create colleges for physical education to portray in a most dramatic manner the role of Christ in the modern world—this carpenter who had to have fine muscles to be able to hack his way through the tremendous amount of wood in front of him. You couldn't really engage in vice if you wanted to emulate the Galilean.

There was a certain similarity between the forces creating black and white YMCAs. The latter met the needs of those

41

Italians, Irish, Finns or whatever, who might otherwise have got lost in a rooming house with questionable landladies. Your 'Y' membership from Chicago made you welcome in New York or wherever your work took you. Now for black boys coming up from the Deep South, or other areas where inter-racial mixing was very difficult, the coloured men's branch of the YMCA was evolved. Strictly speaking, of course, only one Central YMCA was allowed in any town, but you got round this racial difficulty by allowing the formation of separate coloured branches. And the coloured community in turn put a great effort into building up its own branches; there was the concept of the community chest—the putting aside of a day's wages—and then the hope that some great industrialist or philanthropist would help out. When for instance Booker T. Washington and others were trying to raise $25,000 for a coloured men's branch in Wabash Avenue, Chicago, Rosenwald heard of it and was stupefied to know that this community noted for its poverty was coming together to raise this sum.[3] He offered them a challenge to their self-help scheme: 'If you raise $25,000, I shall give you $50,000'. And in ten days' time they were able to raise the original sum. Rosenwald continued with the same principle for the 'Y' in Harlem at 135th Street and 7th Avenue.

Although the branches frequently represented various nationality groups, and had their own Italian, German or black 'Y' secretaries, at the higher level the 'Y' spirit was intended to bring about interracial, and international, harmony. This was the idea of the great 'Y' organizer, J. R. Mott; he did not hesitate to establish the YMCA in Jerusalem, in the belief that it would bring about better relations between the Arabs, the Jews and the Christian elements. There was a definite conviction that the bringing together of various nationalities would make for peace. This was one reason why you found the 'Y' playing the same sort of role during the Great War as the Red Cross—showing Christianity in action. The spirit was one of learning from each other; so when 'Y' secretaries went for instance to China, they discovered they had to know something about agriculture and the other rural sciences, if they wanted to penetrate the peasantry. In fact, these secretaries from places like Cornell were pleasantly surprised that rather than teaching when they got there, they were learning from the Chinese in matters of poultry husbandry and egg incubation.

In America the YMCA would identify the social problems of the area and use them to appeal to industrialists. After pointing to juvenile delinquency, you would say to the financiers: 'What is a city without its "square boys and square men"? '—i.e. men on the level. I remember vividly in my days as a 'Y' secretary in America this was a favourite term; the appeal would go: 'A city may be very beautifully designed with its architectural expression, but what about the boys of the community? It's your square boys who will uphold these things for you. Otherwise when you see juvenile delinquency amongst the coloured boys stretching to such a height, the city won't be safe for anybody. Give to the 'Y'!'

There was also the high 'Y' as we called the high school counterparts. You would go there and conduct classes on the Christian way of life. A high 'Y' club would be established, and in it there would be no emphasis on emotionalism but the boys would train to sing Negro spirituals. And then you could challenge the white community for funds by taking the high 'Y' glee club to the Central 'Y' where these bankers and industrialists would come to hear these nigger boys sing like that. 'Hell, Mak,' they'd say, 'you've done a fine job; your nigger boys deserve a camp.' They saw themselves as bridging a gap between the communities, and were probably sincere men. Take MacFadden, the chairman of the Central 'Y'. He was an oil millionaire with 200 square miles of territory, and probably in his father's day, the family may have had very good nigger slaves. But he saw these nigger boys as doing wonders in their recitations and, being the chairman, he was well able to co-opt other big men to give aid.

You could, I suppose, look at their motives with some cynicism; but obviously they were not indifferent to human values. Mr. Burley, chairman of the Texas National Bank, would not find it difficult amongst his friends to recognize me, wave his hat and speak with some degree of distinction: 'You 'Y' men are broad-minded—you're helping to save our civilization, preventing us from all becoming Ku Kluxers. Otherwise there would be signs all over Beaumont, Texas, "Nigger, read and run. If you can't read, run anyhow".'

The attempt that we secretaries made was to try to narrow the gap between the extreme proletariat and the rich. So we had camps for these boys and took them there for training like scouts. Something of the same spirit was involved in those communities in which I worked around the Magnolia Petroleum Company in Texas. It employed about 60,000 blacks, and the conditions under which they lived were really awful. Now, before long we were able to prevail upon the company to establish a famous high school, and I was also able to get a brass band of sixty pieces given to the workers. You may say that this was really a device to keep them out of trade unions, which it did of course. At lunch time therefore when you had an hour's break, and had eaten your sandwich, you lay down on the grass and heard our boys playing away. Well, it kept you out of mischief; but certainly if you had had any of these radical IWW fellows around, they would have said: 'This is all shit —let's get together and destroy the bosses'.[4]

Still, our black boys taught by their white conductor became quite famous in the community. And subsequently as the band developed, parties were given and despite the laws of Texas, the big boss of the company would come round and shake hands with these fellows. In a way, though, the YMCA discouraged strikes in the sense that it instilled the value of human relations at all cost in industry. Hence you got the involvement of big people like Procter and Gamble of the soap company, and Bell Telephone, becoming involved in the 'Y' movement. They discussed the eight-hour day, and were greatly concerned that the lowering of the day's work would lend itself to too much leisure and a lot of evil. Here you could see how they could be appealed to by the 'Y' people, and it was no accident that they supported a lot of university research on this aspect of labour problems.

Particularly at the university level you found the 'Y' making its way, and frequently you would associate YMCA secretaries with a knowledge of sociology. This was certainly the case with the famous young coloured international secretary, Max Yergan[5]; he was entering a profession which had a high calling and also demanded a deep knowledge of sociology. The need for a good grasp of sociology had been sharpened after the Great War when the blacks from the Deep South flooded into the North, and calamitous effects took place—bad housing, terrible living conditions, immorality, incest and other things.[6] It sparked off the foundation of the Urban League, and forced the 'Y' people to find out what was happening. Especially amongst the blacks in the 'Y' was the fear that these frightful conditions would be used as propaganda against blacks in general. People might well, it was feared, begin to point to these new ghettos, and show how blacks there were resorting to a form of life close to slavery: 'You see these niggers; they never change. You thought that by levelling things up it would help. No! They're all the same damn thing.' These were the factors that brought an awakening in the universities and land-grant colleges, producing basic studies on urbanization and its problems. The YMCA secretaries tended therefore to take this sociology, to help them deal with crime and the breaking up of homes. If you like, they were a new form of social worker.

Soon schools and colleges were established with large endowments to incorporate the 'Y' principles: Lake Geneva, Wisconsin and Boston, for instance. And it wasn't only religion; the Galilean was used as the example of the man who went beyond his own tribal background to assist his fellow men, bringing men from their provincial outlooks to a broader view. And in America we see this principle embodied in the thinking of Mott, Reinhold Neibuhr, Kirby Page and others, rebellious men and international. It was the same type that Mott tried to encourage to join the coloured men's YMCA. So these new black intellectuals had a job cut out to inspire a new spirit of identity in the raw negroes (as they were called) coming up to Chicago and New York after the war.[6] They deliberately set up their homes and hostels naming them after celebrated personalities in black history, like this chaste Negro poet Phyllis Wheatley or like Paul Lawrence Dunbar. These were people who like the Galilean were not narrowly religious.

This was the mould of the new recruits to the 'Y'. They had been to white theological seminaries, and got away from the emotionalism of the Negro Baptists towards the reason of the Presbyterians. They were professionals and to them their work in the 'Y' was the same philosophy that underlay Christian socialism. You can see it illustrated in the invitation to the Duke of Windsor to come and address this body; this was because in a way he had shown some solidarity with the workers in the great speech he had just made in Wales about 'the way I see my people live . . . and I would not tolerate it'. It marked him as having some sympathy with the workers. The same thing might be said of Wellington Koo of China, who could have been merely another banker, but had this international concern, as well as being involved with the nationalist tradition of Sun Yat-sen. Koo's sister was later the wife of Chiang Kai-shek, and had been educated in the famous girls' school of Hunter College in New York.[7] She, like Koo, was able to make appeals for the YWCA, capitalizing on this 'Y' feeling of identity of interests across race. So these white women, bankers' wives and others, felt an obligation upon them: 'Our sister, Mrs. Chiang Kai-shek . . . these are after all the people, my dear, with whom we are linked by tradition and custom, and we must do everything possible to help them in their travail. We can count upon them.' In a way they were right, for Sun Yat-sen became involved with Lenin and others in the Communist affair, while Koo and Chiang Kai-shek maintained the *status quo*. Possibly Koo during his 'Y' period and contact with America had had his conviction strengthened that the capitalist system and way of life would be ideal; that you could have nobility and wealth, provided you gave a little away to the cause of lesser men.

At any rate this internationalism was embodied in all the major YMCA conferences in North America. I cannot remember any conference being concerned only with American affairs. You would never have a conference dealing with segregation in America without bringing out the parallels in England and India, and throughout it all the feeling of trying to bring about accord. This was certainly behind Mott's moves with the irreconcilable Jews and Arabs; I may be maligning him, but he probably even felt that placing this huge Christian investment in the middle of Jerusalem would actually prevent the suzerainty of any single race. There at the one YMCA Arabs and Jews could meet round the same table, play games together and forget; and so you would be able to create a new race of men.[8] With so many of these international scholars like him you had the faith in the possibility of Pauline conversion: that one little point made in conference might divest people of their hostile traditions and they would see the light and become new men.

My own idea during my 'Y' period was to look for ideas, and while digesting them, investigate the behaviour of my colleagues. But then I had come into the 'Y' movement in a rather roundabout way. I had just arrived in America from Cuba in the early thirties, and I was on my way to study mineralogy at San Saba, Texas. When I got to New Orleans I met a man called Moscow from Jamaica. He had bought an old tin lizzie, a Ford, for about $100, and after I had calculated what it would cost me for my train fare to Texas, I decided to be a partner with him in this car. We started from New Orleans, went through Orange, Louisiana, and one afternoon reached Beaumont, Texas. We fetched up in Rampart Street where the Negroes had their own taxis and restaurants. We went in to have dinner in one of these, and a rather charming waitress was very friendly to us all at once. We inquired where we might stay, since there was only the white (or central) YMCA in Beaumont at that time. 'Oh,' she says, 'a countryman of yours (thinking presumably that all these West Indians and Africans are from the same place) is in town', and she directed us to a Dr. Graham.

This man turned out to be a Buxtonian from my own village; I knew his people. He was one of those who had come across and taken his school work at Talladega College, then gone on to seminary at Oberlin Theological College, where he had got his doctorate and become a Congregational minister. He illustrated in his own way the point I was making about the new theology, for he knew all about the sociology of community work, and saw that the community centre with its volleyball and basketball was as important a side of Christianity as the church. This community emphasis was all the more vital in the South, for the prevailing white philosophy was that black boys should not play at anything except picking cotton—meaning that as these blacks sang while they worked, there was no need to build them a place where they could sing and relax in their leisure.

Graham greeted us, and fixed us up with accommodation at a Mrs. Lee's, a Negro lady married to a man who I'm certain was a European but preferred to take Negro status. He owned a filling station and was quite a gentleman. We stayed there overnight, and in the morning went over to see Dr. Graham.

47

He wasted no time in letting us know what he thought about our priorities, and began to lecture me on failing to realize the age I was living in: 'You may be a successful mineralogist, and go back and mark out large concessions. But if you had more knowledge how much more you could do with these material things! Right here in Beaumont there's a chance for you to acquire that knowledge.' It really haunted me. Then he told Moscow; 'There's a job for you here; this community is growing. There are builders but no electricians, and here you are, a state-registered electrician with experience in Chicago and other places.' We hung around town a little longer, and met another West Indian, Dr. Borden from St. Kitts, who was a great Baptist scholar. He was a short stocky man, powerful and linked with the black businessmen in that community. In no time he had converted Moscow to the idea of starting his business there.

I was left on the horns of the dilemma in the face of these other values, until finally Graham took me to meet Hasting Harrison, the white secretary of the central YMCA. My plans were explained, and Harrison discovered in a sort of quiz that I knew all about the YMCA, its philosophy and organization, because those of us in Guyana who were a part of it had indulged a great deal in analysing its workings. As a result of this conversation, I was privileged to walk into the doors of the Central 'Y', and participate in some of their activities twice a week. In the month of June Harrison told me that a conference was to be held during a three months' course at the Lake Geneva YMCA at Wisconsin; a number of outstanding personalities from Asia were to be present;[8] and the Central 'Y' would only be too happy to pay my expenses; it might help me to make up my mind. I was ready to accept, because in the interval I had not much to do, and had been helping Moscow by stretching his wires, and just getting to know some of the local community and even speaking a little in young people's classes. So I went off to Lake Geneva— it must have been 1928 or 1929.[9]

I met so many fine products of the 'Y' there that when I returned I offered my services full-time. And for three years I worked in the community, organizing the activities in schools and the high 'Y' clubs. To begin with we just rented a shop as an office as there was no other suitable accommodation thereabout. I started sounding out a number of businesses like the Magnolia Petroleum Company, and finally with Graham and Professor Tatum (another Negro, head of a primary school), we prepared a budget for the amount of money it would take to launch a YMCA in Beaumont for the blacks. So much for salary, so much for two floors of premises in College Street.[10] Then we worked out a programme for a black businessman's club, to be addressed largely by white speakers, who, it was hoped, would help to pave the way financially. We presented the budget, and it was accepted right away. The 'Y' was launched and in no time MacFadden had actually offered some of his land for a camp site. Well, the news got around that we had launched this project in record time, and I was consequently asked to speak at various Negro colleges—Prairie View, Texas College in Houston, Paul Quinn College, Marshall, Wiley and Bishop Colleges. And a small number of white friends invited me to Bulor College which was the first college that started work amongst the Indians in America. At the same time I was attending the State conference, and it was not difficult to win the concern of people there if you had anything in you. Most of the white 'Y' people I met were Southern boys with the exception of a man Dean from Boston. He was a radical of the first water and would use his radicalism largely in Negro colleges, but when he was with the white boys, he was too scared.

It was at the wider level of the international conference that this 'Y' spirit of concern and radicalism was most marked. When, for instance, we met in Toronto, everything was solemn. Most speakers pointed to the tragedy of the gap between the rich and the poor. The mood of that period reflected the deepening crisis, and this was felt not only in the 'Y' but in the Federal Council of Churches in America. Serious questions were confronting men. What was going to be done with the unemployment problem—the collapse of the stock market? What values, not transient, but a new yardstick, were going to sustain people through a period of crisis? All the great names of the movement were there or were mentioned—Kadara of Japan, Arun, the Christianized Indian and our own Max Yergan. I already knew of the existence of these men through reading the 'Y's Men, where all the work in the field was reported. And the next year I met Max for the first time; I would meet him again later in connection with our pan-African work, but at that time

49

in 1934 (I think) he was still associated closely with developing the work of the 'Y' in Fort Hare, South Africa.[11] He told me something of the tragedy of the Bantu students, and possibly when he met these great thinkers in the 'Y', and saw the drift of the period, he expected some really powerful support. Quite likely it was contact with the rebel element in the churches— people like the Presbyterian A. J. Muste, that made him more rebellious on his return to South Africa, and helped to bring about his break from the YMCA as international secretary.

It was also at that particular conference that Wellington Koo made an observation which I have remembered as summing up the essence of the 'Y' approach: 'Gentlemen, the theme of our conference is Youth Adventure with God, and being adventuresome, anything may happen. But whatever we may do, whatever might be the bitterness that our belief may drive us to, let us pledge ourselves to differ, but while we differ, let us differ to agree. Because if we agree, whatever may be our differences, we shall gain something. But to leave here without some degree of agreement, would be chaotic. And there'll be no place for us in the world when we come to mend bridges.'

NOTES TO CHAPTER 3

1 See further ch. 10, p. 173.

2 For West Indian-African hostility, see ch. 17, p. 277.

3 The operations of the Rosenwald Fund in improving Negro rural schools, and encouraging self-help in education, can be gathered from the Rosenwald Fund Archives, Fisk University, Nashville, Tenn.

4 For an account of IWW (Industrial Workers of the World) activities during the early 1920s, see I. Howe and L. Coser, *The American Communist Party* (New York, 1962 edn.), pp. 12-16.

5 The career of Max Yergan in the YMCA in East and South Africa is referred to in K. J. King, 'The American Negro as Missionary to East Africa', *African Historical Studies*, Spring 1970.

6 A useful account of Southern Negro migration into Chicago during and after the First World War is A. H. Spear's, *Black Chicago* (Chicago, 1967).

7 I am indebted to Professor Cuyler Young for pointing out that while Mrs. Chiang Kai-Shek may have matriculated in Hunter College, she certainly did her undergraduate work in Wellesley. Dr. Wellington Koo was at different times Prime Minister of China, Minister for Foreign Affairs, Chinese Ambassador to Britain, and Chief Delegate to the League of Nations.

8 The records of many of the outstanding international secretaries are retained in the

YMCA Historical Library, New York. See further, K. Latourette, *A History of the World Service* (New York, 1947).

9 According to Talbot, Makonnen was in Cornell during 1932-4, since he came through from there to Talbot's graduation in 1934. Apparently his going to Cornell to study agriculture was tied in with some contacts Makonnen had made during his YMCA Texas period. Talbot believed that after qualifying in agriculture, he had at one point intended to go back to Texas, 'buy land, open a farm and be independent'.

10 Makonnen's exact address at this time was 746 College Street, Beaumont, Texas.

11 Yergan broke with the YMCA co-operative approach to South Africa in March 1936.

CHAPTER 4

WASHINGTON, DUBOIS, GARVEY, AND THE WEST INDIAN DIASPORA

A LL of us had heard about Washington and DuBois when we were growing up in Georgetown, but it wasn't until I had reached America myself that I was able to put discussions about them into some sort of perspective. The controversy between Booker Washington and DuBois is often considered to be about whether Negroes should have industrial or classical education. Generally, however, this argument was carried on in the Negro world without any grasp of what America at large was doing with her revolution in industrial technology. White American leaders had long ago discovered that the country was entering into a new period. Slavery had been abolished, and, in addition, new immigrants were flocking into the country looking for work with pay. The economy had to take on a new form, and much of this was aimed at the mechanization of agriculture, grain preservation, canning and allied industries. There was much talk in the agricultural states of the need for a free flow of goods and commodities. Facing all this, Washington feared that the abolition of slavery had left millions of Negroes anxious to enter the free market, but without the necessary skills to meet the demands; he thought also that foreign labour entering would be a disaster for the Negro. He conceived, therefore, a proposal for a form of industrial education that might prepare the Negro to enter American life. However, the skills he was proposing for Negro youths were already being outdated by the technology of the new land-grant colleges.[1]

There was nothing particularly creative in Washington's demands for industrial education, for all across America the agricultural and mechanical colleges had been trying to cope with the needs of the new technology, just as Bismarck had established his technical high schools to maintain the growth of German industry and agriculture. Nor should we accept DuBois's criticism of Washington as valid; it looks as if he was not concerned with ideas but just assailing the man, because Washington had been more successful than him in gaining the ear of the philanthropists.[2] Whether Washington even understood the philanthropic urge from the North is another matter. For the philanthropic era was in a way a continuation of the Civil War by other means; they had had the fighting first and then the intervention with the Carpet-baggers. Finally in the 1880s and 1890s it looked as if the way to keep the Union together without a further confrontation was for the North to take out of its own pockets the cash for Negro education which the Southern States ought to have been providing. So Washington was really in a cul-de-sac; he couldn't attack Virginia or Alabama and demand equal education. Instead he played along with the White South, as Banda does with Vorster in South Africa, and meanwhile he encouraged the missionary element in the North to come to the aid of the blacks.

There is the parallel with Africa here, for we can claim that the missionary movement in the continent gave tremendous openings to the British lower middle class. People whose fathers were coal-miners could get a little high school education, go to a theological college and to Africa. He would return to tell the story of millions of people who had never heard the word of God. This in turn gave the father a new status in the community. 'That boy George who was with us and might have become a pit-hand, today is helping to clear out some of the doubts of the Empire.' A large number of people entered the missionary field for that reason. And so it was in America; Booker Washington by his appeal for the darkies provided a new outlet for a large class of do-gooders, without realizing the historical realities. The trouble was that the white folk from the North who came to help these poor devils were not as well qualified as the other whites who were teaching mechanics and agriculture to the sons of the white 'crackers'.[3] Often the teachers for the white schools and colleges came from Harvard, MIT or Yale, but what was the status of these white fellows going to the Negro colleges? Like those who went to Africa in the missionary group, perhaps only one in a hundred was highly qualified.

They had their dedication though, and needed it, for the South looked on these white teachers at Fisk, Hampton and other Negro colleges as goody-goody fellows and nigger lovers: 'Why should we tolerate them? How do we know that they are not even niggers themselves—during the colonial days they might have been mixed up with niggers. That's why they are showing so much love; because no decent white man who understands that he is superior could allow himself to teach on a par with these niggers.' This, of course, was the more extreme white approach, but even at the academic level there was the writing of people like Stoddard and others demonstrating that there was no visible evidence of black equality with white. Such writers should not be underestimated; they were very dramatic and bold, and had tried to show that any black who had done anything in America had done so through having a little white blood in his veins. Even the philanthropists who did not come out in the open and accept this race writing, had little islands of doubt lurking in their minds.[4] And the same thing is true today even when the whites in many parts of Africa are actually working under black bosses—the same lurking suspicion about black inability.

So we have to get away from this false dichotomy between industrial and classical education if we are to understand what DuBois and Washington were arguing about. DuBois did not fully realize that the mode of education he was fighting for was widely considered to have been a disaster in India.[5] She had gone all out for it and had mastered the very thing that DuBois felt would be the saviour for Negro training. Finally the other aspect of their controversy was really a personal one—a cultural or mental conflict between DuBois who felt an intellectual contempt for Washington—the contempt of the Harvard and Berlin trained scholar for the mere product of a Negro industrial school like Hampton, where Washington had his education.

Turning now to Garvey, we can see that he, too, was not aware of some of the larger American trends. If he had understood properly he might well have fallen in line with the co-operative movement. I used to tell him this myself much later when Garvey and I were in London and we used to see each other twice a week. This man, I could see, had had a great following, and if only he had been aware of what the co-operative movement had achieved in Denmark and elsewhere, if he had seen that co-operation in the *osusu* was a part of our heritage as blacks, he might have worked towards that, instead of trying to establish a Chamber of Commerce or a Stock Exchange where the black men could parallel white. Garvey looked at American capitalism, but did not see within it a new movement to reform it. In a way he and others like him became more determined to make capitalism work than the very people (like the Jews) who created it.

All he really understood was that the black man had been a victim of slavery, and was a mere appendage to all the things that had been written. Therefore his history and race pride should be built up. But in his work of African renaissance, he somewhat mixed up his facts. Many of the people he claimed as Africans were actually Arabs. He seems to have been unaware of the pillage and tragedy of Africa South of the Sahara by those in the North. He lumped far too many of these North African poets together with the other Africans and conveniently forgot that some of these poets were free from day to day to write their lines only because they had black men—eunuchs— in their fathers' homes who catered to their needs. For this reason I have always been a little sceptical about Garvey and others pointing to the great kingdoms of Timbuctoo and Ghana as a legitimate source of black pride. I've always asked myself; were these really black men? We must never forget that some of these desert or Sudanic people never saw themselves as real Negroes—certainly not the Tuaregs. And even with the Fulani rulers of Northern Nigeria and Cameroon, there is a feeling of separateness from the local Negro populations. They did not see themselves as Negro; they were the special caste that had been lost in the desert, lost in Africa for thousands of years, and they saw themselves as having a great impact in the formation of kingdoms.

So when we are faced with some of these myths about the Negro we should notice rather that Africa has been in a state of change for thousands of years, and many of the spectacular developments have been the results of a mixture of minds and of peoples. Often, too, development was less to do with race types than with the presence of great rivers like the Nile, Niger and the Euphrates around which great civilizations can grow up.

It is just as important if you are thinking about Timbuctoo to ask how far it is from the Niger, as to wonder what people were responsible for it.

Garvey, however, was one of a line of romantic agitators. He built on the traditions of Europe where people like Garibaldi, Cavour and Mazzini had seen that Italy must be united through a great spiritual nationalism. There must be a return to ancient greatness. All this made Garvey's cheeks burn, and he took advantage of the European and American rhetoric about the Great War being a war for democracy. If that is so, how are you going to continue the annexation of certain territories in Africa and elsewhere? Instead, America should use her influence to make sure that Britain toed the line after the war, and broke up her colonies, setting the people free. There had been all these speeches with which to arouse the white soldiers, that this was a human crusade; away with imposition, away with suppression! A new charter. In other words go back to the French Revolution with its call for man to be unfettered. So Garvey took up this brief, and applied it most logically to the blacks: 'Didn't we fight too, man? Our boys died in Flanders field, in Mesopotamia and other battle-fields. So are we to continue to have our chains? No.' He proceeded therefore to arouse the black people to this injustice, just as Poles were doing at the same time, or the Pan-Slavic movement against the domination of the Austro-Hungarian empire.[6] This was the gospel that Garvey carried around Nicaragua, Puerto Rico, Cuba and even down in Venezuela, making his kinsmen aware that they should not be peons under the little Spaniards.

This movement of black men around the Caribbean countries is important, and before long it will be necessary to chart the history of the Americino Negro (as the Spanish called the English-speaking blacks) in countries like Cuba. Even in the recent revolution in Cuba, quite a number of black people fought, and some of these may well have their antecedents in the long line of blacks imported from the other islands into Cuba from the time of the first war. Importation became vital once American capital had begun the rationalization of the sugar industry there, and Henry Ford had been given the exclusive rights of exporting his trucks to the island, and there had been agreement on developing communications.[7]

56

But the involvement of American capital in Panama, Cuba or elsewhere really had its greatest effect on the labour-exporting islands. Let us take Barbados which, immediately after the Great War, was still continuing a primitive form of agriculture. There were still the great estates, English-owned, with the niggers living there. Admittedly the products of the estates had diversified a little, but not sufficiently to take up the increase of population. It became impossible for many Barbadians to continue on this little island 150 square miles, but with a larger population than the whole of Guyana. So it was no accident that large numbers went to the Panama and to Cuba, while others found themselves in San Salvador or in Maracaibo in Venezuela once the oil industry started there.

Wherever you go in the world you will find a Bimsha— a Barbadian. He finds himself on a ship and gets off in Japan. At the end of the Second World War, a number of Barbadians were found there with their Japanese wives. Also in China. Through this wandering they have been called the black Jews. This made them the migrant workers *par excellence*, and they were some of the first to respond when the Americans had the fare to Cuba from Barbados reduced from some £30 to one dollar. There was then no need to recruit for the sugar plantations of Cuba; people were ready to come and submit to conditions there when there was no work at home. And all of this naturally was advantageous to the British government. It couldn't provide any work itself for its nationals, so was quite prepared to turn a blind eye to conditions in Panama or Cuba, or, for that matter, the new orange industry near Key West, Florida, which was also worked by West Indians.

One of the key roles of West Indians therefore was to work outside the West Indies. Thus you had some 90 per cent of the clerks employed in Northern Nigeria during the first war coming from the West Indies. And there were others in India and Ceylon. Two of these I knew rather well later in London. They were remnants of the many West Indians who had been taken to India in the 1890s when there was still amongst the British a legacy of suspicion of using Indians. There they had tended to marry women who were largely Christian, and the children consequently felt they had some status because their fathers had been in the civil service. Both the men I knew, Cox and Cedric

Dover, had been born in India. Dover was particularly talented; he had published some of his poems and writings on the coloured problem when he was in India, and his famous *Half-caste* and other books he brought out after settling in England and was working as a proof-reader for the Oxford University Press.[8] He was a very good geneticist, and set out in all his work to debunk all this race superiority business. Later partly through my aid he went to Fisk University to continue his studies. Before, however, they had given up India for Britain and other countries, a number of these West Indians had tried to capitalize on the withdrawal of the British Raj, by setting up an association to ensure their position once the British had left. But Nehru soon put a stop to that. Anyone who wasn't prepared to identify himself with the new society was made unwelcome. Hence a man like Cox was transferred to colonial office work within Britain itself. There he worked and looked a complete gentleman with his Anthony Eden hat and his umbrella, but black as they make them.

Trinidad was somewhat different from Barbados. By virtue of its position near the South American mainland it became a natural entrepôt for the Latins on the continent. And in any coup it was an obvious place where they were able to run to and find an asylum. Some of the sophistication of the Trinidadian was the result of this melting-pot. Typical of this was Captain Cipriani who played a leading role in the trade union movement in Trinidad, but was originally a Venezuelan mulatto boy. The island's development was also probably a little different because Trinidad remained Spanish longer than Jamaica and some of the other islands, and so continued to attract that rebel element from the mainland, and also an important mercantile class from Europe.

A number of people from Trinidad and even Guyana used Barbados and then Cuba as stepping-stones to reach America. For by this time America was beginning to have a strong pull; it was now known that even if you did not have much money you could go there, could work your way and get a college education. So many of the poor 'buckra' boys whose fathers had been working on the railways or at Prostons decided to try it. They hadn't the money for England, but had realized that if they could get the fare to Barbados, they could then reach

58

Cuba for one dollar. If they could weather working conditions for a time there, they hoped to proceed later across to Key West or New Orleans.

In fact I found a number of Guyanans doing just this when I travelled via Barbados to New Orleans. When I reached Barbados with my American visa, I met about fifty Guyanans, people like Barnwell and Mittelholzer (whose fathers were noted citizens back home). They had got so far but the money they had saved up to reach America had run out, and they were stranded. I came fresh and said, 'To hell with it! Let's break out.' So instead of my paying the $ 50 or $ 100 for my single ticket to New Orleans, I bought tickets at this cheap migrant-labour rate for all of us to go to Cuba. I did not at that point realize that it was a sort of semi-bondage we were heading to. After all, I had my two trunks, my three or four new flannel pants and my blazer. When we arrived these Spaniards came swaggering up with their two pistols: '*Vene Aqui!*' they shouted as they began to get their twenty or thirty Negroes and put them into trucks to drive them off to the plantations. It seemed just like the old slave-pens, with these Spaniards examining this latest batch of slaves, and the Negro old-timers hanging around them, giving advice on which ones looked rebellious like the Coromante slaves.

The Barbadians and the Spanish immediately identified us as a rebel group. I called the captain of the ship and said to him, 'What is this nonsense? We are not slaves, you know; we have a British passport marked student and we have a legitimate affair.' We consequently demanded that Mr. Black, the British Consul, should come, and pointed out that our taking the cheap fare did not mean we should become bondsmen on arrival. The Barbadians and other migrants simply resented us. 'These niggers trying to make trouble. We came here to get our bread and these Guyanese fellows, they're funny people coming here trying to make trouble.' So we took this very legalistic line, and I personally demanded a telegram to be sent to my father or uncle for money. Not just for myself, because the whole group of us felt solid. Some of them had been my old classmates at Queen's, and others like Greenwich and Mittelholzer had lived quite close by. They had slipped out of Guyana without my knowing it, when I was up in the hinterland in the mining business.

At this point most of us scattered from Oriente Province, after deciding we would try to meet ultimately in America. I and a number of others reached Havana, and while I was waiting there a ship came and its bo'sun, Gomez (a Portuguese who had spent some time in Cardiff) smuggled six of the boys aboard. I subsequently got a letter from them that they'd got across to Key West, Florida, and were on their way.

I have emphasized some of the differences felt between island and island, and especially between the continental Guyanan and the men from the islands. But sometimes West Indians were unable to see the forest for the trees; until they finally realized that whether they were from Guyana, Trinidad or Jamaica, they were still all subjected to the same colonial rule. This meant that at times you got a common and therefore uniting feeling among them, that, historically, they had been opposing the same white man. So the Maroons with their fighting tradition in Jamaica would feel something in common with people who had stood against the British in Guyana. But the wounds were remembered perhaps more than the things in common; so that years later in England Coromante men from Ghana would come to us West Indians and say: 'You damned West Indians; you aided the British to defeat the Ashantis'. These feelings are morbid—this bitterness originating from a period that is so distant.

The black man's attitude in the British West Indies towards Haiti was strictly intellectual. When you started digging into your history you took pride in Haiti in rather the same way you did with the Ashanti and their great military history. But there was very little physical contact. In a way also, the past record of Haiti was rather more admirable than the present, as we looked across to that island in the 1920s. It seemed to us as if they had taken on the tendency of the Spaniards of having a revolution every three or six months, and deposing their leaders. Sometimes it was embarrassing if you were sitting in a street-car in New Orleans reading your American Negro newspaper, to see the headlines: 'Another Revolt in Haiti'. You felt it to be something of a reflection on yourself. You thought it would prove to the white man that these blacks are all just a bunch of anarchists; that they cannot manage a stable government.

Quite a number of West Indians also managed to land up in

Canada, especially from the smaller islands of Grenada, St. Kitts and St. Vincent. Many of these found themselves working on the Canadian-Pacific Railway. But originally they had very often managed to reach Canada through the Nova Scotian ships taking timber down to the Caribbean. Stowing away was relatively easy. Then, once you were in Canada it was common to try to bring the family over afterwards. The other attraction of Canada was the ease of access to America, and in many ways America had more appeal to the West Indians than Canada—apart from the larger cities. Remember this was the era in Canada of 'Go West young man', with people going off to carve out their own little empire so many days from civilization and without any neighbours. But to many darkies this was not their game at all. They sought out the cities.

This lack of adventure can be explained in terms of the insecurity the Negro felt in those new surroundings. He felt happier if he was the only black man in town. Many of them in a place like Manitoba would make the calculation, for instance, that there were too many niggers coming into town, and where there were too many niggers, then segregation was sure to start. 'But if I'm the good old nigger in town, I'll be able to go to the Methodist church, and even be asked to be the altar-boy.' Still, there were quite substantial nuclei of blacks built up in university centres like McGill, where a tradition was established of West Indians doing law and medicine.

Certainly the majority preferred to migrate to the States, but there were complications both from the black and white Americans when West Indians came. The whites liked his hard work, but realized also that these 'King George niggers' (as they were called) were saucy and would fight back. They would answer back to a white American as no American Negro would do. And if there was any trouble down in Florida, these King George niggers would immediately try calling for their consul. This was not particularly palatable to the whites, and they would explode: 'I have a nigger here who has just told me he is a British nigger and wants to call his consul. What's all this about?' This was especially annoying to the Americans who thought they had finished with Britain back in the 1780s, and suddenly to have a West Indian flourishing his British passport at you in the Southern States was awkward. Many of them,

61

if they could, deliberately held on to dual citizenship in the South as a form of protection, and they would use the business of being British to excuse their being on the wrong part of the Jim Crow train and so forth.

Others who had some language ability, say, Spanish, made use of that. In fact I got away with it myself with my '*Que tal?*' '*Que dices?*' Even to speak in some Creole which the American did not know might convince him that you weren't a Southern nigger, and that he perhaps better be careful with the treatment. All the African students used to do the same thing, and later you had people like the Sudanese businessman Duse Mohamed Ali making use of the fez to great advantage.[9] Once you had discovered this American folly, you would put on your fez and 'pass' like any white—even ride on the Pullman. People might think you were an African prince.

It wasn't everyone who took this line. Many West Indians who had gone over to Florida wanted nothing better than peacefully to set up little restaurants and hotels to serve the black community. It was always the wandering scholar or the bigoted ex-civil servant from the islands who tried this stuff about being a British subject. The majority however were the plantation workers who were prepared to take on the hardest work for a period. They had been attracted by wages of $14 a week instead of ten a month at home. Even though there was a lot to lose by insolence they were more prepared to try the protection of the laws than the American Negroes. And the white labour officers wouldn't take too many chances with them either.

The idea, therefore, behind a lot of the West Indian attitudes in North America was to try to avoid being circumscribed. I did this myself in my YMCA secretary period when I was constantly having to move from place to place. Often one's greatest barrier to having access to the Pullman cars was not the white man but the black porter. He, too, would then relent and decide I was not a nigger. The trouble was that this kind of tactic did not do much good to West Indian/American Negro relations, especially at the lower echelons of society.[10] The American Negro might come back at you with: 'What the hell you are trying, you monkey-chaser? You come in from the bush, you African (or West Indian). You come in here jumpin' from tree to tree catchin' at things like monkeys, tryin' to enjoy more privileges in my country than I do.' There was certainly this stigma, and people used to go on, 'Don't mind that goddam home-country man. He's just full of bull. He's tryin' to pass for everything like the son of God.'[11]

Even at the level of the professional classes it created friction. And many of the local black doctors who had graduated from Howard and other universities would say: 'These damn fellows from the West Indies are living too well. They enjoy privileges by saying they are West Indians, trying to escape Jim Crow laws and at the same time pretending they are part of us. Well, what sort of damn thing is this? Either we all experience the same thing, the same bitterness, or we'll never hold together.' The same attack would be made later against some of the Kenyan Africans who came across to study after the hell of Mau Mau, in the 1950s. Say you asked some of those East Africans who went across through the Tom Mboya scholarship scheme how things were in America, how did they find things amongst the American Negroes? You would be told: 'Well, I can't tell you what things are like in the black community. I went to a little white school and all my friends and guardians were white.' This is the sort of thing that really embittered me. I would have thought that going through the Emergency in Kenya would have prepared one to be a better pan-Africanist—to seek out and sympathize with the black man in the New World.

The interesting thing is that a number of American whites would try the same sort of thing. They would make use of this alleged distinction between Northerners and Southerners, and point out to blacks that they weren't Southerners, but then you might find out that he had only been out of the South for one generation. It is just the same mentality which allowed an American to kick his blacks around in America, but when he landed up in Scotland or Britain, and saw a black man in King George's uniform, would say, 'Hello buddy'. Back home if he saw an American Negro in the same military uniform, he would tell his friends, 'This fellow has got a tail, and he never wore any shoes until Uncle Sam put them on him.'

Another feature of the early West Indian experience in America was that because of the grimness of life in so many of the islands many West Indians developed a kind of thrift and the approach of 'It's a hard world, son': every man for himself. Consequently in some of the ghettos of America, they were able to make their way with little shops, and sometimes the Jew boys would be quite pleased to move out and let the West Indian take over the shop, and pay him so much. Gradually, therefore, the West Indians built up a substantial economy in insurance and taxi businesses, in apartment houses in Harlem, Philadelphia and in Florida. Really the only other non-white who built up comparable wealth was the Georgia peach—as we called the mulatto woman who had a white husband. Hence we used to say in my days in America, that there were only two free people in America: the white man and the black woman.

Some of these attitudes I have outlined were certainly there amongst those West Indians who foolishly decided to be carried away by their own special identity, and who never let anyone forget they were different: but even when you did not want to try to separate yourself from black Americans, something of this early training in Guyana or Jamaica made you the odd man out. Once, for instance, I had been asked by a girl I had met to spend Christmas with her family in San Saba, Texas. So in order to demonstrate that I was a big guy, I got myself some plus-fours, and some golf sticks (I used to play back in George-town). I bought a train ticket, but to my surprise once the train was some hours out of town, the conductor came round, and I found that the man on the platform at Houston had taken the wrong half of my return ticket. The conductor contemptuously asked me what the hell I was doing with the wrong ticket. And I, being a King George nigger, started to argue with him, pointing out that the onus was on the man at Houston who had given me the wrong half and so on. He said, 'Nigger, you are talking to a white man!' I said, 'So what?' As there was a reverend gentleman, a Negro, who had got on with me at Houston and had seen the whole affair, I turned to appeal to him. 'Rev . . . ', I began. 'I don't want to know about it,' he said. He dissociated himself from me at once. In fact it was only two years later that I found out that these clergymen were allowed to travel on the trains at half price, and he was therefore safe-guarding his position.

The man pulled the cord, and the train stopped in some place in the wilderness of Texas. It was a Sunday morning, and I got off with my plus-fours and golf sticks in the desert, just a few villages full of 'crackers' with their corn-cob pipes and a bunch of kids running around me and shouting, 'Here's a Bobby Jones—a nigger Bobby Jones!' Finally a good Samaritan came, and put me in the boot of his car—he said he dared not put me in the car with him—and eventually I reached San Saba.

NOTES TO CHAPTER 4

1 On the general industrialization of Negro education during the age of Booker Washington, see K. J. King, *Pan-Africanism and Education* (Oxford, 1971), chs. 1 and 2

2 cf. A. Meier, *Negro Thought in America, 1880-1915* (Ann Arbor, 1963), pp. 85-99. Also, W. E. B. DuBois, *Souls of Black Folk*, pp. 42-54.

3 DuBois has, however, pointed in his chapters 'Of the Dawn of Freedom', and 'Of the Training of Black Men' to the very high quality of a number of the white college teachers who came South in the immediate post civil war period, DuBois, op. cit.

4 For an analysis of the race factor in the philanthropic funds see King, *Pan-Africanism and Education, passim.* On the emergence of the racist literature of Stoddard and others, see Meier, op. cit.

5 cf. A. G. Fraser, *Village Education in India: A Commission of Inquiry* (London, 1920).

6 For Garveyite parallels with other European 'pan' movements, see Langley, op. cit.

7 The involvement of American capital in Cuba is referred to in R. Scheer and M. Zeitlin, *Cuba: An American Tragedy* (Penguin, 1964), chs. 1 and 2.

8 cf. C. D. Dover, *Cimmerii? or, Eurasians and their Future* (Calcutta, 1929); also, *The Kingdom of Earth: Ten Essays* (Allahabad, 1931), *Know this of Race* (London, 1939), and *Half-caste* (London, 1937).

9 cf. G. Shepperson, 'The African Abroad or the African Diaspora', in T. O. Ranger, *Emerging Themes of African History* (Nairobi, 1968), pp. 171-2. See further Ian Duffield, 'Duse Mohamed Ali and the Development of Pan-Africanism' (Ediburgh University Ph.D. thesis, 1972.).

10 A controversial assessment of the role of West Indians in black American politics is contained in H. Cruse, *The Crisis of the Negro Intellectual* (London, 1969 edn.), pp. 115-46

11 Roy Ottley, *New World A-Coming* (Cass Reprint, 1968), pp. 44-8.

CHAPTER 5

BLACK AMERICANS AND WEST INDIANS: POLITICS AND RELIGION IN THE TWENTIES AND THIRTIES

THE physical setting of North America is in some ways so spectacular with its modern towers of babel that it used to make me wonder whether the Afro-American was really capable of feeling truly American. What, after all, does it mean to feel like an American? What is it that has made people separate Americans as a distinct category from the French, the English and other Europeans? Can the Afro-American really be thought part of this American milieu, or is he a completely different type, outside the mainstream? Historically, if you think over the stereotypes of the American Negro in advertisements, in the old minstrel shows, or the later Amos and Andy style, you would notice that it was not even Negroes who played the roles, but anybody who was prepared to put on black make-up and earn his keep. We never knew whether the blacks doing the Brother Kingfish advertisements for Pepsodent, or other products, were black men at all. This kind of stereotype made the NAACP and other organizations object to this particular representation of the Negro. But my question is, if this was the stereotype what was the correct image? And I doubt if we can say that the black man was an American in the sense that he was just another one of the many ethnic groups that made up this composite nation.

In the early decades of the twentieth century the Afro-American could not have the same attitude towards Africa as, say, the Japanese-American had towards Japan, because at that time all the films still showed the African or Negro in the motherland chasing a gorilla; in the media the African was a person so close to nature that no Afro-American could identify with the image.[1] Consequently with nothing to be proud of from their background there arose a shared feeling among the blacks of resistance against oppression in the New World, whether they were from the West Indies, North America, or Spanish America. Blacks from the West Indies never dreamt of regarding the black Americans as Afro-Americans; they didn't believe these blacks had participated in the American civilization. So it was relatively easy, despite the occasional jibe about monkey-chasers, for all blacks to find accord through this community of suffering that four centuries had given us all. The people therefore who regarded themselves as something special, as did some West Indians, were simply closing their eyes to the fact that all blacks in the New World were in a state of continuous emergency. It didn't matter whether you were a wealthy doctor, you were still segregated and discriminated against; it didn't matter if you had served as a soldier in the First World War, you still had to fight your way through white mob-riots on your return to Chicago or Houston.

It was never the case that the Afro-American was having it so good that he was able to feel that the African was much lower than he was. Quite the contrary. Africa was used by the early Afro-American scholars to improve the security of their own status in America. DuBois and Carter G. Woodson[2] began to discover the grandeur of Africa after being continually challenged that the black man had never created anything. These scholars saw clear past the white man's Tarzan image of Africa, and showed that there were elaborate systems of government, and that certain features of black literature in North America had been taken from Africa through the slaves. There began to be a scholarly appreciation amongst black intellectuals of African ways of life and thought.

On the whole this awareness of common origin and suffering meant that there was no substantial gap between the various black communities in North America. Those, however, from the West Indies or Africa who did feel superior and different to American Negroes, make an interesting psychological study.

What was it that actuated such people to feel superior to someone who had done so much in the creation of universities, colleges and separate black churches? Even these attitudes should not be overemphasized, for, as far as I know, they never resulted in the two communities coming out into the streets to fight it out. Differences certainly existed, but they were more on the level of the verbal animosity between the Scots and the English than two groups openly hostile to one another, like the Irish, the Poles or the Italian communities in North America. A place like Harlem was therefore a conglomeration of all kinds of blacks, a ghetto which cut across these superficial differences.

Such differences quite often stemmed from the West Indian having the edge on the Southern Negro in education, and also from his being used to rubbing shoulders with whites on a plane of equality. So what was natural in society in Guyana suddenly became revolutionary when transferred to the Southern States, making the Negro in the South sometimes exclaim: 'Hey, this darkie is not afraid, you know. He talks to the white-man boss, and makes me so proud.' It was similarly the educational factor that allowed many West Indians to take leading roles in black American religious denominations. This was particularly true in those sections of black America where people were striving for middle-class status, and where they wanted to get away from the emotionalism of the Southern Negro churches.

Many of these churches had congregations that liked to get the gravy—to moan and shout and get happy—but it would be very difficult to find a West Indian preacher doing that sort of thing. Often they were products of old world Christianity in the Methodist or Anglican churches in the West Indies. They proceed-ed to America and had theological training in the northern white colleges, and then ministered to this new middle-class aspiration. In fact, I believe that Carter G.Woodson has shown in his studies of the Negro Church and Reconstruction that a number of the black preachers and state representatives were of West Indian origin.[3] Of course one of the most obvious examples of this trend towards American training by West Indians in the early period must be the Reverend Edward Blyden from the Danish West Indies.[4] He didn't stay in America after his education, but many of the West Indians with this headstart were attracted to the land-grant colleges which were opening up in the late nineteenth century. Frequently also they turned up on the faculties of Tuskegee, Hampton, Virginia State and Alabama State universities. These were people like Maloney and Maloney, the two Trinidadian brothers who dominated the field of biochemistry at Howard at a certain period.[5] But they were not necessarily college heads, because that was a job that required someone who was not prepared to stand up to the white man in the south. He had to be something of an Uncle Tom if he wanted to continue getting grants for his school. Taken all in all there were a large number of West Indians in the university world, and they did constitute a certain leaven in the dough with their tendency to stress the equality between the blacks and the whites.

It was this same tendency which drew a number of West Indians into the Garvey movement in the early 1920s, and this perhaps caused some ill feeling between the NAACP and Garveyites. Because a number of NAACP people began to identify the Garvey movement in this way, and said, 'These damn West Indians, these monkey-chasers, why have they come here to disturb our good relations with the white folks.' The West Indians for their part saw the NAACP as an Uncle Tom organization where the big white folk would pay contributions to help the Negroes but at the same time refuse to have them eat at their tables; and they proceeded to attack this attitude. Yet this was quite largely because DuBois of the NAACP had already led the charge; he had wanted people to know that this blackamoor, this Garvey, was a big-mouthed ugly Negro from the West Indies, who wanted to stir things up. Instead, therefore, of DuBois dealing with Garvey at the level of personality or ideology, he tended to resort to these ethnic attacks.

Although the Garvey movement was clearly not a British West Indian affair as some have alleged, undoubtedly many of Garvey's lieutenants were West Indians because they had been given to meeting the white man on an equal plane.[6] The requirements of the rostrum or the soap-box inevitably favoured those who were prepared to damn the white man. Even if they had not had the opportunity to question their position in the West Indies, this ire came out in the Garvey meetings. 'I know what this bastard white man has done in the West Indies. I know how he has treated the black man—how he would rather deal with the mulatto than with the real black man.' From there they would go on to make the relationship with Africa, the motherland, and say they were proud to be linked to that continent.

Although the Garveyites did come out against a variety of Uncle Tom organizations, from the NAACP to the Negro church leaders, the *Crisis* of DuBois was usually careful not to launch any attacks upon West Indians in general. For it was not the policy to split the ranks. But Garvey's *Negro World* was adamant; it gave no quarter and asked for no mercy. Most important, it addressed itself not to West Indians nor to American Negroes but to all Negroes across the world, preaching: 'This is your century. The black man has been a victim of circumstances for so many years. But remember your past, the historic period of Egypt when you dominated the scene at a time when these white men were cannibals. Awake to self consciousness. Don't forget that you have dentists, doctors and lawyers in your midst whom you should support, for this will cleanse you of your dependency and degeneracy, of your willingness to listen to the white man. And if you must go to a white man for treatment, then go to a Jew, because he at least has been kicked around like us; he is looked upon as a threat to society in the South. He is not allowed either in certain colleges. So the two of us should get together. We are both hated by the Anglo-Saxon. We both have been alienated from our homeland and for centuries like gypsies the Jews have wandered over the world. We must have an alliance with these people who have suffered equally.' There was in this way an aspect of pro-Semitism in the centre of the Garvey movement, especially in the recourse to Jewish lawyers in some of the great trials. Garvey also used Jewish advisers when he had amassed sufficient capital, and wished to invest it in the *Black Star* shipping line.[7]

However, this alliance with Jewish lawyers in defence cases and for financial aid went beyond mere Garveyism, and could be found also in the NAACP attitude. It, too, never despised Jews because of the generous gifts from people like Julius Rosenwald. The same was true of the Scottsboro case, when Jews aided in the defence of those being tried for the supposed rape of the girls in Alabama.[8] In fact, it is an attitude which has lasted down to the present time, and may help to explain why blacks who support the Organization of African Unity still find it hard to side with Egypt against Israel. Partly this must be understood in terms of the long domination by Jewish lawyers of the struggle for civil rights in America.

Even at the social level you had quite a number of alliances between Jewish girls and black boys, particularly amongst the communists and socialists. And there again you had considerable intellectual militancy amongst many of these Jews coming from Poland and elsewhere; they tended to be found in the Cigar Workers Union and the Printers Union, and were in the front rank of the union struggle generally.[9] In a way they provide something of a parallel with the West Indians, for a number of people have assumed that Jewish-black relations were not good in the ghettos. Yet I don't know that we have had clashes between the Jews and the blacks in the way they occurred between the Irish and the blacks. It might be thought that the Jew was exploiting you in the ghetto, but at least he was giving you a job, and if he went too far you could always say: 'Don't go too far, Moses, because the white man is after you, the Irishman don't like you. So we better stick together.' A bit of a love-hate relationship, since the Jew was often your master, and yet often came to your rescue.[10] There was certainly nothing in Jewish-black relations to equal what the immigrant Poles did to blacks in the Detroit lynchings during the Second World War— at the very time Poland was groaning under Hitler. This particular paradox had such an effect upon me that when I opened the Cosmopolitan restaurant in Manchester during the war, I had a special plaque executed on the wall showing the Pole coming straight from suffering Europe and leading the charge against the blacks of North America.[11]

Something of the same alliance with Jewish girls was true of blacks in England. Many of these girls had become ashamed of their fathers' petty bourgeois shopkeeping existence, and imbibing some Marxist doctrine were prepared to work in with the blacks, to demonstrate that landladies were discriminating against coloured people. Jews in general were seeking allies against the menace of Moseley, and this again made them ready to side with the blacks in a common cause. Marriages took place between a number of blacks and foreign Jewish girls, some of them highly intellectual refugees escaping persecution in Vienna under Hitler. And these alliances were much more balanced than those which a number of our early African doctors had contracted in England or Scotland, when some white women, often intellectually inferior, had shown an element of courtesy to the poor darkies. Things were better in the very early period when the missionary type of Negro in Britain was able to find a certain type of English woman within the church, who was prepared to go back with them to Africa or the West Indies and give service there as nurses or teachers.

The alleged separateness of the West Indians as a community did not, any more than it did in other immigrant communities, disappear at once. But you got a gradual indigenization. Thus many West Indians would explain away their accent by saying that they were Geechies—referring to this group of people you found in pockets along the Sea Islands and the Georgia coast who spoke a language which had a number of African elements still in it. (Lorenzo Turner did research on this phenomenon.)[12] The point about America, then, was that it was not a melting pot, but most of the immigrant groups from places like Finland were very closely integrated, and continued to practise some of their customs from the homeland. America has always provided all and sundry who came with the opportunity to hold on to their own belief—especially in the religious sphere. The Ukrainians, Poles and Italians all managed to maintain their own particular religious outlook in their watertight compartments.

The blacks did the same. Originally in the North, those who had come under Wesleyan or Congregationalist influence might try to maintain a presence in the white churches, slipping in behind all the whites at the back. But gradually the process of elimination and group consciousness forced the blacks out to create parallel churches, or set up black schools and seminaries like Talladega with its northern links. Some of these separate black churches had their roots back in slavery like the Ebeneezer Baptist Church. Others, such as the Baptist Convention, split away from the whites later. The process of secession went on until by the 1920s, in a place like Harlem there were as many separate churches in one block as there were with the whites. In fact probably more, for in the segregated and depressed black communities, a clerical career provided an opportunity to become a member of the privileged class. So by Garvey's time there was almost an excess of black Christianity.

Garvey realized this, and saw that the Negro had found escape in the church. He couldn't therefore avoid supporting a national black church as a wing of the Universal Negro Improvement

Association. Again, there may have been a conscious borrowing from the Jews who had demonstrated the unifying element of religion. At any rate, this urge produced the African Orthodox Church under Bishop McGuire.[13] He was actually an Anglican priest in the West Indies, and brought some of this element into Garvey's church. But the name 'orthodox' is interesting. A number of blacks had undoubtedly found out about the Syrian and Greek Orthodox Churches by working for various Greek and Syrian shopkeepers in the ghetto. They discovered that their master belonged to a religion different to that of many Americans, and being sharp boys looking for a safe berth somewhere had borrowed the forms. Fine regalia and a wonderful sceptre are acquired; they rent a few rooms and start a new religion. And they tell the story of the wee bird whispering in their ear and saying: 'John, you must give up fornicating and all sorts of evil and lead your people.' Only later on they would discover about the schism at Antioch and accept this as a premise of their own denomination. And the name 'orthodox' was particularly attractive since it seemed a more ancient form than the Methodists, Anglicans and other bodies the Negroes might be breaking away from. 'We are orthodox—the only people who were born into this thing. And if you feel that you are reborn, come and I will baptize you into this too.'

Rabbi Ford was a good example of this. He was a Barbadian, a sound scholar in Latin and Greek, and also a great musician and composer. In fact he became for a period the musical director of Garvey's Liberty Hall in Harlem.[14] But like others, in his search for some basis whereby he could be treated as a man, he discovered he had become a Jew. Shortly after, he was part of that early Garvey delegation that went to visit Haile Selassie (or Ras Tafari as he was then) to intercede for land for his African Communities League. There were along with Ford a lawyer, a geologist, a Jewess and an engineer. Their aim was to point out also that there was a vocal group in America who could help Ethiopia.[15] It is said, however, that a number of the influential Ethiopians like Martin and Heroui refused to identify themselves with the delegation, for they considered themselves as not being Negroes. In fact, Ethiopians were said to have betrayed the same attitude when, after Haile Selassie's coronation, a delegation came to America. Dr. Workineh Martin was on it, and he refused to lecture even at Howard University.[16] And when the delegation took with them back to Ethiopia only two or three very fair-skinned Negroes, this again seemed to prove that they thought themselves to be white people.

This apparent preference for mulattos, and the Emperor's refusal to receive the Garveyite delegation, made Garvey bitter about Haile Selassie until the time of the former's death. It was one of the issues that George Padmore and I used to fight him over, because at that time in London, Haile Selassie symbolized our unity in Europe. And yet from the time of the Emperor's arrival in England, Garvey castigated him as a man who, instead of dying on the battlefield in the tradition of Ethiopian leaders, had slunk away to England to find refuge; how could such a coward, Garvey alleged, be the leader of such a great nation?[17]

I think the rebuff over Ethiopia affected Garvey more deeply than the episode with President King of Liberia. There, at least, he had managed to extract from Liberia a document promising the African Communities League some million acres—and they had already shipped about £60,000 worth of machinery to start sawmills when the agreement was broken. It was actually DuBois who was used to turn King against this fiery Negro who they alleged would stir up trouble in Africa. But DuBois was only building on the pressure that the British and French governments had already brought to bear on King. However, once the Americans had staked out their Firestone concessions in Liberia, DuBois rather regretted his action, and saw it was a great error against Africa.[18]

What makes both of these affairs more tragic is comparing them with the Jewish enterprise over Palestine at the same period. They had already set up a tremendous fund to buy land from the fellahin, and they acquired other land through sale from the Mufti of Jerusalem. This readiness of the Arab leadership to sell land to these Jews would make things awkward, for the Jews could claim that they did not steal the land; they had bought it. 'If your leaders had not been playing some double game, they would not have given away what you claim is your inheritance. We don't want conflict, we want to settle down and farm in peace. We have a tremendous religious attachment to this land, and like you, the land has been strongly identified with us. After all we are part of the same people; we are only two branches of the same family.'

This Jewish and African awakening of consciousness could have come together in Ethiopia where there was actually a historic community of black Jews—the falashas. The Jews were probably already aware of them in the 1920s, and certainly a man from Ethiopia, Tamrat Emanuel, was. After the expedition of Swiss missionaries, he was taken to Basel in Switzerland to prepare himself for work amongst the falashas; and he also spent some time in Palestine presumably to understand more of the Jewish language and faith, before he returned to Ethiopia with his printing press. I would be speculating now, but it seems not impossible that Rabbi Ford might also have been attracted during his time in Ethiopia to investigate these other black members of his faith.[19]

Right across the board, black American interest in Africa compared very unfavourably with Jewish American commitment to Palestine. There were admittedly a number of Negro missionaries of the Baptist and other churches who came across to Africa, but it seems that they reflected more of the American expansionist spirit than of fervent black Zionism. I do not know in detail of their achievement in South or West Africa—especially Liberia—but I am convinced that more could have been done if there had been a less provincial attitude.[20] I remember reading early in 1931 some statistics of the Baptists, that they had spent over a billion dollars in churches in North America. So most of the money they got from self-help was ploughed back into these towers of babel, show-off churches with organs and the usual circus. All to satisfy this limited goal, instead of copying the outreach of the Jewish groups.

When we turn our interest to Islam among black Americans, we have probably to trace its emergence to the Somalis. Of course there were also Indian Muslims in America but they were highly accomplished, and never really associated themselves fully with the Negroes. They only did so to the extent of selling their charms and advertising their astrologers through the Negro papers like the *Chicago Defender* and *The Boston Chronicle*. The Somalis on the other hand when they got off the ships at the ports in the North and South were immediately conspicuous as a self-reliant and disciplined people, who stuck to the Koran and had their particular hours of prayer. They quickly became a reference group for certain black Americans who admired their lack of racial inferiority, and had noticed that these chaps would walk into white stores with their fez and long white robes wherever they had decided to settle. The feeling was that: 'This man is black like I am—even blacker—yet it's easy for him to walk into my own country and be served when I am not. So, how can I too find a way?'

It has often been assumed that blacks embraced Islam only in the lower echelons of society. But I have met outstanding Afro-Americans who posed exactly the same questions, and who changed their names to Ali or something like that. Take Billy Eckstein, the celebrated singer who was making about a million a year; he entered Islam, and when he used to visit me in Manchester from time to time, I would attack him for this as an act of cowardice; why should a man become a Muslim when they were still enslaving us in various parts of Africa? For the first time in his life he said he didn't know, but what could one do in the circumstances? 'I have seen fellows without my wealth who were able to go to the best hotels with just a little turban on their heads; it was for these privileges I changed my name, because it's hard, Mak. It isn't easy.'

It wasn't only for privileges; people like Elijah Muhammad had discovered back in the 1930s that American Negroes were devoid of discipline, while in Islam there were certain rituals and performances you could use to make for solidarity, and allow you to build up a commercial community around the religion. But there was always the danger, illustrated in the case of Malcolm X, that Islam might be used for political purposes. Consequently I had to take Malcolm X to task when he visited Ghana in the mid-sixties[21]: 'What is all this business—this Muslim business? We are fighting a hell of a rearguard action here in Ghana against them, because these Muslim fellows are all over the place, and Nasser may be using them against the Party at a certain point.' I was referring to the presence of these Zongos, watertight Muslim communities which you got just outside some of the principal towns like Accra and Kumasi.[22] Within these they had evolved their own chieftainship to suit themselves, possibly even paying some tribute to Nasser. But they are hardworking, vigorous people, who trade in magic, and are consequently able to build up fabulous wealth in a short time.

Although they had married local women, and adopted some Ghanaian ways, in the eyes of some of us, the Convention Peoples Party (CPP), they had been politically infiltrated by the Cairo-based Muslim Brotherhood. Because of the need to have a single, strong, one-party state, we felt we couldn't allow these fellows to belong to the party and at the same time be working with Nasser's UAR ambassador, who was building up Muslim schools and offering scholarships to go to Alhazar University. 'We can't lodge together', I told Malcolm, and he admitted too that he had been learning a lot on this African trip. His views on this were not static.

People usually associate the beginnings of Black Muslim influence in the 1930s with some of these shady characters like Duse Mohamed Ali and Prophet Fard;[23] but it is important not to neglect the possible influence of the celebrated scholar Blyden. He did not hesitate to point out the virtues of Islam, especially for Africans. I am not sure how open he was with this preference for Islam in North America, but he was certainly asked in many learned societies in England to expound his views.[24] I have even heard that Queen Victoria knew about him, and invited him to Buckingham Palace to hear his views. What one can't find out is how many of these later Muslim claimants had actually read their Blyden. But a great number of blacks were influenced by his message. I was touched myself, but being politically a black man more than anything else, I have never been able to embrace his cult; I'm too jealous of the black man becoming a prisoner in any other camp. I feel he must evolve his own '-ism'. Once you have found the particular truth appropriate to your people then, like Mahatma, you can train up your disciples to accept and cherish the sacred principles. But the moment we Negroes move into a field that has already been well ploughed, we continue this stigma against us of being imitators. 'Come and hear my nigger. How well he's been able to imbibe this religion.' That's why I personally kept out of any denominations in North America, even though a number of my uncles were of the cloth in Guyana. The YMCA nonconformist approach appealed to me with its absence of mysticism, but I have always been sceptical of the various religions and cults, especially when so many of our people have fallen for them.

Typical of this religious fascination was the Father Divine movement in the 1930s.[25] His origins are lost in obscurity, though some claimed that he was a Southern Negro. His philosophy is difficult to untangle, because it looked almost as if he had been attracted by this Muslim harem affair, and yet nobody ever attacked his morals. It seemed however that he had to find a white woman as the angel of his cult. Some of us also thought that the city fathers in New York were inclined to encourage his movement for, by building up these nunneries of single women, he was doing a lot to cut down the birth rate of the Negroes in the ghettos. For large numbers of women came and changed their names to those of saints, and there were also some wealthy blacks who sold off their possessions and gave the money to Father Divine because they felt he was God. We also felt that the city fathers found it easy to support him through his chains of restaurants, on the principle that it was cheaper during the Depression to subsidize these chicken meals in the Father's restaurants than to have these people on the dole. In fact I've gone to many of them with some of the boys, and you got a damned good chicken dinner. His women were doing the serving, and as his disciples came in they would greet each other with the salutation: 'Father is God, and Peace; brother, Peace.'

Finally in America there was the rolling, singing element of religion. This derived ultimately from the plantation in America, where even the master was moved to hear these fellows singing together. And naturally the plantation owners discovered that it was a good way of keeping these slaves out of mischief; they were able to find their god through singing, and not have time to reflect on the evils of the system which worked them so hard. But it's strange that one doesn't find these spirituals in the West Indies; it may have been because the slaves were so beaten that they had no time or inclination to evolve something of their own. You cannot really compare the Rastas of the Ras Tafari movement with the American phenomenon, although this movement was the nearest you could get in the West Indies to Southern Negro Christianity.

The Ras Tafari cult arose from the coronation of Haile Selassie in 1930 in Ethiopia and was built up with the threat to Ethiopia in the Italian invasion.[26] It seemed then that Negro fortunes had fallen to the depths, for Ethiopia was seen to be the last citadel of African collective security—the last piece of land that was still left to us. The Rastas were therefore determined to go to its aid, and gradually out of this conflict came the belief that the black man had through Ethiopia belonged to a race that for 5,000 years had not been conquered by anybody. The Italian affair was consequently make-believe; Ethiopia and the Emperor would never be conquered, for the Emperor was God: 'Good luck to you! I support Ras Tafari. The man is in exile but I am one of his subjects. The Italians think they can deceive us, but they'll fail. To hell with the British King. I am a Ras Tafarian; my King of Kings is Haile Selassie; so I'll follow him to the last. Manley and all of this Bustamante, these are nothing but jackals to me, sir. I have a king. I am a black man, and I belong to the throne of Sheba. My ancestors—you can't find enough paper to write my pedigree. So don't talk to me about these things, man.' The Rastas did not have any '—ism' beyond their pride in nobility and their desire to go back to Ethiopia. But actually more went to England as Bevin Boys to become skilled technicians during the Second World War, where I met a number of them. One noticed even there that they lapsed into smoking *ganja*, or pot, since they felt that this stuff grew wild naturally in Ethiopia. There was therefore a lot of fantasy involved, but at least, unlike so many of these New World cults, they did actually meet their god when Haile Selassie personally visited the West Indies in 1966. I was in prison in Ghana at the time, but heard afterwards about the wonderful reception—how despite this earlier propaganda about the Emperor regarding himself as not being a Negro, he was delighted at the reception, and was moved to know of this Ethiopian movement in the New World.

NOTES TO CHAPTER 5

1 On the question of Afro-American images of Africa, see H. Isaacs, *New World of Negro Americans* (New York, 1963).

2 C. G. Woodson was the founder and director of the Association for the Study of Negro Life and History, and editor of the *Journal of Negro History*. See further, his *History of the Negro Church* (Washington, 1921).

3 It has not been possible to document adequately the West Indian element in Negro church movements, but it is clear that with the exception of Cruse's somewhat polemical piece, almost no serious study has been made of the West Indian diaspora.

4 Blyden was in the United States between May and December 1850, but was refused entry to a number of colleges on racial grounds. See further, Lynch, op. cit., ch. 1.

5 There were large numbers of West Indian students also at schools like Tuskegee and Howard. In fact it must be assumed that the majority of the 150 British colonial students in Howard in the late twenties came from the West Indies. See further, J. R. Hooker, *Black Revolutionary* (London, 1967), p. 6.

6 Cruse has suggested (op. cit., p. 124) that Garveyism was '*not* an Afro-American nationalist movement' . . . but was 'Afro-British nationalism'. See further below, ch. 7, pp. 96–7.

7 For the view that Garvey entertained strong prejudices against Jews, see Cronon, op. cit., pp. 199–200.

8 For Jewish communists involved in the Scottsboro case, see Cruse, op. cit., p. 148.

9 The role of Jewish immigrants in the cigarette industry, and in the International Ladies' Garment Workers Union, is referred to in H. R. Northrup, *Organized Labour and the Negro* (New York, 1944), pp. 103 and 124. For Jewish labour radicalism, see Howe and Coser, op. cit., pp. 343 and 403.

10 Cruse has a further polemical chapter on Jews and Negroes in the Communist Party whose conclusion is that 'solidarity was never a real fact down below among the black or Jewish masses, and it is misleading nonsense to claim that it was ever so', pp. 169–70.

11 See further ch. 9, p. 137.

12 The results of Lorenzo Turner's researches are his *Africanisms in the Gullah Dialect* (Chicago, 1947).

13 A brief biography of George Alexander McGuire is contained in A. C. Terry-Thompson, *The History of the African Orthodox Church* (privately printed, 1956), pp. 49–52.

14 Rabbi Arnold Ford has been something of a shadowy figure. Howard Brotz, in *Black Jews of Harlem* (New York, 1964) has suggested that he went to Africa, possibly became a Muslim, or reappeared as W. D. Fard.
   However, an interview with his wife, Mrs. Mignon Ford, in Addis Ababa in 1970 has helped to clear up some of the difficulties. A Barbadian, he was principally a musician, and taught music for a time with the British Navy in the West Indies; he was then a clerk for a spell in Bermuda and proceeded to America. Attracted by Garveyism, he became the musical director of Liberty Hall between 1920 and 1922, and was responsible for the *Universal Ethiopian Hymnal* (published by Beth B'nai Publ. Co., New York, n.d.). At this time he was Rabbi of the Congregation Beth B'nai Abraham, New York. In 1930 he emigrated to Ethiopia, opened a night school, but gave lessons in music during the day. He never visited the Falashas deliberately, but met a number of them in Addis Ababa. Ford had met Tamrat Emanuel in Addis before the latter left for his trip to Europe and the States, and seems to have put him in touch with a number of West Indians and black Americans in the U.S. He died during the Ethiopian-Italian war of 1935-6.

15 It is not possible to document this particular delegation to Ethiopia, but it is quite clear that a number of Garveyites found their way there independently. At the time Mrs. Ford arrived in Addis in 1932, there were several families, mostly West Indian, already settled. One was in animal husbandry, some farmed, one was involved in dam-building on the Tana lake outlet, while another was a carpenter. All in all the following islands were represented: Barbados, Virgin Islands, Jamaica, Trinidad (also British Guiana). For further evidence on black Americans in Ethiopia, see J. Robbins, 'The Americans in Ethiopia', *American Mercury* xxix, no. 113, May 1933, pp. 63–9.

80

16 For details of Dr. Workineh Martin's fascinating career from the time of the Napier expedition of 1867-8 down to his service to Haile Selassie, see *New Times and Ethiopia News*, 21 November 1936. Martin was first in Harlem in November 1927 with a message from Ras Tafari welcoming to Ethiopia skilled American Negro artisans. But according to a clipping of that date, this message came as a surprise to American Negroes who till that time were under the impression that 'the black empire was not desirous of making contacts in this country'. (M. N. Work's files on the Negro, Tuskegee Institute archives.)

17 A typical example of Garvey attacking the Emperor's 'cowardice' can be seen in 'A Discordant Voice', excerpt from the *Daily Chronicle* (Georgetown), reprinted in *New Times and Ethiopia News*, 19 December 1937 (hereafter *New Times*).
'Unfortunately the Emperor did not believe himself a Negro, and at the start of the conflict he turned down many offers of American and other Negroes to help. . . . I think Haile Selassie is the first African chief who ever ran away from his people at the time of crisis. . . .'

18 The story of Garvey-Liberia relations is told from Garvey's point of view in A. J. Garvey, op. cit., part III, pp. 351-412. See also DuBois, 'Liberia, the League and the U.S.' in *Africa as seen by American Negroes* (Presence Africaine, 1956), pp. 329-44, cf. also, Cronon, op. cit, pp. 124-32.

19 Beyond what has been mentioned (note 14 above), more must be known about Tamrat Emanuel's aims in America and Europe before it will be possible to exclude Ford from a planning interest in the Falasha mission.

20 The factor of discrimination against Negro missionaries in Africa must be borne in mind, however, see King, 'The American Negro as Missionary'.

21 For mention of the meeting, see *The Autobiography of Malcolm X* (Penguin, 1968), p. 471. See also, W. Scott Thompson, *Ghana's Foreign Policy* (Princeton, 1969), p. 8.

22 For Zongos, see E. Schildkrout, 'Strangers and Local Government in Kumasi', *Journal of Modern African Studies*, viii, 2 (1970), pp. 251-69.

23 E. U. Essien-Udom, *Black Nationalism* (Chicago, 1962), pp. 43-46, contains a useful summary of the speculation about prophet Fard.

24 E. W. Blyden, *Christianity, Islam and the Negro Race* (London, 1887), *passim*, for Blyden's attitudes to the two religions.

25 The Father Divine movement is considered briefly in Essien-Udom, op. cit., pp. 32-3.

26 One of the most valuable comments on the Ras Tafarians is G. E. Simpson, 'Jamaican Revivalist Cults', in *Social and Economic Studies*, v, 4 December 1956, pp. 320-442. I am grateful to Dr. Richard Pankhurst for mentioning this article.

CHAPTER 6

PERSPECTIVES IN BLACK BUSINESS: AFRICAN, WEST INDIAN AND BLACK AMERICAN

WITH the recent interest in things African by young black Americans, the impression is sometimes given that most American Negroes in the 1920s and 1930s had a totally negative attitude towards Africa. But we must not confuse the presence of the stereotyped white image of Africa in the media with any belief in that image amongst the thinking blacks in the States. When I was there myself I found a great interest in Africans and in things African, and along with my colleagues we treated all such Tarzan films and books against Africa as mere propaganda and mud-slinging. And for all the existence of the stereotype, we never considered for a moment that Afro-Americans actually believed that Africans were naked savages running wild like beasts of prey, with no idea of social or economic or moral advance. Young people today who suggest that their fathers or grandfathers believed all this are really suggesting that blacks of the earlier period were gullible children who swallowed anything they were offered on the white media.

I think it is clearly unhistorical to suggest that the majority of black Americans in the inter-war period would rather be called niggers than Africans. Remember the tremendous impact of the Garvey movement with its African programme, and remember, too, the influence of the great scholars writing on Africa such as DuBois, Kelly Miller, Walter White, R. R. Moton, Carter Woodson—even Booker Washington.[1] And poets such as Countee Cullen, Claude McKay and Langston Hughes[2] all kept an African awareness very much alive in their period. Like the Jews, the members of the African diaspora could not ever completely forget the land of their origin—even though the blacks were never Zionists to the same extent. They did not have a religion to bind them in exile like Judaism or Hinduism amongst Indians abroad; nevertheless, we all did have these peculiar racial characteristics, and we could not therefore run away from our common heredity. We were bound together also by the universal proposition that the devil was black; that evil was characteristic of blackness. To combat this you did have a movement which, if not a religion, was certainly a powerful intellectual ferment. Pan-Africanism. This is still in its infancy, but its scholars are beginning to chart the full dimensions of blackness at home and abroad—in the New World, in Indonesia, New Guinea, the Philippines and India, and soon enough the picture of our dispersal will be complete.[3] Then, with the full evidence of our past, it will be possible to create a new concept. We shall be regenerated, and more ready for the great tasks awaiting us. Naturally, as a pan-Africanist, I firmly believe that we as a people have a distinct contribution to make to the good of mankind.

The treatment of the Africans who reached the States in the twenties and thirties was evidence of this early pan-African spirit at work. Apart from the African students, the few from the continent who reached America at that time came on ships, and could be found in most of the harbour towns like New Orleans, also in Maryland or New York State. Invariably they were taken to the homes of local Afro-Americans and made to feel at ease, and were encouraged to participate in whatever social functions there might be. The Negro churches played an important role here, and if you were a visiting African, the social round was never complete without your appearing in the local church. And the preacher would make use of the event to elaborate on the oneness of black people: 'Here we have a son from Pappyland, folks, and we ought to be mighty glad to have an occasion like this to feel part of that great brotherhood. Four hundred years has in no way impaired our sense of oneness with each other. He's here to tell his story; and what I'm afraid of is that he may be more enlightened and know more about the Book than those of us who have lived in this civilization, and who have sometimes been told that millions of them in Africa have never heard the word of God.' This is how it would go, and I know because it happened to me on occasions, and to a number of other West Indians who might have to pass as Africans in certain circumstances.

Another aspect which should not be neglected was perhaps the impact upon Afro-Americans working for white Americans of seeing in these big houses large African works of art from the 1930s onwards. Many valuable pieces were brought across, especially from the Congo region, and naturally a number of black Americans began to wonder, 'If the white folks bossman can have all these things and attach a lot of importance to them, how can we reconcile that with the notion of Africans being wild people running through the trees?'

So this loose talk today about the negative attitude of earlier black Americans towards Africa is misinformed. People forget that the 1920s was the period of the Negro (or African) Renaissance. DuBois had shown the way earlier with his doctorate linking Africa to America through serious research,[4] and he was followed by the poets of Harlem who expressed this African awareness through their writing. You also had others indulging in a vein of African glory such as Maliet, this Jamaican, who identified the Egyptian achievements as African, and pointed out that the first people to indulge in moving thousands of Africans for labouring jobs were not the plantocrats of the New World, but the Africans who engaged so many hundred thousand workers for the building of the pyramids. Also in this more popular style, there were writers like J. A. Rogers, the Afro-American historian and journalist, originally from Jamaica, who wrote several books on these grandiose African themes. He would attempt to show how in so many European households black people had emerged, pointing to people like Pushkin, and using him to show how even in a Czarist household the black man had come to the fore.[5] Naturally a number of black historians of his time were embarrassed by his rather extreme form of chauvinism, and felt he was a little too close to the Nazi historians who were doing the same sort of thing in this period. Nevertheless, he did point out the influence of the blacks in the early Portuguese period—the Negroes who were taken from Angola to replenish the manhood of Portugal and Spain. For his volumes he used to select photographs and drawings from museums in Rome and Paris showing the black Pope and other proofs

84

of his thesis. I met Rogers myself, and used to take him to task
for his defensive attitude, all this desperate searching for evidence
that the Negro was actually a man. This was when he was
coming through London on his assignments to report from Addis
on the Ethiopian-Italian war in the middle thirties. The point
is, however, that he was not alone in that period, even ordinary
church members of the Baptist Church and other denominations
were aware of Africa through their missions there. Indeed,
when I was in the Southern States, I found a number of Afro-
Americans who were well informed about the very early period
of North Africa through reading Gibbon's *Decline and Fall*.[6]

I think we would not be going too far to say that even at the
unconscious level the African continent continued to dominate
New World blacks in their sense of colour, dress and behaviour;
the bizarre manner in which we do things; the way blacks would
wear those funny straw hats, which was very difficult for a
white man to get away with. Then, also, the music hall, with its
atmosphere of banjo music, and the Negro dressed up with
painted lips and black face. Long before musical expression was
formalized into jazz, and became a more intellectual affair,
you would have early informal types of the charleston, and both
in slavery days and afterwards, the party would never be considered complete until the old black granny had come up and
done her little strange jig. So the African influence kept going in
this sort of way.[7]

All this means that we should take a very suspicious look at the
use of phrases like 'I ain't lost nothing in Africa', which whites
have said were commonplace with blacks in the inter-war period.
These would often be said by Afro-Americans, not because
they were rejecting Africa, but because they resented whites
coming to them and telling them to go off and serve there.[8]
The blacks who would retort with that phrase were very likely
thinking to themselves: 'What the hell is this son-of-a-bitch
coming and telling me about my own fatherland? What is he
up to? Likely he has a programme to dissociate me with this
land and get me out of here.' So there is more than an even
chance that whites appealing to blacks to serve in Africa actually
brought out in the Afro-American the old suspicion of the
American Colonization Society; it had after all been making
the same suggestions to blacks back in the nineteenth century,

and they had then reacted in the same way.[9]

Turning back again to the Africans who came to the States in this period, we should remember that Azikiwe and Nkrumah were the unusual type who actually went back into the struggle.[10] Quite often Africans were not great successes in themselves, and preferred not to return. They would use the excuse that if they went back they knew what the colonial government would do to them. But the real reason many stayed on was that they were ashamed to go back home empty-handed; so they would frequently be saying at the same time, 'Nothing is going to keep me in this country', and 'You know, if only I can first become a doctor, it would be better for the family and its reputation.' Consequently I would compare them with the West Indians, and say that perhaps not more than twenty per cent of either group ever returned to their own countries. They simply found that America offered too many opportunities, just as Africans in Paris or London would feel the same. Much of their talk about the African family structure, lack of money for the fare, and the possibility of the missionaries and government discriminating against them on their return were therefore mere excuses. It was much easier for an African to live in the States, remember, than for an Afro-American to live in Africa. Nobody troubled you about what tribe you belonged to; you were part of a community. You married an American Negro woman and you settled down happily with your children.

A number of them tried their hands at business even, and in the process took a lot of whites and other blacks for a ride. They would float companies aiming to import African products such as kola nuts, cocoa, and monkey skins, people would support them, and then nothing ever arrived.[11] Although some were obviously honest, a great number fell by the wayside, and after their spell in an educational college, became slickers, turning to fortune telling, wearing some sort of African dress. Some of the best at this game were the group of French Africans, who had come across through Garvey contacts, often married white women, and pretended they were completely involved in this French culture.[12] In fact I met one man, Diop; he was probably an English-speaker from Gambia, but after he'd got across to America with his English passport, he refused to speak English at all. Real slickers. They had picked up some of the feeling of the salons in Paris, and spent their time in Harlem and elsewhere making their living by conversing with Bohemian groups about Cubism and other matters.

Now Tete Ansa, this Gold Coast business man in America, was a different cup of tea; more honest, for one thing, and consequently he was able to set up his company, just as he had created the National Bank of Nigeria. He moved here and there across Europe and America, taking advantage of the interest shown by both black and white Americans in breaking the English cocoa monopoly of Cadbury and Fry. His operations were thus at a much higher level, and his contacts were much better. Through the Brazilian element in Lagos he had that link with South America, while in America he was able to move with the best, living sumptuously, wielding his big cigar, and discussing affairs with bankers.[13]

The trouble was that people like him expected there to be a considerable class of black businessmen in America with which they could ally. But in reality, what black business was there is North America? True enough, you have had certain institutions like undertaking parlours that go back one hundred years. Then you had a new line introduced with the hair-straightening business, which made Madame Walker a millionaire. But outside of that there was only a little real estate and insurance. In the case of insurance what allowed it to flourish was simply that the big white companies regarded the Negroes as a bad risk; it was part of the stereotype that blacks were riddled with syphilis and T.B. So the Negro insurance companies capitalized on this discrimination, and one of the most famous, the National Benefit Life Insurance Company of Washington, which started shortly after the Reconstruction, built up a tremendous organization.[14] The same was true of banks, and here, too, a number of rather outstanding Negro bankers emerged with their own banks in places like North and South Carolina. One of the more remarkable men was Spaulding with his bank in Carolina.[15] But with insurance and undertaking, you could often see a link between the two, since it was the insurance company which allowed blacks to be sure of having a big showing-off funeral; and it didn't matter if you had been a gambler or a cut-throat, you could still get a blessing given you in the undertaker's chapel.

However, the term Negro business was usually used to dignify concerns like barber shops, hairdressing shops with shoeshine parlours attached, or the many little restaurants where some white folk were to be found eating this fried chicken. In fact eating in such little Negro restaurants was much more common before the influx of Jews, Greeks and Italians made competition too tight. Even what some considered the biggest Negro business —real estate—was very dependent on the movement of Negro people within the United States; so it had one of its peaks during the migration of Southern Negroes up to the North in and after the First World War. It was a time when fabulous profits were made, because even the passages were used as rooms, so great was the overcrowding.

But one could see the real weakness of Negro business on such occasions as when, I remember, the Haitian government made attempts to sound out whether black business in America would have strength to buttress their own finance, through loans and other means. But of course like all Negro enterprises at that time, they did not have enough liquid cash, and even if they had, they were cast in the conservative mould, and doubtless felt that no American government agency would be prepared to guarantee the security of their investments in Haiti. Even in Liberia, where you might have expected a measure of black financial co-operation, it seems that banks were too vulnerable to risk their capital over there. And so it was also with these businessmen from Africa like Tete Ansa; they found more readiness to invest from the Jews than from the black Americans.

The point, therefore, to be made about Negro business is that, with the exception of the occasional enterprising Negro individual, there is after all these years nothing spectacular to show for it. Instead there was merely a scattering of rich doctors who made their money by practising and invested it in real estate, some of them becoming really wealthy. One of these was R. D. Nurse, a Guyanan whose father was fabulously rich, and had about forty children from his various wives. In fact the Nurse household and ours were quite close, and one of my first little experiences of being in love was with one of the Nurse daughters who had been educated in England. And it was her brother R. D. who followed his father's profession, went to the United States and became an outstanding member of Tammany Hall.

As something close to a millionaire he played a significant role in the Republican Party in Harlem, and established a hospital there. Another man who was substantial in this kind of way was Savory, a Jamaican, who worked in the Liberty Life Insurance Company.[16] But he, like many others, took a very hard knock when with the Depression you had the tremendous fall of the National Benefit Life Insurance Company, and the extreme vulnerability of all the rest was also shown up. Indeed the limits of Negro finance in this sphere have been mapped out by Abram Harris in his study of the Negro capitalist.[17] This is what makes me very hesitant about using the term Negro business loosely.

However, with that as a caution, we may look at people like W. A. Domingo who was a good example of the smaller businessman. He was a Jamaican, and had a business of about $25,000 during the 1920s.[18] It consisted of importing from the West Indies the ingredients for pepper sauce, and in his own little factory in Harlem he would chop them and produce the various chutneys and sauces. You can see something of his ability by the fact that Woolworths took his products—and they don't play ball with anybody who doesn't deliver goods on time. This economic base put him on a level to meet with the Socialist Jew boys of the period who also combined business and radicalism. It was a combination that I noticed was also quite common amongst Jews in England when I was there later.

One reason, I suppose, why some of these West Indians established themselves rather faster in this type of business than the black Americans, is their background in Trinidad or Guyana. In some of these islands, as we discussed earlier, you had a living tradition of craftsmanship. People were involved in boat-building, shoe-making, tailoring, and naturally when they transferred to Harlem they dominated the tailoring trade. Many of their customers were admittedly other West Indians, who because of their English background refused to buy a suit off the peg (or 'in the bag' as they used to say). But there were also whites who used to come and be tailored. The West Indies, then, was littered with this kind of skilled man who was consequently able to play in Harlem and other centres a role quite similar to the Jews. They also paralleled the Jews through maintaining their own habits in exile. Certain dishes such as pig-snout, salted fish and pigs' tails were available wherever there was a West Indian community established, just as the West Africans who have gone to Britain to settle have maintained their various dishes of yam and rice.

I think it would not be saying too much if we attributed something in the rather unique quality of the International Ladies' Garment Workers' Union (ILGWU) to this skilled element from the West Indies. It was not only from the Protestant missions that girls were coming over, but also we must not underestimate the influence of the Catholic Church in places like St. Kitts, Puerto Rico, St. Vincent and Jamaica, where the Sisters had been teaching crocheting, knitting and sewing for a long time. There was therefore a pool of skilled people to be taken up by the millinery, needle trades, and particularly by the ILGWU, at a time when the rural worker from the Southern States had very little to offer. People like the ILGWU head, David Dubinsky, were possibly better able to fight for their case of equality in the union for black and white by the fact that the blacks were certainly likely to be as skilled as anyone else.[19] It was also because the ILGWU had attached to it some rather remarkable men like Morris Hillquit, and David Saposs, the outstanding theoretician of the labour movement, who wrote that incredible book on left-wing trade unionism.[20] There was also the very progressive educational wing of the ILGWU, where people like Mark Starr, a Scotsman, gave a great lead in workers' education.

However, before we leave men like Domingo, it should be noted that they also had their hand in a small way in the publishing business. Along with this other Jamaican, Maliet, they had published a number of Claude McKay's poems.[21] Maliet with his job in the British High Commission was regarded as a stooge by many of the blacks; nevertheless he did co-operate in this small publishing business. And again with one or two notable exceptions such as Robert Abbott of the *Chicago Defender*, there had not been in North America the same tradition of interest in printing and publishing as amongst a number of the West Indian group. The outstanding example here must be Garvey with his *Negro World* because he could edit and he had also picked up the details of the printing trade through working with Duse Mohamed Ali in London.[22] But remember that, as in West Africa, you had in a place like Georgetown a tradition of newspaper ownership amongst certain blacks. I'm thinking of the *News Chronicle*, the *Argosy* and others which were edited by black men like A. A. Thorne.

Even if the tradition was longer in the West Indies, there were still in Negro America a large number of papers owned by Afro-Americans, and if we could consult the Tuskegee *Negro Year Book* one would find more than two hundred names listed, such as the *New Orleans Bulletin*, the *Houston Informer* and many others.[23] Also making a valuable contribution were press agencies like the Associated Negro Press, and we made use of this agency in particular once we were in London, and felt the need to find an outlet and an audience for George Padmore's articles and others. We would send them off, and Claude Barnett of this agency would then distribute them to all the interested Afro-American papers. Even though they took some of Padmore's and Wallace-Johnson's[24] dispatches, most of these Negro newspapers were not read by the serious student of Negro affairs. In our day you would turn to the *Crisis* or the *Opportunity* for serious comment; the average Negro newspaper was merely a wastepaper basket (you'd find everything in it) or a gossip sheet. The *Chicago Defender* was different simply because it approximated more to the sensationalism of the Chicago white press. This is what got the *Defender* banned from time to time in the Southern States through its sensational comment on lynchings. But the same thing did not happen to Garvey's *Negro World*, because for all its incitement to race pride, it gave some Southern whites the satisfaction of thinking that the black might indeed go back to Africa, as Garvey was suggesting, and that at least would get him out of the way.

Another aspect of Negro business which I had a little to do with during my Texas days was trying to encourage black grocers to take advantage of the competition amongst the big chains of manufacturers. In those business luncheons which I organized, I got leading white businessmen to state why they would be quite willing to build up the small black grocer if he would market the ninety products, say, that his particular firm produced. I felt blacks should take advantage of this inauguration of the chain store to build themselves up.

Slightly later the mood changed, and then the theme became

that of consumers' co-operatives. In *Opportunity* and most of the Negro Press in the mid-thirties you can find articles about wonders of the co-operative movement, exhorting Negroes to study the examples of other groups such as the Hungarians or Rumanians in Massachussetts, or the classic example of the Scandinavian agricultural co-operatives in Wisconsin. People like George Schuyler, for instance, plugged this for all their worth, demonstrating how capital could be amassed co-operatively.[25] And I suppose it was really from that time that I became interested in the co-operative movement; my socialism grew by degrees through concern with this collective aspect of the economy. But for all the interest in this theme, you could not point to any single embodiment of the co-operative movement. It's difficult to say why. It's not that blacks could not co-operate because they would do so fast enough to build a church, and they would let a preacher get away with murder in capital accumulation.

In lieu of organizing your own business, one thing you could do was at least make sure that you spent your money where you could work; that was how the slogan went in the Depression years. So you had picketing and speech-making to ensure that the big stores employed blacks—and real blacks, not just very light-skinned salesgirls. This was the nearest we got to involving the masses in action over the economy. I took part in this myself, and in speaking from the soap-box about this, we were really re-enacting the Garvey demand that a large ghetto population should not allow itself to depend entirely on Italian, Greek and Jewish shopkeepers, especially if they did not even bother to employ a few blacks as window-dressing.

At the same time this group of left-wing Communist and black national elements was also engaged in protesting against rents which were astronomical for the sort of services you got. During the school holidays from Cornell (where I went after my YMCA secretaryship), I used to go down and stay with Dave Talbot who was now living in New York, and studying at City College of New York. We did a bit of piecework, taking in suits to press, but in our free time we went around explaining to people what was happening about their rents; that people were taking advantage of the Negro. He was the last to be hired and first to be fired, and yet he still paid these steep rents. And we could see quite well that this high rent was precisely the reason why

so many blacks were forced to turn their houses to other uses—
for prostitution, making illicit beer and drinks—simply to make
ends meet. It was a vicious business because consequently the
police would raid the Negro areas, and the courts would be
full of Negroes caught engaging in illicit affairs, and so a whole
lot more would be thrown out of their jobs. For us it was a
moral question, and we spoke in churches in Harlem about it.
In fact I remember speaking in Powell's father's First Abyssinian
Baptist Church on this very business—why we should picket
and strike over this rent.[26]

It was during this period in Harlem in the early thirties that a
number of us added a continuous African interest to our other
protests. People like Talbot, and Crawford from Barbados,
as well as a handful of Guyanans, began to meet a few African
students in a regular way. We called ourselves the Libian
Institute—Libian because we felt we should see in Liberia a
Garvey style image of Africa Irredenta. And we accepted
the necessity to get down to the roots, to find what was the basis
of our Africanism. Hannibal and these other North Africans
were critically examined to see whether they could be called
black men. I remember this sort of thing consumed a lot of our
time, and it was partly because so much of this early literature
on North Africa was in Arabic or Greek that we decided to set
our feet on terra firma, and concentrate first of all on Liberia.
Talbot became the institute's secretary; there were also people like
Setrum (he's dead now) and a man Shepherd who subsequently
became fabulously wealthy with a taxi-fleet of 200 cabs. The
two most regular African attenders were Zik and another
Nigerian, Paul Cardoso.[27] We used to meet in Harlem either in
the Schomburg Library or in the Ebeneezer Baptist Church, and
we would read learned papers on aspects of Africa. I remember I
read one myself on the Kru-man, the coast man of West Africa.
It was all very interesting, and it went on right up to when
Zik was called back to take up his newspaper work in the Gold
Coast. But you could hardly view it as a very virile affair; it
was simply a few chaps who had the vision and ability to dare.
In this respect it was very close to the relatively small nucleus
of people who would later make up the Pan-African Federation
or the International African Service Bureau in our London
days.

NOTES TO CHAPTER 6

1 For Washington's interest in Africa, see, *The Story of the Negro* (2 vols) (New York, 1909). The Negro history movement is well discussed in A. Meier, *Negro Thought*, pp. 257-78. See also, St. Clair Drake, 'Negro Americans and the African Interest' in J. P. Davis (ed.), *The American Negro Reference Book* (New York, 1966).

2 Examples of the African orientation of Langston Hughes and Countee Cullen can be seen in Alain Locke (ed.), *The New Negro*, pp. 141, 144, 251.

3 The recent burgeoning literature of pan-Africanism includes much more amongst G. Shepperson and T. Price, *Independent African* (Edinburgh, 1958), and 'Pan-Africanism and "Pan-Africanism"': Some Historical Notes', *Phylon*, xxiii, 1962; St. Clair Drake, 'To Hide my Face? An Essay on Pan-Africanism and Negritude', in H. Hill (ed.), *Soon one Morning* (New York, 1963); J. A. Langley, 'West African Aspects of the Pan-African Movements (Edinburgh University Ph.D. thesis, 1968); V. Bakpetu Thompson, *Africa and Unity* (London, 1969); J. R. Hooker, *Black Revolutionary* (London, 1967); and K. King, *Pan-Africanism and Education* (Oxford, 1971).

4 W. E. B. DuBois, *The Suppression of the African Slave Trade* (Harvard, 1896).

5 See, for example, his *World's Great Men of Colour* (New York, 1947) and, *From Superman to Man* (privately published, 1924). See below ch. 10, note 20.

6 Meier has noted significantly (op. cit. p. 264), 'The interest in African history was part of a larger identification with Africa shared by the majority of Negroes, however attenuated the feeling might be.' Writing as early as 1925, Arthur Schomburg, the black Puerto Rican, recognized a Negro counterpart to the race writing of white supremacists: 'The blatant Caucasian racialist with his theories . . . has bred his Ethiopian counterpart —the rash and rabid amateur who has glibly tried to prove half of the world's geniuses to have been Negroes and to trace the pedigree of nineteenth century Americans from the Queen of Sheba.' (*New Negro*, p. 236.)

7 An interesting contemporary view of African survivals in black American culture of today is Julius Lester's *Look Out, Whitey* (New York, 1968), pp. 83-93.

8 For a wider view of black American reactions to Africa, see Harold Isaacs, *The New World of Negro Americans* (New York, 1963); also, King, op. cit., p. 80 ff.

9 See further, Hollis Lynch, *Edward Wilmot Blyden* (London, 1967).

10 For Nkrumah in the States, see in more detail chapter 10, *passim*.

11 An example of this type is a gentleman who was going by the name of the Rev. Prince U. Kaba Rega of Bunyoro, Uganda. In 1919 he was touring America trying to raise money for steamship purchase, and claimed to lead the Ethiopian Enterland Interdenominational Missionary Society.

12 Little work has been done so far on contacts between French-speaking blacks and blacks in the United States; see, however, J. Ayo Langley, 'Pan-Africanism in Paris 1924-36', in *Journal of Modern African Studies*, vii, I (1969), pp. 69-94.

13 Information on Tete-Ansa can be found in A. G. Hopkins, 'Economic Aspects of Political Movements in Nigeria and the Gold Coast, 1919-39', in *Journal of African History*, i (1966), pp. 133-52. Another fascinating figure in the world of West African/ North American produce trading was Duse Mohamed Ali, see further, I. Duffield, 'The Business Activities of Duse Mohamed Ali' in *Journal of the Historical Society of Nigeria*, iv, 4 (1969), pp. 571-99.

14 For an exhaustive directory of Negro banks, see Monroe Work, *Negro Year Book*, *1925-6* (Tuskegee, 1925), pp. 393-5.

15 ibid., p. 395.

16 P. M. H. Savory, see Ottley, op, cit., pp. 47-8.

17 cf. Abram L. Harris, *The Negro as Capitalist* (Philadelphia, 1936).

18 See Domingo's own analysis of the West Indian role in North American business: 'Gift of the Black Tropics', in Locke, *New Negro*, pp. 341-9.

19 For a critical retrospective analysis of the role of Dubinsky in the ILGWU, see M. Myerson, 'ILGWU: Fighting for Lower Wages', *Ramparts*, viii, 4(1969), pp. 51-5.

20 See Hillquit's *Socialism in Theory and Practice* (New York, 1909) and D. Saposs, *Left Wing Unionism* (New York, 1967 edn.).

21 A. M. W. Malliet, 'Some Prominent West Indians', in *Opportunity*, iv (1926), November, pp. 348-51, is one of the few available writings of this little known figure

22 Duse Mohamed, a pan-Africanist of Sudanese and Egyptian descent, had Garvey working on the staff of his *African Times and Orient Review* in 1912; see Cronon, *Black Moses*, p. 15.

23 Monroe Work, *Negro Year Book*, pp. 465-72 contains a useful breakdown of the Negro Press.

24 Valuable biographical information on this Sierra Leonean trade-unionist and pan-Africanist is contained in Hooker, *Black Revolutionary*, pp. 51-2.

25 For the interest of black Americans in group economics during the mid-1930s, see Cruse, *The Crisis of the Negro Intellectual* (London, 1969), pp. 173, 177.

26 For details of Adam Clayton Powell (senior and junior) in the political and religious life of Harlem, see J. Hendrik Clarke, *Harlem, U.S.A.* (Berlin, 1964), pp. 18-19, 188-9. Also R. Ottley, op. cit., ch. 16.

27 For the reflections of this Nigerian student, Cardoso, on North America, see, 'America and Nigeria' in *Southern Workman*, liv (October 1925).

CHAPTER 7

THE WEST INDIAN IN NORTH AMERICA —RADICAL OR CONSERVATIVE?

I T is necessary to go rather more deeply into the question of West Indian politics in North America, particularly as it has recently been suggested by Cruse that they were an extraneous and confusing element.[1] This talk of alien influence in North America reminds one of the rifts in the Communist Party when there was this search for 'true American types'. Men like Michael Gold[2] were in the late twenties and early thirties suggesting that all the people with communist ideas were really foreigners, just as Cruse points to the West Indians as very much involved with this foreign ideology in the 1920s. But of course this quest for the true American is pointless, for apart from the American Indian and the few Virginians who claim descent from the early fathers, all the others have been relatively recent arrivals. Indeed, I suppose the Afro-American has as good a claim as any, since with the exception of some admixture from his white masters, he has maintained his stock in America without being propped up by new infusions from outside like the European immigrant groups.

Whatever the stupidity of hunting out aliens in North America, there was certainly this period when the communists were deeply divided into two camps; those around Foster, the Irish Roman Catholic union leader, and the group around Jay Lovestone, many of whom were Jews and Poles.[3] An attempt was made to show that the Irish despite their Catholicism were more American than the Jews with their exclusivist religion, and their strong commitment to Europe. Attempts, however, to denigrate such great Jewish theoreticians of the Left as Sidney Hook, Max Eastman, Bressenden, Gitlow and others, by imputing foreignness to them, were seen by us at the time to be mere opportunism within the factions of the Communist Party of North America—each section trying to out-manoeuvre the other in catching Moscow's ear. There was a parallel, too, amongst the blacks in North America at a certain stage, for the factions in the party began to apply the same criteria of foreignness and Americanness to them. So it was no accident that at the time Foster became accepted instead of Lovestone, it was likely to get a local southern Negro preferred to some of the West Indians who had been quite dominant in the party. Hence in the elections to the American presidency in 1932 the communists fielded Foster, and this originally southern sharecropper, James Ford, was to run for the vice-presidency.[4] I have nothing against the communists making alliances with the blacks, but this sort of move was much more often based on opportunism than on any consistent policy towards blacks in the New World.

Cruse's other thesis that the West Indian is a hopeless conservative at home and an agitator abroad is also a dangerous one. Firstly it does a great disservice to the blacks in North America, if you suggest that outspoken movements like the Garvey affair and the Communist Party (at least the blacks in it) were all West Indian-dominated. You give the impression that the local American Negro is therefore a docile type whatever the circumstances, and like the old colonial governors in Africa you point to the dangerous outsiders coming in to disturb the good relations between 'our good black boys' and the local whites. If we are to believe this kind of thing, then we shall have to begin regarding DuBois as some sort of freak, or Frederick Douglass as someone who did not conform to the stereotype of black American docility. What, too, about all those slaves who had use of the Underground Railway escape route from the slave States, many of whom were fed up and were prepared to resort to armed combat? Was this in keeping with the American spirit, or was it perhaps borrowed from some West Indian exiles? Or going right back to the beginning of things, how shall we treat Crispus Attucks who has always been thought to be the black in the front line of the Boston Massacre.[5] If we take the argument to absurdity, we shall have to say that people only revolt because of their ancestry, and that if we come across some slave revolt in the United States, it will have to be put down to the Coromante element in the plantation.

The other point is that it makes a lot of difference what you class as 'conservative' at home. You have to take into consideration the reverence for the lawyer in the West Indies, and decide whether these black boys in Port of Spain, Georgetown and elsewhere who can quote their Blackstone (the eighteenth century English jurist) are necessarily conservative. The tradition is there right from your exposure to Cicero in the secondary school, and you have to realize that amongst certain people in the West Indies the best entertainment was not actually cricket, but going along to the Law Courts to observe some young man quoting the law and putting the judge on the spot. People positively admired the art of using literature to make one's case whether it was an outstanding lawyer or a preacher who knew several languages such as the Reverend Dingwall. It wasn't all show either; the role of the lawyer in opposing colonialism must be examined in all fairness. It's not good enough to dismiss a group as conservative because they are men with the legalistic approach. Historically both in the West Indies and in West Africa, lawyers have been very quick to champion the rights of the people, or to point to some particular abuse. As a boy in the West Indies I remember the celebrated case of over fifteen black lawyers defending Critchlow over his strike action within the union movement. Amongst these were Edmund Fitzgerald Fredericks, Elmore Edwards (from Grenada), the young Sharples, Eleazor and Davis, the solicitors. All of them were out in the open confronting the governor and the judge over this affair.[6]

Of course there is an element of truth in the suggestion that West Indians may behave differently out of the West Indies but that is nothing to do with the West Indies only; it is a general characteristic of people moving from a relatively small self-contained community into a quite different environment. Remember the sense of certainty in a place like Buxton; all the family and relations there; the family church, the burial ground. And even if there is poverty in certain sections there is always a strong feeling of belonging and identity. This is quite lost in America. The prevailing feeling there was: 'Hell, no. This is my life now; I'm not that big man's son any longer. This is a country where all people are equal. You have no caste, no class. Mark you, I may be poor today, but tomorrow my number may turn up and I'll be rich. I am not conditioned any longer by the folkways and the mores of the old community. I am in America. So I can get on a soapbox and follow Garvey's pattern, even though we would not have thought of it back home.' This kind of change in style is common of many groups coming into America, and it's tied up with a new individualism, and a new reach for possibilities. It's not West Indian *per se*, but equally you could make the point about many an Englishman or German who got a new fillip when they entered America. And certainly there are a number of formerly priest-ridden Italians who on entering the American scene found themselves committed to activities like leading a strike, which would have been unthinkable back home. The same phenomenon would be true even within the British Isles, where the Dubliners who had been working in England would go back quite changed to their own country—often quite fearless.

Another way of examining the subject would be to take one of the more famous examples of the West Indian radicals abroad: George Padmore.[7] Here we have an ideal example. His father was an outstanding government official, and as a relatively noted botanist his circle would naturally include some of the other professionals in medicine, law and government service. You could almost say the same of Eric Williams; although his father was of the lower middle class in his post office work, he was still a respected member of the community.[8] With both of them, there would be strict observance of the village norms. Even after George (or rather Malcolm Nurse as he then was) had graduated to his job as a newspaper reporter, there was still a standard to be adhered to. You could go to the reporters' rumshop, but God help you if you got drunk: 'Malcolm, you are a disgrace to the family of the Nurses. Fancy a son of Nurse in this condition!' So it wasn't until you left the country and became free of these patterns of restriction that you could really expect different behaviour. I remember sometimes in America or England he would reflect on this difference: 'As a boy, I remember the struggles at home if anything was done out of step. The family would come to you wanting to know if you had gone mad; if, like now, I began denouncing the government and denouncing the imperialists. The police would come and arrest me, and my family would be subjected to all sorts of inquiries.' So back home there were things that for the family's sake you would never do unless you wanted to become a jailbird, or unless you didn't care a rap, like my aunt Margaret.

Her behaviour simply underlined the prevailing norm; she was such an exception. She would fight a dozen policemen at one time, and had her own method of dealing with them—kicking them in their tenderest parts. Also, just as soon as there was any carnival or festival (or even without any excuse) she would start to jump about and get happy as soon as she heard the music. It was very shocking to village respectability; or in the town, if she was seen approaching our three-storey building on main street, you would get the shutters closed, and not a voice heard, so that she might go on by, and the neighbours would not find out that she was actually your relative. This was very much the pattern—the closed society, especially in the period before the town and village culture of the blacks was disturbed by the influx of the Indians from the plantations.

You have therefore these two elements to keep in mind: the village community's conservatism, and the proud legalistic group. Padmore's uncle, Sylvester Williams, would be one of the latter class; Padmore used to talk of him, and say that he maintained this high intellectual level after his return from England.[9] But also in Trinidad, there was a very famous example of this constitutional protest at a time when Padmore was only a boy. It was on the occasion of an attempt by the islanders over a period of months and years to collect enough money to send one of their bright men over to England to write a book as a retort to Froude's attack on the West Indies. It became almost a legend—how this black boy had mastered the white man's language and had gone to England to attack the great Froude, who was almost on the same rung as Macaulay. The man was Thomas, and he put Froude to flight in his book *Froudacity*.[10] Here, then, was indigenous West Indian protest, and elements of it could be found in most parts of the area. So it seems to me there is no need to impute conservatism to the West Indian at home, and suggest that it is only the Jews and the West Indians who have radicalized the Afro-Americans abroad. One should be aware of the recent research which has shown how outdated the concept of the American Uncle Tom is. A good deal has been written showing quite the opposite.[11]

You can't make any very valuable generalization from noticing that there were a number of West Indians in the Communist Party of North America. It's more important to understand the communist strategy. In America they realized that it would be very difficult to bridge the gap between black and white at the level of the proletariat. They knew very well that the trade unions had never showed any disposition to call the Negro a brother. It was very hard to put across the Marxist idea of all workers being brothers, because the blacks would retort: 'This man my brother? If so, then how is it that this is the person who lynches me, and who prevents me from joining his union?' The communists had therefore to look to the universities and hope to find young men who would be malleable, people you could gradually turn away from their Burke and Descartes to more earthy considerations. They would keep their eyes on the blacks who wrote little pieces here and there in the newspapers, take their names and addresses and follow them up. Often enough you did not know till much later that one of your friends was actually a member of the party; this conspiratorial side to it meant that your friend in the party would not reveal everything: 'You, Mak, you talk too much. There are lots of things you could know, but people don't know whether you would give these things away. Not that you are a traitor, but there are moments when you must be quiet.' So there were certain things that you learnt about your friends' activities maybe five years later.

This was so with our relationship to Padmore. We knew him as a militant certainly at Howard, and he did not hesitate to take action against any interference with the college from outsiders.[12] He saw the university as a place of consciousness, not just a place where you subject yourself to individuals because they are professors. 'You should have the right to question them, because they are merely consulting textbooks here and there, and you and I have access to the same books and we may come to different conclusions. So don't treat them as gods.' In other words he had not forgotten the Greek or Socratic approach to learning, and would advise us not to let the professors merely create mirrors of themselves in the students. This much we knew of the man, but didn't know that he was already in communist employ. He was, however, always pointing out our need for 'eternal vigilance', and getting us to be critical of people like Professor Kelly Miller. 'You can't allow this buffoon Kelly Miller to insult Africans like this: "Are you from Africa? I thought so. Can't expect anything great from you".' But in contradistinction, George would say that as long as the students had people like Professor Alain Locke they would be safe.[13] In all this we never suspected that George's links were so great with the communists.

I didn't realize myself the links until the rather important occasion when I got my first copy of *The Life and Struggles of Negro Toilers*.[14] The name on it was George Padmore, which I did not know before, but I just had a feeling that this might be a pen-name for someone else. So I went to the party's New York headquarters near Times Square on 42nd Street, and knocked at Jay Lovestone's office. This was at the time when Lovestone was still in charge of the party but both factions were awaiting the verdict of Moscow to hear which wing would be allowed to continue as representative of the Third International.[15] Already the Trotskyists had been expelled from the party, and this meant men like Weisbord, Max Shachtman, Cannon and others, some of whom were really outstanding intellectuals. At any rate, I went along this unlit corridor, and into a room where Lovestone was. I mentioned that I would like a copy of this particular book and I should like to see the author to find out if it was possibly my old friend. Naturally I was treated cagily with a certain amount of suspicion. They might well have thought I was some kind of agent, and they wanted to know what I wanted with Padmore. 'I don't even know if it is the same man', I told them, 'but I read this book and I couldn't sleep. It's the first attempt to place things in perspective about the whole conflict between the classes.' After talking to Lovestone for some time, he told me that Padmore was not there, but had already gone to Europe. It was clear, however, that Padmore was the Malcolm Nurse I had known.

This was quite a remarkable experience for me, and when I eventually left, Lovestone gave me a few books, took my address, and said that they would continue to supply me with literature. Most of this did not compare with the quality of Padmore's writing. His language was entirely different, and a revelation to me with its new approach. It was almost as if he had invented a new dictionary of terms with which he could burlesque the chiefs and yes-men of the various colonial regimes. And I felt here was a change from the measured pace of the lawyers in the West Indies. At that time he seemed to have a magic weapon in his hands which I had not yet mastered. I can still hear his descriptions of those chiefs in their top-hats as black toads. There were others, however, with whom I came in contact after this, such as Cyril Briggs. But a man with whom I had much closer links was this black socialist from the island of St. Thomas, Frank Crosswaith.[16] He was another of those spellbinders, distinguished on the platform winter and summer with his red carnation. I was ready to expose myself to the dialectic of question and answer that the communists carried on in their meetings, and they made quite a trenchant analysis at times of the Negro position in the United States. However, I never became a party man; I borrowed a lot from them, just as they had from Marx and others, but I felt I could do this without carrying the magic party card.

NOTES TO CHAPTER 7

1 Cruse, *The Crisis of the Negro Intellectual*, pp. 115-46.

2 A very hostile assessment of Michael Gold at the period when he was the driving force behind the *New Masses* is contained in Howe and Coser, *The American Communist Party*, 274-6.

3 The detailed manouevring of these two groups, leading to the eventual eclipse of the Lovestonites, is ably presented in Howe and Coser, op. cit., ch. 4.

4 Some of Ford's principal writings on the international aspects of the American Communist Party can be found in Hooker, *Black Revolutionary*, p. 157. See especially, J. W. Ford, 'Two Readings', in A. C. Hill and J. Kilson, *Apropos of Africa* (London, 1968), pp. 368-75.

5 A revisionist account of the too often idealized work of the Underground Railway is Larry Gara, *The Liberty Line* (Lexington, 1967). See W. J. Simmons, *Men of Mark* (New York, 1887; reprint Arno-Cass, 1968), ch. 4 on Attucks'First Martyr of the Revolutionary War'.

6 The West African counterpart of these lawyers is well analysed in Langley, 'West African Aspects of the Pan-African Movements'; see especially sections on the National Congress of British West Africa.

7 At the moment the only study of Padmore of any length is Hooker, *Black Revolutionary*, which concentrates on Padmore's American and British periods, but has very little on his last years in Ghana.

8 For Williams's background and early education, see E. Williams, *Inward Hunger: the Education of A Prime Minister* (London, 1969), pp. 26-33.

9 Apart from a brief sketch here and there (see Shepperson, *The African Abroad*, p. 169,) Sylvester Williams has remained a mysterious figure; however, a biographical study of him by Hooker is due to be published shortly.

10 The book giving offence was J. A. Froude, *The English in the West Indies* (New York, 1888). The retort to this is J. J. Thomas, *Froudacity, West Indian Fables by James Anthony Froude Explained* (1st edn., London 1889; 2nd edn., London & Port of Spain, 1969).

11 Typical of this new writing on slavery is Sidney Mintz, 'Slavery and the Afro-American World', in J. Szwed, *Black Americans* (Washington, 1970), pp. 31-46.

12 Padmore organized a protest against the visit to Howard of the British Ambassador to the U.S., Sir Esme Howard (Hooker, p. 6); earlier when at Fisk University he had been involved in similar student protest over segregation; see Rukudzo Murapa, review of *Black Revolutionary* in *Africa Report*, xvi (Jan. 1971), p. 36.

13 Locke's intellectual environment at Howard University and the larger black American scene, is sketched out in Eugene C. Holmes, 'The Legacy of Alain Locke', in H. Clarke ed.), *Harlem*, pp. 39-55.

14 G. Padmore, *The Life and Struggles of Negro Toilers* (London, 1931).

15 There seems at first sight a dating discrepancy here, since Lovestone's party had been ruled out of office by Moscow in May 1929, and Padmore's book was not available until two years later. However, although the Lovestone faction had lost the favour of the Communist International, it reconstituted itself as the Communist Party of the U.S.A. (Majority Group), and was doubtless still projecting itself as legitimate when Makonnen first made contact with it.

16 Brigg's involvement in the Communist Party along with other West Indians is gone into in Cruse, *The Crisis of the Negro Intellectual*, pp. 133-6. Crosswaith was much less prolific; see, however, his 'An ex-Slave who Fights for the Next Emancipation', in *Messenger*, November 1926.

CHAPTER 8

INTO THE ETHIOPIAN ARENA

B
Y 1932-3 I had moved from Texas to Cornell University, and through the summer vacations which were spent with Talbot in New York, I was able to come in contact with further elements in the white Left. One of the most notable of these was the Presbyterian pastor, A. J. Muste, who was also deeply involved in the Brookwood Labour College. He followed Norman Thomas's Socialist Party, but at this time when people were much concerned with the workers, he responded to the call that went out for teachers to aid in workers' education. This was a general call to the universities and churches to realize their obligations, and I, too, responded along with a number of others. We went to Brookwood as instructors and lived on a communal basis.

My first task was to help prepare a primer on American history, slanted towards the needs of the working class in the way that Mark Starr had done for England. Then I also worked on a dictionary of terms essential to the workers' movement. The aim was, by explanation to show the workers what lay behind some of the terms loosely used by the bosses in the trade union discussions. We had a close examination of terms like strike-breaker, blackleg, and anarchist—going right back to the case of Shelley's father-in-law who was an outstanding anarchist.[1] We would proceed to examine the nature of the bureaucrat, trying to get to the root of what typifies the creature, seeing whether a labour leader could be called a bureaucrat. What sort of thing did one mean by saying that a person had bureau-cratic tendencies? In all this we kept plugging the students with practical examples; how, for instance, could you classify John Lewis of the Anthracite Trade Union who was a Greek scholar, yet had created a parallel trade union organization to the American Federation of Labour in the Committee on Industrial Organization?[2] Then what about this frequent use of the phrase 'rationalization of the means of production' that the owning class was always employing to confuse the workers? We felt it was necessary to show people the implications of such terms as obsolescence, a sinking fund, so that they could deal with the managers on an equal basis.

The majority of workers who came for these three-or six-month courses were from white unions, anthracite workers and miners who were being prepared to speak out from the soap-box on their return. But we also had a few coloured women coming over from the ILGWU, and men from the stevedores or the printing organizations. The idea being to give the various unions a scattering of serious representatives at the level of the proletariat. You had to get out of people's heads the notion that they were merely outsiders to the whole question of dispute settlement; they had to be brought in and attempts had to be made to see things from the inside. It was going to be much the same approach that I would later bring to the courses of the Ideological Institute in Ghana[3]; there, too, most of the young Ghanaians were members of the party without having any substantial ideology for their membership. And in rather the same way, I would help to expose them to a six-month course on some of the crucial books, like Padmore's *How Britain Rules Africa*, or the parallel book by Saposs on the trade union movement—so that they might have a firm way of looking at Africa as a whole.[4]

But back in Brookwood you could say that the spirit most manifest was the romantic socialism of Eugene Debs: the idea that in this world of plenty one can attain happiness with little provided others are not without. All in all we tried to set the record straight on all the major issues that touched on the worker. For instance, when the New Deal was ushered in, and a number of us were inclined to believe that it was a panacea, that the government at last seemed to be giving up its traditional *laissez-faire* attitude, we teachers were ourselves educated by hearing a man like Scott Nearing, the left-wing economist, reinterpreting the Deal as a fraud[5]; in his eyes this closing of the banks and re-conversion of money was simply a device to save the Federal government so many million dollars.

Brookwood was not the only point of contact with the radical Left. There was also this fascinating Rand School which was similarly connected to the Socialist Party of America. Here, too, there were a number of committed younger men like Paul Blanshard, the student secretary of the Socialist Party, and someone who later developed important links with Russia. If you like, he was in his way, along with his black colleague Crosswaith, the socialist equivalent of the John Mott and Channing Tobias group we mentioned in the YMCA.[6] Although they were socialists, you could not say that Blanshard and his associates were jump-ups with no background; often enough they were noted Phi Beta Kappa students from Yale and Harvard. So they were able to appeal to others in the big universities and ask them to come down in the summer to attend lectures at the Rand. And the lectures were worth attending. There was Professor Franz Boas, for example, giving a novel explanation of the relationship of the family through the genes.[7] Then with the Dolfuss tragedy in Austria we had a number of the leading European socialist exiles giving us lectures on the whole problem of socialism, its history and contradictions.[8] They created through their presence a kind of university in exile, in the tradition of the ancient communities of wandering scholars.

We had to pay to attend these, but somehow most of us around the left were the sort of people who knew how to save money, or we were never out of a job. In my own case, I had quite a bit saved up from my Texas days, and when I got to Cornell, I managed to take over a job in the library from a middle-aged Englishman who had actually been born in India, and had started at Cornell as a freshman. I got quarters, too, above the library; so I was not hard up for a penny. Consequently, I spent a lot of my time following the various trends on the Left, and the few Africans that I saw like Zik and Kalibala would make a joke of it.[9] 'Mak, what are you up to now with your white friends up in New York? What are you about?' I naturally felt that they were rather missing out on what America had to offer by concentrating only on their degrees. I think, though, that Talbot, who I introduced to a number of these white radicals, was more sympathetic and continued meeting them for quite a time after I had left America.[10]

Cornell was itself not isolated from some of these critical questionings from the Left. How could it be when you had a fellow like Laski across from England lecturing on government and showing us that even in such an ancient citadel of reaction as England there were new forces at work? We were also fortunate to have Professor George Catlin visiting in the department of government—with Laski he had been one of the early Fabians but they had subsequently broken away. In this way there was a continuing cross-fertilization of ideas—part of a long tradition in American university life of worshipping at the English shrine It wasn't just a question of ideas either, because on the occasion of the early Hitler crimes—the burning of the books and certain libraries—I and one of my Jewish friends, Spizer, whose father was mayor of Yonkers, held a meeting at Sage Hall. There were about fifteen of us altogether, and I said, 'Tom, I think it would be a damned good thing for us to have a demonstration and ape the Nazis with their goose-stepping.' Well, we practised for a few days behind the Cornell armoury (in those days you all had to be members of the Officers Training Corps). Then we marched with a display of all these great German work by Heine, Goethe, Schiller, Hegel, Mann. We knew quite well that the majority of students were reactionary chaps belonging to their fraternities, and that any form of demonstration would arouse them, but we succeeded in getting about two hundred students finally to join in with us. Soon enough there was the inevitable faculty meeting about our action but fortunately we had very strong support from this liberal professor, Black This we followed up by getting a number of our friends who worked on the *Cornellian* to publish an attack on the reactionary professors who would like to see liberty castrated, and we rounded it off with a quotation from Ezra Cornell, the founder, which you saw as you came into the university: 'I shall found a university where anyone in quest of knowledge shall find a place to study.' That wasn't quite the end of it because when the old graduating classes of 1904 and 1907 came up to Cornell a couple of months later, the word got about that there were some reds loose on the compound, and one 'red black'! However, not all these old boys were the reactionaries they looked; one or two old radicals would come up to me and say, 'I hear you are the Satan around here.... Well, keep it up! Don't mind those old conservatives.'

On the campus there were two serious social gathering points; the Sage Philosophical Society and the more recent International Club. The latter reflected the international complex of Cornell at that time; it had so many Chinese, Koreans, Japanese, Indians— in fact some fifty nationalities. We had John R. Mott's son as secretary in our time, but by this period it was harder to hold to the optimistic idealism of the 'Y'. Crises were looming up all round the world. But it was in this milieu that I established firm links with my Ethiopian student friends. There were about eight of them there doing animal husbandry—Mulugeta, Yohannes and Yasu to mention only a few.[11] But it was a period which made for serious discussion, for the Ethiopian crisis was clearly building up fast. Even so it was hard for me to make them see the situation as it was. Indeed I remember once I had found an article written by an Italian journalist which showed just what was being planned, and I took it over to Yohannes to thrash it out seriously with him. 'Oh, you're a Trotskyist,' he broke out, 'you don't understand this affair.' I replied that it wasn't any longer a question of philosophy but of history. The article pointed out quite distinctly that the Duce had made his plans, and, more important, the Italy of 1934 was very different from the Italy of 1896. Men were being shipped out to Massawa at a frightening rate, and it looked as if this time Benito would accomplish his aims.

I tried therefore to explain to Yohannes and the others that the few platoons of soldiers we had in Ethiopia would be insufficient. Moreover, this would be a very different war from Adowa in 1890s. There would be the element of camouflage, and the traditional Ethiopian soldier with his white *chama* would be the target for any fool. Any conceited concept about 'we beat them once, we'll beat them again' would only bring further doom. Mulugeta had respect for my ideas, but the others were too deeply traditionalist to believe, unless someone from their Foreign Office came and told them to their faces. If only they had made more contact with the Chinese students and listened sympathetically to their fears of the Japanese, and understood the Manchurian incidents, they might have seen the link with their own situation. That's why I told them I wished they were as sophisticated as our Chinese friends. 'Oh you're a Tigre,' they threw back at me. 'You Tigres always have fantastic ideas.'[12] 'Yes, but the trouble with you Amharas is you're too conceited.' So the argument went back and forth.

By this time I had, you see, changed my name from Griffith to the Ethiopian Makonnen. But in any case no one doubted my Ethiopian origin. The real difficulty was to get them to see the imminent danger, and the need for a different approach. Perhaps the most realistic of the Ethiopians in the States was this man Makonnen Desta who came over one holiday from Harvard, and we two found agreement. It was obvious that playing up to the moral gallery at Geneva at the League of Nations would not allow us to escape from the fundamental threat to the country's sovereignty. So in all these debates, I was at least treated as an insider, just as I was always involved if any Ethiopian delegation came over to the States. This was the way in fact that I originally met Dr. Workineh Martin when he was over in the States seeking technicians.[13] But to me it was an interesting reflection on Garvey, that just a few years after his plans for technical advisers had been turned down, here was Ethiopia actually pleading for precisely this type of aid. To do the Ethiopian students justice, they listened with interest to my description of Garvey, and felt that this might well have been the kind of help they needed. A number of them had of course met Rabbi Ford in Addis, and had been able to see the seriousness of interest from the New World. And even though the original Garvey scheme had fallen through, there had still been a number of blacks from the New World who had gone out individually to serve. Typical of these was Miss Bastian, a Jamaican woman who had been involved in the Garveyite enthusiasm in New York. As a trained nurse she had joined Garvey's Black Cross nurses, and then in due course she had gone to Ethiopia, where she ended up working as nurse to Dr. Martin's children. This was the whole point of the Garvey scheme, of course, that he would only think of sending over people who had something definite like this to offer.

It was also the lack of solid information on the Ethiopian crisis that was one of the factors that made me ready to move to Europe; also there was the feeling that it was in Europe that things were coming to a head with the eclipse of Austria and other threats; so I began to think that I should see things for myself; and as far as a particular country was concerned, I was tempted towards Denmark. It had already become known as a refuge for many European exiles from fascism. In America I had always found a great degree of tolerance from the Scandinavians, and then, of course further back, we all knew that they were held in esteem by having abolished slavery earliest in St. Thomas. I actually was helped to get there by Muste and J. R. Mott's son in Cornell, and also through a Professor Warburton whom I had known when he was working for his doctorate at Cornell, but who had afterwards gone to Denmark. He invited me to come across, a place was arranged for me at the Lanbo Højskole—the Danish Royal Agricultural College in Copenhagen— and I set off right away. It fitted in very well, because I had been studying agriculture and animal husbandry at Cornell, and had become very interested in the co-operative movement;[14] so here was a chance to take both things further.

I passed through London briefly on my way there, and made some important preliminary contacts. Altogether I must have spent perhaps a year and a half in Denmark, travelling to Sweden and Norway. Sometimes, I had a lot of contacts with the radical student world through my links with the Studenterforeningen, and the Norse Student Association, also with some of the many radical exiles from Europe. And in the radical paper *Politiken*, there was a cluster of other left thinkers, such as Peter Rode and Rasmussen whom I also knew quite well. This paper focused on the progress of the Ethiopian war, and every act was publicized to the thousands of Danes who would congregate outside its offices to watch the newsflashes. But it was through my protest on this war that I was eventually made to leave. It concerned the question of Denmark exporting mustard to Italy, which I felt was being used for the mustard gas employed in the war. As you know, Danish farmers are highly enlightened about market demand, and they can shift from one commodity to another to meet world needs. So they were just producing mustard because it was required. I wasn't suggesting in my exposé of this that Denmark was deliberately conniving with Italy, but merely pointed out the tragedy of a nation that paid lipservice to peace while not realizing the relationship between peace and war. Modern warfare was so interrelated that you needed to be very careful to avoid your market products going to the wrong side. How did we know whether the Italians were also thriving on Danish eggs and bacon? Well, the night after I made this statement, I went home after a party at about 2.30 and had just got to bed when the Danish police arrived. I was taken to the police station and deported the next morning. My time there was not completely forgotten because about two years later Jomo Kenyatta and Padmore would be invited up there to address some of the radical elements I had known earlier.

Interestingly enough the boat on which I was deported to England had Paul Robeson as a passenger. By this time he had left the American scene and was particularly making a name for himself at the Unity Theatre in London.[15] So we met and discussed matters, and he asked me to come and look him up any time I liked. However I didn't take this up for some months, since there were two very pressing issues at the time—the Spanish Civil War which was boiling up and the Ethiopian crisis. And of these the most pressing then was Ethiopia. Now, already by the time I had arrived a small group had been formed around C.L.R. James called the International African Friends of Ethiopia (IAFE).[16] He had made a considerable mark on England by this time through his writing. His special field was cricket, and he had written a number of books and articles on the subject— in fact for a time he was the cricket correspondent of the *Manchester Guardian*. But not only that; in the general field of letters he was also noted. He had a number of plays to his credit, and being a Shakespearean critic, he was quite at home in the controversies of the day. There were also other works like his nostalgic *Minty Alley*. This was the name of a famous alley in his native Trinidad, and that particular book conjured up the whole atmosphere with its scents and powerful images.

At a certain point, however, it became difficult for such obviously talented and cultured blacks to stand idly by. Gandhi and his followers had shown the way to anti-imperialism, and there were people like Harold Laski, Creech Jones, and Nancy Cunard who were stridently taking up the burden of black injustice. People began to look at you to see if you had something to say. If you had, then the best place to say it outside the liberal element was with the Independent Labour Party (ILP), or the working-class movement—especially if you didn't want to risk the disgrace of being a CP-er (member of the Communist Party). Very soon therefore C. L. R. James became an imporant force in the ILP, making forays to Scotland, writing frequently for the *Glasgow Forward* and *New Leader*. Also his intelligence instantly put him on a par with the other outstanding ILP-ers such as Fenner Brockway and Jimmy Maxton, and this was a tremendous advantage over some of the new acquisitions of the Communist Party.[17] There it was all too obvious that behind these working-class frontmen like Harry Pollit you had the big dogs of the party—the Horrabins and others; in this way you would contrive to give the party a working-class aspect but in reality a man like Palme Dutt was operating as a commissar from behind the scenes. No real equality.

It was on my first brief visit to London en route to Denmark that I first came across James and some of the people involved in the IAFE. I had noticed in an evening paper an announcement of a big meeting in Trafalgar Square the next day, so I went along. A number of people spoke, including Jomo Kenyatta representing the Kikuyu Central Association, and I still remember the part of his speech where he was dealing with the Ethiopian policy of Sir Samuel Hoare, the British minister[18]; it was a crude satire: 'Sir Samuel Hoare . . . you wonder about him? Well, what else can you expect from a whore? A whore's a whore. He will buy anything, sell anything.' It was after him and a few others had spoken for a time, that I passed my card forward saying that I was an Ethiopian and would welcome an opportunity to speak. At once I was invited to come forward, and from the plinth at Trafalgar Square I dramatized the whole scene. I linked up the struggle in Ethiopia with the larger struggle against imperialism in Africa. Across the square I pointed to South Africa House and linked its significance with the present conflict. And what else does one see from the centre of the square? Napier, Kitchener, outstanding British war-lords, and towering above them all was Nelson. But what of the English that the black and brown colonials knew about—the Shelleys, Byrons and Keats—all tucked away in some gallery or church? So one could see that Britain had really glorified those who had made its empire, and not its scholars. I proceeded to show that it was not in Britain's interest to assist Ethiopia, and pleaded the supreme necessity of sanctions against Italy. For at that time sanctions were only being applied to one side. Ethiopia had quickly realized the need for arms after the initially successful Italian strike, and there were a number of people like the Greek merchants in Ethiopia who were quite ready to organize a supply. It was these and other supplies of arms for the Emperor that were not allowed in through Djibouti by the French, while up further north at Asmara nobody was stopping Italy from bringing in as many munitions as she required.[19] I rounded it off by stressing that the world had become very small, and that people should not regard as isolated the incidents of Japan and Manchuria, or the fact that Franco and his group were just waiting. As the Emperor had said, there had to be some positive force for collective security, otherwise it wouldn't only be Ethiopia who would suffer.

After the meeting people came up and we introduced ourselves, and went off to Lyons Corner House for the usual tea. Three days later I had gone to Denmark. But I was there long enough to see that the Left was in some difficulty over the attitude to intervention in the Italo-Ethiopian War. You have to remember the great Peace Pledge movement of Dick Shepherd was at its height, and there was still the legacy in the ILP and other leftist groups of their period of conscientious objection to war during the Great War. It was complicated even more for a man like James by the fact that he could be attacked as a Trotskyist who yet found it possible to campaign for Haile Selassie: 'How can you, a convinced Trotskyist, support a bourbon? Is it not like someone trying to combine support for both the Russian Revolution and the Romanovs at the same time?' He therefore decided to differ from the rest of us, and followed the ILP line that sanctions policy against Italy would simply lead to another bourgeois war which would not benefit the working classes in the slightest.[20]

It was a difficult question for George Padmore also; for he had only relatively recently broken with the communists, and still firmly held to his old anti-chief, anti-emperor position. But he was gradually won round to a position close to my own[21]: I was a blatant nationalist on this question, and whatever you might think of the rights and wrongs of the Emperor's position *vis-à-vis* the subjects, that was an internal matter. 'We will settle that amongst ourselves', I used to say, 'I am not going to expose his internal policies in the world forum.' And once I was back from Denmark, I was able to dig much more deeply into the relevant history of Ethiopia to illustrate the case. George and

114

I spent a good deal of time in the British Museum digging out some of the ancient history of Ethiopia. It was then possible to discourse at Hyde Park and at more serious meetings on the medieval period of Ethiopian history, the significance of Teodros as a unifier like Cromwell, rather than as the barbarian the British thought they were defeating in the 1860s. One would then discuss the social structure, the hierarchy and the church, and attempt to educate English public opinion, rather in the way that Sylvia Pankhurst was doing with her *New Times and Ethiopia News*.[22]

Once Haile Selassie was in England, it was obvious that the British government was embarrassed by his presence, and gave him minimal attention. So this allowed one to make the point that it seemed strange for the British Royal Family to be holding itself back in the face of a royalty several thousand years old. If Britain felt in some way that she was successor to the Roman Empire, then I felt Ethiopia could even more legitimately claim to be the lineal heir of the Jewish Empire of Solomon through Sheba. There was a barrage of propaganda all round, and it was greatly helped by the activities of a man like Professor Jevons or other scholars writing learned letters to *The Times* over some particularly flagrant breach of treaty by the Italians. Now as far as the Emperor himself was concerned, I think he felt it more appropriate that he and his Minister, Dr. Martin, should operate at the highest level, for instance by using *The Times* or operating at the diplomatic level if they came out in the open at all. I believe they thought that would bear more fruit than having people like ourselves to propagate the cause. But whatever the Emperor's position on this may have been, we felt it crucial to make some sort of stance when he arrived in Britain; otherwise he would simply give more fuel to this man Garvin, the Editor of *The Observer*, who, despite his classics, saw Benito Mussolini as some sort of new Caesar, but considered the King of Kings in Ethiopia nothing but a part of the decadence of this antique Amhara monarchy.

So I organized a group in order that when the Emperor arrived we would meet him. We had orginally thought of going down to Plymouth, but as he had to come up to London, it was decided to welcome him there. We picked out the daughter of Chris Jones, this leader from Barbados of the Colonial Seamen's Union, and also Dr. Dingwall's little girl; they were both

115

dressed up fine and had lovely flowers ready. Finally the imperial delegation came out on to the platform, with Princess Tsehai in the lead. We were there in strength, but really had to push our way forward.[23] We were determined, however, not to be kept away by these imperialists who were pretending to be in sympathy, shedding their crocodile tears. And it is of some historical interest to record that almost exactly thirty-four years after his arrival, Haile Selassie was to record during a visit to Kenyatta in Kenya that he had been extremely touched by the welcome he had felt from Africans and other black groups in the London of that day.

It's very important to put the response of the black world to the Ethiopian War into perspective, especially since it is easy to get the impression that pan-Africanism was just some type of petty protest activity—a few blacks occasionally meeting in conference and sending resolutions here and there. But the real dimensions can only be gathered by estimating the kind of vast support that Ethiopia enjoyed amongst blacks everywhere. We were only one centre, the International African Friends of Ethiopia, but that title was very accurate. Letters simply poured into our office from blacks on three continents asking where could they register. 'I've got money; I can pay my fare across to Ethiopia, and I'll buy my own rifle even.' Indeed, if researchers would care to consult the columns of a paper like the *Chicago Defender* of that year they would find countless letters from ordinary blacks all over North America.[24] And the same was true of Africa. When the Italians entered Addis Ababa, it was reported that school children wept in the Gold Coast. Also in June 1936, the month the Emperor reached England, my colleague Wallace-Johnson and Azikiwe wrote that article, 'Has the African a God?' which had them both charged with sedition. But it was sparked by the spectre of the Italian Church of Rome blessing the final victory of the troops in Ethiopia.[25]

It brought home to many black people the reality of colonialism, and exposed its true nature. They could then see that the stories of Lenin and Trotsky, or Sun Yat-sen, must have their African counterparts. Those who had disregarded in the past and felt that this fellow Padmore with all his talk about imperialism was just a commie stooge, could now see things straight. It was clear that imperialism was a force to be reckoned with,

116

because here it was attacking the black man's last citadel. Those blacks who had thought thet the era of gunboat diplomacy was at an end, that imperialism was just a schoolboy phrase from the past, suddenly now saw for themselves how it operated with a nation hacking its way towards empire at the cost of everything sacred. Now that communications were developed, no part of the black world was able to indulge in indifference. So this was a call to arms to all black men in the world, to realize that wherever our people and heritage are threatened, we must be prepared to move against that menace.

To a number of us it was evident that this kind of exploitation of man by man could only be halted by a new form of social system worked out by ourselves. This was crucial. It must never be felt by the masses of black people that people like ourselves were simply operating as agents of some other imperialist power like Russia. We were out to create a movement that was free from any entanglement; and any black man coming into our camp who had one foot in the communist camp, we would deal with ruthlessly. People, we knew, would call us fascists, but we were simply not prepared to compromise, we were not going to have any European leadership. All help from that quarter we would accept, for we knew that historically there had always been groups in the white world which had been prepared even to risk their own lives for this type of idealism. These would be our comrades-in-arms, just as we would in turn aid the Indian and other groups who might benefit from such an alliance. Whether it was with Scottish nationalists, Indians or Welsh, the policy would be to fight together against the common foe, but we would refuse to merge.

These were the sort of feelings that lay behind the creation of the International African Service Bureau shortly afterwards. Two other influences impinged; firstly the fact that the existing African and West Indian organizations in England at the time were very mild, and also one could see a useful parallel in the Indian League with its powerful expatriate Indian nucleus working in close conjunction with the Labour Party intellectuals. We had naturally considered the possibility of reviving DuBois's pan-African movement, but it seemed safer to operate under the umbrella of service rather than risk a frontal attack by taking a bolder pan-African title. The idea therefore was to emphasize

service to people of African descent in as many ways as possible—
educational, economic, co-operative and political. The constitution
was actually written by me, and this stress on co-operatives was
also my doing. I had been conscious for a long time of the need
for our socialism to be informed by the economic system most
appropriate to it. By now one knew the various strands that had
made up the co-operative experience of America, Scandinavia
and England with its Dr. King in the 1780s down to the Fabian
thinking of the early twentieth century. And it seemed plain
that this should be linked with the co-operative tradition (the
osusu) of West Africa and the West Indies. Really it was the only
sensible move for a people that lacked any primitive accumulation
of capital.

But we cannot see it as a large highly-organized movement.
Like the Libian Society of New York, it came together in an
informal way. Padmore was there, James, Babalola Wilkie from
Nigeria and perhaps another thirty fellows.[26] But there wasn't
any clear membership. A lot of them came around simply
because we provided a base and a talking point where the coffee
pot was almost always on the stove. This flat from which we
launched the Bureau we obtained in a curious way; there was a
chap, Bresiando, from the Gold Coast in London at this time.
He was projecting himself as the leader of an independent
African orthodox church, and his parishioners were cocoa
farmers. His purpose in England was to try to break the cocoa
squeeze and find independent buyers for his parishioners' cocoa.
Well, he rented a building next door to *The Sketch*, and as he
wasn't using the basement, George and I rented it off him for a
year. Upstairs Bresiando with his Seychellois colleague, Louis,
an Accra businessman, carried on their business in quite an
impressive way.[27] They seem to have borrowed some of the
techniques of Tete Ansa; but really they were in a lost cause,
since they were up against the big alliances of Unilever and
Cadbury's. Then the *News Chronicle* began to create some kind
of scandal about the two of them (of course the *Chronicle* was
a faithful servant of the Cadbury interests), and downstairs we
were just hoping that they might try and point the finger at
us and we would then be able to take them for libel.

The movement gradually proceeded. We organized a rota of
speakers for Hyde Park, and experts who could be called

to address any one of the numerous meetings then going on in the Left circles. We also brought out this paper, *International African Opinion*, and James and Padmore would ask me what I wanted them to write up. With the paper printed I would then look up all the halls where leftist meetings or peace meetings were on that night, and sell this thing illegally at the door on the way out. I would make pounds and pounds this way, because many an old English lady would give me sh.10 just to get rid of me. The other place I sold a large number was after speaking at Hyde Park. That was an interesting set up. I made use of this chap Monolulu to help draw in the crowds. He was a tall outstanding Negro, a race-course tipster, but a big draw for the crowd because he had a kind of Rasputian tone. He was crude in all his references, but knew the British psychology, and traded in subtle vulgarity of a high order. I would let him start off. So he would set up his platform with his two flags, one Jewish and the other the Union Jack, and then he would begin his funny talk; 'God bless Lyons Corner Shop: two veg. and roast beef. . . . When I came to England forty years ago, the English woman was something to look at; she was built for speed and comfort. She had a powerful roast beef and two veg. But look at them now! They are just all speed, and you've got to run like hell, like a gazelle, to keep up with them.' Then he'd turn round and say 'God bless the Jews. If it wasn't for the Jews you wouldn't have Christianity now, despite the fact they're the ones who are anti-Christ.' Then he would go on to his anti-Hitler piece.

As soon as he was through and this huge crowd was around, I would dissociate myself from this 'buffoon,' and try to present a different type of Negro: 'We, unlike those of you who are praying for peace, are asking for war; it's the only way we are going to get our rights.' Then after stirring them up for an hour, one would end with, 'Now you know it is against the law to sell papers or to ask for aid, but all the things we have just been talking about, and much more, are right here in our paper *International African Opinion.*' So sometimes I would clear more than £20 worth in a single meeting. After paying the printers, there would be still large savings, and I gradually built up capital without the other fellows noticing. Even a number of Europeans sent in money unsolicited after reading the *Opinion*. I was soon able to open an account in the Bureau's name, and really try to come to grips with the thing. But then like many papers in this early stage, we would sometimes concoct letters purporting to come from the Congo and many other places, or Nancy Cunard would write in to show that there was a branch of the Bureau here and there in Africa.

Another source of money at that time was the cache of 2,000 copies of Padmore's *Life and Struggles of Negro Toilers* which we managed to extract from the Communist Party basement, and, since the book had been withdrawn on George's expulsion from the Communist Party, we were able to sell it later at great profit.[28] There were so many of these protest meetings every week in Livingstone Hall, Conway Hall and other places, that we would just turn up and advertise the book. And often enough people would give sometimes ten shillings or more—especially if you were well dressed. George always was. Spic and span like a senator, and his shoes shone so you could see your face in them; his trouser creases could shave you.

So this whole movement towards the IASB derived directly from the Ethiopian crisis, and although our interests now became broader, a link was maintained with Ethiopia right through the period in London.[29] I knew particularly well Ato Emanuel Abraham, the first secretary of the embassy there, and at a certain point he was round at my house, seeing me every day.[30] He was an interesting case. If you like, *he* was an example of Dr. Workineh Martin reliving his own history, for the latter had been picked up by one of the officers on Napier's expedition, and educated entirely at his expense. In turn, therefore, Martin picked up a number of young men and educated them in his own household, and one of these was Emanuel. I saw very little of Dr. Martin myself because he always had a lot of Europeans calling on him, and also I don't think he attached much attention to our grouping.

NOTES TO CHAPTER 8

1 Shelley married the daughter of the early anarchist, William Godwin; see further, James Joll, *The Anarchists* (London, 1964), pp. 37-8. See Mark Starr, *A Worker Looks at History; Being Outlines of Industrial History Written for Labour College - Plebs Classes* (London, 1919).

2 For John Lewis and trade unions re-organization, see Howe and Coser, *The American Communist Party*, pp. 368-73.

3 For the Ideological Institute at Winneba in Ghana, see below, pp. 205–6.

4 For Makonnen's view of the significance of *How Britain Rules Africa*, see below, ch. 11, p. 194.

5 See further, Scott Nearing, *Black America* (New York, 1929).

6 Channing Tobias succeeded J. E. Moreland as senior secretary of the coloured YMCA in 1929.

7 For Boas's writings on race, see M. Work, *A Bibliography of the Negro in Africa and America* (New York, 1928; reprinted 1965), p. 571. Boas had close relationships with a number of African students, including James Aggrey and Kamba Simango from Portuguese East Africa.

8 The factional struggles in Austria leading to the death of Chancellor Dolfuss are usefully dealt with in G. D. H. Cole, *Socialist Thought: Socialism and Fascism* (London), pp. 159–66.

9 Kalibala, a Ugandan student who attended a variety of white and black colleges in America, is treated in some detail in King, *Pan-Africanism and Education*, pp. 228–30, 240–9.

10 Talbot edited a paper, the *Voice of Ethiopia*, in the period after Makonnen had left New York.

11 This was a period when the Emperor's policy of sending young Ethiopians abroad for training was producing a number of Ethiopians in both black and white colleges of North America. At Howard University, for instance, between 1931–3, there were Haile Makonnen, Melaku Bayen, Ingida Yohannes and Zawdi Bayene. There were other Ethiopians in Muskingum College, Ohio in the early twenties. There is further evidence of Ethiopian student interest in USA in Richard Pankhurst's article in C. Scanlon, *Church, State and Education in Africa* (Teachers' College, Columbia, New York, 1966).

12 Note that Makonnen's grandfather was said to be a Tigre in ch. 1, above.

13 Dr. Martin's first trip to solicit technicians was in 1927; Makonnen must have met him on a later mission.

14 A portion of Makonnen's library on agriculture and animal husbandry is with Talbot in Addis Ababa; all the books date from the 1933–4 period in Cornell.

15 For Paul Robeson's period in England, see his *Here I Stand* (New York, 1958).

16 The influence of the Ethiopian crisis upon pan-African thought was critical. See Langley, 'West African Aspects', pp. 447–82. The black American reaction to Ethiopia at this time is usefully drawn together in W. R. Scott, 'The American Negro and the Italo-Ethiopia Crisis 1934–36' (M.A. dissertation, Howard University, 1966). Also, S. K. B. Asante, 'The West African Response to the Ethiopian Crisis' (University of Ghana, forthcoming Ph.D. thesis).

17 Makonnen's attitude to Brockway is expanded on in ch. 11 below.

18 There is very little material available on Jomo Kenyatta's seventeen odd years in England; see, however, D. Savage, 'Jomo Kenyatta, Malcolm Macdonald and the Colonial Office, 1938–9', *Canadian Journal of African Studies*, iii, 3 (1970), 315–32. For Kenyatta protesting over Ethiopia, see plate III.

19 A useful commentary on the diplomacy of sanctions is George W. Baer, *The Coming of the Italian-Ethiopian War* (Harvard, 1967).

20 The changing line within the ILP on attitudes to the Ethiopian War can be followed in the *New Leader* during 1935 and 1936. See especially C. L. R. James, 'Is this Worth a War?', 4 October 1935; also 'The Abyssinian Debate,' 17 April 1936.

James's own account of his break with IAFE is instructive: ' . . . early last year (1935) I offered myself through the Abyssinian Embassy here to take service under the Emperor, military or otherwise . . . . Unfortunately, Dr. Martin, the Minister, told me that he thought my work with the International Friends of Ethiopia would better serve the struggle against Italy. When, however, that body decided to support League Sanctions and possibly lead British workers to what Marxists knew from the start would be an Imperialist war, I broke at once with the Society.' (Letter to *New Leader*, 5 June 1936.)

21 Padmore's restrospective account of the relationship between communism and black nationalism is to be found in his *Pan-Africanism or Communism?* (London, 1956) ch. 16.

22 The *New Times*, beginning publication in the month that the Italians entered Addis Ababa in 1936, continued for many years afterwards to be the most authoritative single source on the Ethiopian question. In particular it seldom failed to document the many pro-Ethiopia meetings in England and to note black participation in these.

23 For the Emperor's reception in England, see the *New Times*, 13 June 1936, 'A Right Royal British Welcome', which notes the attendance at the reception of the following black groups: 'Pan-African Federation, International Friends of Ethiopia, Gold Coast Aborigines Protection Society, Negro Welfare Association, British Guiana Assoc., League of Coloured Peoples, UNIA, Gold Coast Students Association, the Somali Society, the Colonial Seamen's Assoc., and the Kikuyu Association of Kenya'.

24 cf. Richard Pankhurst, 'Ethiopia and the African Personality', in *Ethiopia Observer*, iii, 3 (Feb. 1959), p. 71: 'Thousands of letters still extant in the possession of the editor of *Ethiopia Observer* bear witness to the extent to which ordinary Africans and peoples of African descent gave their support to the Ethiopian cause.'
There was considerable interest amongst non-Ethiopian blacks in volunteering for service with the Ethiopians; cf. the resolution of the Kikuyu Central Association of 28 September 1935, quoted in Padmore *How Britain Rules Africa* p. 364. See also, 'Negro Army for Abyssinia', *News Chronicle*, 26 August 1935. However, the British Foreign Office placed a ban on British subjects serving with the Emperor.

25 Wallace-Johnson ended this attack on European Christianity with, 'Ye Christian Europeans you must "Christianise" the pagan Africans with bombs, poison gases etc!', quoted in Pankhurst, op. cit., p. 71. See also Azikiwe, *Renascent Africa*, pp. 220–3.

26 For more detail on the formation of the IASB, see Hooker, *Black Revolutionary*, pp. 49–50, and Padmore, op. cit., pp. 146–7.

27 It has not proved possible to document Bresiando's church as yet. For the organized pressure groups of Gold Coast Africans in London over cocoa issues, see S. Rhodie, 'The Gold Coast Aborigines Abroad', *Journal of African History*, vi, 3 (1965), pp. 389–411.

28 The story is told in more detail in Hooker, op. cit., p. 23.

29 The intimate connection between the IASB and Ethiopia can be seen just two months after its foundation in March 1937: 'The African Bureau had a particularly good meeting in Hyde Park on Sunday May 23rd, some thousands strong. Wallace-Johnson, Ato Makonnen and Miss Mary Downes were the speakers. The case for Ethiopia was put . . .', *New Times* (29 May 1937).

30 Emanuel Abraham, presently the Minister for Mines in Ethiopia, put 'The Case for Ethiopia' in *Journal of the African Society*, xxxiv, 1935, pp. 374–7. In an interview of April 1971, Ato Emanuel said that he fed a good deal of the information used by Kenyatta and Makonnen for their protest meetings on Ethiopia. Of the two men, Makonnen was the real 'go-between', and was 'the closest to the Ethiopians' of the various blacks in London.

PLATE I. Dr. W. E. B. DuBois, wearing his delegate's badge to the 1945 Pan-African Congress in Manchester.

PLATE II. Dr. Peter Milliard with Anne Van Laer, whose mother was a Mancunian. Her father, after student days in England, became a judge and an ambassador.

PLATE III. *Jomo Kenyatta, a frequent demonstrator with Makonnen, seen here as a delegate to the 1945 Pan-African Congress.*

PLATE IV. *Session of the 1945 Congress in Manchester Town Hall, with (from left to right on the platform) Dr. Peter Milliard, Mrs. Amy Jacques Garvey, the Mayor of Manchester and I. T. A. Wallace-Johnson.*

PLATE V. *Delegates to one of the 1945 Pan-African Congress sessions: note Jomo Kenyatta in the third row from the front, centre.*

PLATE VI. *Delegates to the 1958 Positive Action Conference in Accra, Ghana. Makonnen is front right.*

PLATE VII. Makonnen (extreme right) in attendance at the funeral of George Padmore in Accra.

PLATE VIII. From left to right, Gaisey (Ghanaian businessman), Nkrumah and Makonnen, pictured in Accra.

CHAPTER 9

BLACKS IN BRITAIN

B UT what was the English background like, when we were operating such organizations as the IASB?[1] What was it like to be a black man in the Britain of the 1930s? Certainly we were not rich; far from it. But we were generally happy in our lot—just to know that we were challenging one of the greatest empires in the world. Imagine what it meant to us to go to Hyde Park to speak to a race of people who were considered our masters, and tell them right out what we felt about their empire and about them. Despite the suffering of our people, there was never a gloomy moment, particularly when we realized how much we could do in England: write any tract we wanted to; make terrible speeches; all this when you knew very well that back in the colonies even to say 'God is love' might get the authorities after you!

Those of us who had come to Britain from America felt the contrast quite strongly during the 1930s, and we were going to feel it much more once America had entered the MacCarthy persecutions, and people were being taken to task for utterances they had made perhaps twenty years earlier. It made us reflect that there were certain things that would not be possible in England, because of the historic link with freedom of expression. You could find plenty of highbrow and noble jurists, but they wouldn't be prevented at a certain stage from coming back to the defence of the people. For us Lord Hailsham was an example of just this; he had attained all the heights moneywise, but on a matter of the rights of the people, he would not hesitate. Britain had committed her crimes all right, especially in the colonial arena, and yet, as George Padmore would say, 'There is something to be said for these people, Mak. Imagine, you were

123

abusing that white man today in Hyde Park, and his own people came round afterwards and spoke to you. In America do you think we would have been able to do it to the same extent? There you would have to talk about some nebulous class, without naming names; so there's a lot to be said for them. Look at the people who send us money for support, knowing that we are trying to wreck their empire. Then the security people, they know we are here; they come into our offices pretending to be buying books or magazines, and sometimes when we're returning from a trip to Russia, they hold us back after crossing the Channel. But you can joke with them and say, "We've just been across to get some Russian gold, and we're coming back to enrich the old country". Instead of giving you the American cattle-prod treatment, they laugh it off. Where else but in Britain would you get Lord Bridgeman's son heading the League against Imperialism, or the daughter of Lord and Lady Cunard—Nancy—associating with people like George Padmore??'[2]

The other main difference between America and Britain in this period was that there was no specific 'Negro problem' in the latter. The few West Indians, West Africans or Somalis who worked in the ports or in London were certainly living under terrible conditions but these were not different from those of the Welsh miner, or the appalling area of the Glasgow slums. You did not get to the same extent these tight clusters of national groups that we have noticed on the American scene; rather there was a levelling, and we were able to see the worker, the struggle of the proletariat much more clearly than across the Atlantic. This was also true of the social level, for wherever individual West Indians or Africans found themselves in various communities, they simply became part of the Methodist or other Churches, or joined whatever political party was appropriate. There wasn't this question of racial hostility, whether in Poplar or elsewhere, because they all sat together on the same bench getting public assistance. Their poverty was the same, and there was none of 'You darkies, get away from here; you're getting something that belongs to us.' The proletarianization was so pronounced that there was no room for this attitude; so you just had the two darkies sitting with perhaps forty white boys in the pub. This is why the attempt to internationalize the Scottsboro case of the black boys from Alabama being tried for rape came as quite a shock to English race relations.[3] Many of the blacks in Britain were embarrassed to have this stuff about race positions imposed on them from America; it seemed in a way an artificial affair arousing them to feel a conflict between black and white. That might be so in America, but the prevailing mood in Britain, whether you were a cockney or a black seaman, was to look at the American scene as just a bunch of barbarians. We might have our little conflicts occasionally on this side but never to the same extent.

The other important distinction from America was that in Britain blacks were at that time so few that there was none of that social stratification within the black community that one had seen in Harlem or Boston; there the few West Indian or American doctors and lawyers tried to create a false rich stratum on their own. In Britain on the other hand if there had been some outrage in Accra or elsewhere in West Africa, and a constitutional delegation came across to England, its members were not removed from the local English black population. So when your Danquah or Sekyi[4] came over to hold some brief before the Privy Council the locals saw this as prestigious for themselves: 'Our big man is around, and I put on my black suit and go to Mayfair to see these big fellows.' There was therefore this strong kinship link amongst West Africans, and even with the West Indian community in Britain, although it wasn't so obvious, you could see there were links between the visiting Fredericks, Bruyning, or Cipriani from Trinidad and many of the black boys in England who had perhaps failed their examinations and settled down with some white girls[5]; they would meet up in the Strand and have a meal or a drink.

The other distinguishing characteristic of the English scene was its charity, and we could see a historical continuity of charitable organizations from the anti-slavery days down to 1930s and 1940s. In the early period money had been set aside in a typically English way through cellular organizations in the various towns, and these foundations could be used to help blacks in various ways. Originally it was to provide certain sums in relief of blacks stranded in Britain who wanted the means to go back to Africa. But we were able to tap the same funds much later; there were a number of fellows who came to England and couldn't stand it, got mad and believed that the *ju-ju* had followed them there. Instead of being disgraced we would provide money to pay for their passages from these funds, and there were literally hundreds provided for. The English scene was thus noted for its charity, and sometimes it could take surprising forms; you would even get members of the white West Indian commercial community who might not be able to do anything for the blacks on their plantations ('The moment I have to give six pence more on the wages of the proletariat, I am toeing their line, and not being the boss'), but in England, away from the scene, they would ask the clergyman in the community to do something for individual blacks whose clothes were tattered.

An extension of this charitable tradition was the League of Coloured People (LCP). As its name suggests it was not primarily for Africans, but naturally included the Indian element. Its president initially was Dr. Harold Moody, the Jamaican physician then resident in Britain, and he set its tone through his effective links to church groups. Indeed he worked his church connections like a lay preacher, keeping close to the SPCK and other missionary circles. It was involved in mild protest, or, if you like, harassing the goody-goody elements in Britain. It was therefore interracial, and you could notice this through the title of ts publication, *The Keys*. This was a direct reference to the message of James Aggrey, the Gold Coast man, who had popularized the idea that you couldn't have harmony unless you employed both the black and the white keys on the piano. This was a nice image but obviously Aggrey did not realize that the colour of the keys made no difference to the achievement of harmony![6]

At any rate the LCP had quite a hold over the loyalties of the blacks who had settled in Britain. You see, there were little outcrops of black professional types all over England, some with a little property in the West End, or a lucrative practice in Liverpool. Many of them had served with a company like the United Africa in West Africa,[7] and on retirement had come 'home' to the mother country. Naturally they had gravitated towards each other through such an organization as the LCP. There was also a pull because the LCP had managed to establish close links with the Colonial Office; and if there were any garden parties attended by the King, you would always find a few invitations for members of the League. For many of the leading lights of the LCP were what you could call representative of the coloured people;

126

they had had the stamp of approval from whatever community they were practising their profession in.

Look at the people closest associated with it. Arthur Lewis the economist from the West Indies had an honorary position; Sam Morris, who was later a journalist in Ghana, had been full-time secretary once. Dr. Mitchell of Trinidad had then been secretary Moody had been president right through to his death in 1946, and then there was Leary Constantine who had built up a tremendous reputation through his cricket, and then combined this with welfare work. But many more people were welcomed or given parties by the LCP than were actually members. Gandhi, for instance, received official treatment from it on his visit to England, and interestingly enough that was the occasion when Kenyatta first met Gandhi.

Now, as far as our relationship with the LCP was concerned, it was one of convenience. We recognized it as a powerful organization amongst the liberals, but it had little effect on us, because we had already mapped out our own independent course. Our only hesitation was that it tended to divert from a more radical line. We would attack them on these lines: 'You obstructionists, you are using this balm of aid, and garden parties to seduce these young men. So instead of their leaving England after their studies ready to embrace the principles of the age of revolution in which we live, you are giving them rather a mild dose of something—the belief that their good friends in the Colonial Office will ameliorate things all in good time.'

Rather more outspoken than the LCP was the West African Students Union, or WASU as it was called.[8] It provided much more of a social outlet also, for WASU House was a homely place where you could always get your groundnut chop, and there would always be dances on Saturday night. The LCP was much more of an administrative centre with its two offices on St. Andrew's Street, near Buckingham Palace. WASU, however, was much more suspicious of the Colonial Office than the LCP, and this was illustrated in the notorious affair of the projected Aggrey House, when it was discovered that the new hostel for WASU was going to receive financial aid from the Colonial Office.[9] What is less well known is that Marcus Garvey (who was currently trying to make a comeback on the English scene after being rejected in America) was the man who made

the really generous gift to WASU. He gave that house of their
in Camden Town, and of course this put a number of the more
conservative members in a difficult position; they were no
sure whether this rabble-rouser Garvey was an even more
dangerous person to associate with than the Colonial Office
The more political committee members of WASU such a'
Solanke realized, however, this debt to Garvey.[10]

Not that WASU was completely cut off from the Colonia
Office people. It may not have been a respectable enough place
for the King to visit, but you did get a man like Hanns Vischer,[11]
the Secretary of the Colonial Office Advisory Committee
sniffing around to see what these Africans were up to: 'We hear
some new things are happening, and that some chap Padmore
has been publishing documents that have been reaching West
Africa. Now, what do you fellows know about this?' Of course
they were right up to a point, for WASU had been developing
a number of links with the more radical left. People like Dorothy
Woodman, the wife of Kingsley Martin, were well known in
WASU circles and this facilitated publicity for West African
causes in the New Statesman. Really, though, there was no very
definite line followed by WASU; many of its members had
one foot in the LCP or in our organization. One explanation
for this was that it was an omnibus movement, and was open to
anyone from West Africa, or other spheres, who wished to join.
And you've got to remember that many of the so-called West
African students of that day in London were middle-aged.
Often they were men who had served well in the colonial
machinery, or in some large expatriate company, and now they
wanted to take on another job like law. Naturally as they had
been saving up money for years to get this qualification in the
minimum time, they were not disposed to risk their chances by
dabbling in politics. So a number of this generation of African
lawyers were old dodgers—policemen who had done good
service around the 'stools' or the courts, and now they had
decided to become members of the ruling class as a judge or a
magistrate. They were not types you'd expect to rebel like the
younger generation of students such as Eric Williams.[12] There
were plenty of jobs to be filled in West Africa, so they would
run back home to their niche just as soon as they were
qualified.

Another grouping of blacks at this time in England was the Colonial Seamen's Union led by Chris Jones; it was one of the commonest occupations at that time for West Africans, and had risen quite naturally from the white seamen's fear of West Africa being a white man's grave. Hence the tendency first of all to take on local crew when your ship entered West African waters, and then gradually as the fellows showed merit they went further and further afield. Finally they found their base in England, specially in Cardiff, Liverpool or London. It became one of our jobs along with Chris to persuade such people to join the union; otherwise we were attacked by enlightened white trade unionists who were afraid that the blacks would act as scabs. So the Colonial Seamen's Union was not really a union in the strict sense—we did not want a separate black union—it was more of a welfare and propaganda grouping which would get the colonial seamen together and persuade them to join the white union. They would be shown the weaknesses of staying un-unionized: that 'if you do not join the union you'll always be paid lower wages by the bosses, and this will separate you from your comrades.' Chris's role as leader of his 'union' was to act as a mouthpiece if there was any injustice that needed taking up. He had his contacts with the Labour Party and with us, and if there was any case with, say, the Greek shippers not paying some of these black boys' wages for nine months or more, he played an important role as a go-between. So he was looked on as a leader in the same way as some of the outstanding Irish dock leaders in New York.[13]

On the more narrowly welfare side, some of these seamen had the services of this fellow Pastor Eckhart.[14] Following in the tradition of the whites who had always had some sort of outreach to the seamen through missions and hostels, Eckhart found a need among the African seamen, and gradually created a little world for himself by building up this little shanty for seamen in the slums of Liverpool. It's difficult to analyse the role of such welfare workers; some would say that they tend to magnify the suffering of their people and create a bureaucracy to deal with it. And certainly a number of white seamen were suspicious of the power base a man like Eckhart could build up against unity: 'You with that collar round your neck, you're not playing the game, mate. You don't know we are all together

129

in the same bunker in the bowels of the sea; yet you come across here, and with your damn collar you try to divide the black from us.' Despite this, a man like Eckhart could make himself indispensable by his ability to deal with West African languages and even the more class-conscious people like Dorothy Woodman and Nancy Cunard were therefore tolerant of Eckhart and felt 'We have a very good man in Liverpool who is helping to solve the problems of the coloured fellows.'

A rather different tie between some of the working-class black and the wealthier stratum from abroad was provided through the arts. Jazz had by this time in the early thirties projected itself powerfully in America, and you had your Louis Armstrong and Duke Ellingtons coming across to tour round the provincial capitals in Britain. Unlike the situation in America there were very few black entertainment areas where the whites could go to hear this stuff as they could in Harlem. However, when these big black entertainers went their rounds, it gave the local black boys a little prestige, because the whites thought that they, too, might have this jazz thing in them. Naturally, therefore, you found the black seamen and others going backstage and shaking hands, even though they came from the most terrible slums

It wasn't only the big-timers; there were vaudeville groups like the Black Birds doing their act in England and Scotland or a more serious set like the Fisk Jubilee Singers with their Negro spirituals. There were also a few personalities—mostly Afro-Americans—who had opened up little clubs in the West End of London. This was allowed by the censors for they recognized the group-consciousness of the West Indian and West African and accepted that there should be places of relaxation. One of the most famous of these was the Florence Mill Club, manned by Amy Ashwood Garvey (Garvey's second wife); you could go there after you'd been slugging it out for two or three hours at Hyde Park or some other meeting, and get a lovely meal dance and enjoy yourself. Then there was the well-known West Indian club—The Caribbean. And in these places you always got a chance to hear some of the up-and-coming composers or players like the famous Cuban musician, Carl Bareto, Hike Hatch the pianist, or Sammy Davis and others.

The other type of club was a much more dubious business You had the occasional unscrupulous black who wanted permis-

ion to open up low clubs, and as there was always the difficulty
of licences for that sort of thing, you created what were called
Negro Welfare Associations—a string of these joints, where
the intention was not welfare but simply to bleed the fellows—
in Cardiff, Liverpool or wherever. I felt this sort of thing was so
damnable for the Negro image; we had a duty to people on the
Left like John Strachey or to the Communist Party for that
matter, to show there was more to us than dancing the Black
Bottom along with a bunch of whores. Typical of this 'welfare'
organizer was Jimmy Taylor; his father had been a big man in
the Gold Coast around the United Africa Company; he had
sent his son to an English public school, Charterhouse, and then
on to Oxford. He could hardly conjugate a verb, but he got his
M.A. He could never make a go of anything until he resorted
to these things. And as I say this inflamed me, and made me
determined to provide only the very best when I turned later
to this restaurant business.[15] I wanted no part with this image
of the Negro club with its bunch of women packing the place
from morning to night, catering to the black Americans and
later the Bevin Boys during the war. Their attitude was simply:
'Bombs are dropping and England is going up in smoke; so
let us also hack our way through, get drunk and fraternize.'
Well, I thought too much was at stake. If we were really
ambassadors of our people, we should be able to portray our
manhood without any regrets.

This shady business was close to another damnable activity
you could see at work amongst blacks in Paris or London—what
I call social sex imperialism. In addition to straight political
imperialism there was this other form which had been operating
since the days of slavery, and had been suggesting through the
newspaper and novels that this Negro was a curious human
being with strange capacities. Always in the Tarzan and related
strips there was this white man coming to rescue the white
woman from being raped by the black man. Why this fascination
about black sex? Then, especially as the marriage tie loosened
in America and Europe, and people began to say that their
marriages had never been consummated as they should, the
Negro was again projected as a sex demon, full of this and that.
It was even more noticeable in France than in England, and when
we used to go across there, we would talk to our boys there

about it; that this consorting with blacks was a form of sex imperialism, and you didn't hear the whites comparing notes afterwards, or see these blacks being thrown on the scrapheap once the spark and vitality had gone out of them. Unfortunately, too many of the Negroes saw the immediate rewards in the system and capitalized on it, walking about the West End with a big cigar and owning a little specialized salon.

I've even been put in this situation myself. In Manchester I had a number of close relationships with some of the girls, and there was one in particular from a Jewish family that I knew quite well. As a matter of fact they thought I was a falasha with my tie-up to Ethiopia. Anyway, this girl at eighteen developed a strong sex-obsession, and she would come across to me and tell me what she had been doing—not across the colour line but with Jews and other businessmen who would exploit her to the hilt. She reached a stage when she did not know her limit, and would tell me the excesses of her performance (she subsequently married a wrestler, so you can see the mentality). Finally she began to ask me, 'Mak, what about some of your boys; I've heard of their performance . . . .'

All this made many of us very careful in associating with white women; otherwise you could have terrible things said of them and of yourself. Sometimes if you were walking down Piccadilly with a white girl, some white drunk would shout 'white bastard' at her. Some people also would immediately identify this white woman who was walking with you as someone loose, because no outstanding woman would be seen with a nigger. So against your will you took up a defensive attitude, and managed to let the woman be a little in front of you—the excuse being that Picadilly was so full of people! One had the same tactics with the older woman, who felt you were a missionary boy, and would take you into coffee shops with some sort of pretentious English smile. Here one could see the great injustice being done, often unconsciously, by many of these fine women who were dedicated to establish Negro rights.

We shall return to some further aspects of this London scene later, but for the moment my own base changed to Manchester. A lot of our London group had split up with the onset of the Blitz, and the attempt to recruit blacks, through invoking 18B, to some form of war effort. We refused. 'There is only one

war we will fight. It is the war against Britain. So don't tell us
about Hitler. We are not interested. We are only concerned
about the man who is on our shoulders now.' We sent these
enlistment forms back with these sorts of words on them, and
we expected all the time that they would come and put us away.
They didn't, however, so we dispersed. Kenyatta went to the east
coast.[16] Padmore, however, had a throat infection and it was
feared he would never be able to speak. So one fell back once
again on the great conspiracy of white men against black. Indeed,
it was this anxiety about white medical men that led most of the
African students to put themselves in the charge of Dr. Clarke,
this Cambridge man from the West Indies.[17] I suppose all
of us, steeped as we were in the revolutionary tradition, magnified
our importance out of all proportion, thinking that we were
wanted men.

The reason I chose Manchester was that Peter Milliard was
there, and I was able to room with him for a time.[18] He had built
up his medical practice and like the doctors of the pre-National
Health era was more of a shopkeeper. He had his panel patients,
as they were called, and they paid their three shillings. At this
period most black doctors worked amongst the poorer black and
white patients, with the exception of a few rich Indians who had
established themselves already on Harley Street.

I registered then in Manchester University for an advanced
degree in history—the Anglo-Saxon period, because I noticed
that there were certain defects in my knowledge about the
growth of the realm. I was particularly interested to investigate
the blackout that was alleged to have happened after the Barbarian struggle against Roman domination. I kept this side up
because I felt there would be important parallels for the process of
colonial freedom. However, I maintained my close contacts with
the co-operative movement, and along with my Sierra Leone
colleague, Reverend Jones (or Lamina Sankoh as he was later called), we created an organization to embody our beliefs—the African Co-operative League.[19] Previously in London I had had close
contact with the co-operative movement; I had known Lord
Rusholm, the secretary of the movement, and he did not hesitate
to give me the names of the various individuals and guilds in
the North which might be crucial. As a result of this interest,
I was asked to become a lecturer at the Co-operative Union in

Manchester, at the time when John Thomas was principal.

Through this position I gradually accumulated savings because I would go out in the late afternoons three or four times a week getting £2 and my fares, to speak to the various women's co-operative guilds. I soon knew well all the people in the co-operative movement in Balloon Street, Manchester, and I began to point out to the meetings some of the contradictions I saw in the movement. It was all very well all the people in the co-operative party being in favour of peace and denouncing imperialism, but the movement did not question the fact that the wholesale side of the business was doing over £20 million worth of dealings in tea from Ceylon.[20] Our line here was that the movement should try to change the exploitative nature of the tea plantation, and instead make them into co-operative producers' unions. This would ensure that the English would still get their tea, but would remove the imperialistic appearance which the old relationship between the metropolis and the colonies had engendered. And the democratic nature of the co-operative organization with its cells and branches meant that you could get these sorts of points across quite easily. So it was not difficult to convince some of these women to feel that 'my money is helping to exploit people over there.'

We didn't restrict the attack to a single item, but also entered the African field through our analysis of the palm-oil background to margarine. I was able to show, from my experience of the co-operative movement in Denmark, that there, too, it was not free from contamination. At that time the big Danish movement was selling all the butter and bacon it could for export, and the population was eating margarine. But to get this margarine they had to rely either on the exploitative United Africa Company which was an octopus over West Africa, or the Dutch companies in Indonesia and Java. So there were these networks of alliances between the European powers which had to be exposed. This meant that one had to operate on a similarly broad front if one was attacking certain aspects of the movement; which was why at many meetings I would not restrict myself to one subject but would use the occasion to point out certain things about Italian imperialism, handing out copies of Sylvia Pankhurst's *New Times*, or speak on Dutch imperialism. 'You fellows may fall for the myth that in Holland there's equality, but in Java and other places it's hell!' I had been greatly helped in my knowledge of the international co-operative movement by my time in London for there the offices of the Co-operative Union were just round the corner from the IASB. I knew this famous Englishman, Strickland, who had played a role in many parts of the world, and in particular had set up a series of co-operative banks in China.[21] And Mrs. Digby, who worked there in the London office, was very close to me, helping me to consult a number of invaluable documents on the movement. But, as I mentioned earlier, my main reason for projecting these ideas through the African Co-operative League was that I wanted to get away from the ethics of some of these African businessmen who came over from West Africa to Europe and America robbing their own people through cocoa and other commodities.[22] It seemed absolutely necessary to adopt the high British ideal of morality in the co-operative movement and link this with our traditional African form of co-operation in the *osusu*. Here I think Padmore with his demolition of colonialism really lacked anything positive to substitute; it wasn't just a question of independence, but how were we to organize our activity thereafter?

After a time in this work in Manchester, I got involved in the scandal over the Finnish co-operative movement. It was at the time when the movement, with its strong links to the British, was deeply involved in combating Russian aggression; and there were also moves afoot to switch the war against Germany to one which would back the Finns against the Russians. Now as a good socialist I could not reconcile this sort of thing; so when Tanner, the Finnish Foreign Minister, came over to Britain and addressed the Manchester union, I attacked him: 'You Tanner, who are you? You are a stooge of the imperialists. I have no objection to your fighting as a nationalist in defence of your country, but when you are prepared even to come to terms with the Germans against Russia, then you are guilty of high imperialism.' I attacked him on these lines, and got my chips.

A lot of the blacks were frustrated in Manchester at that time; those at the University had no facilities beyond the bar for relaxation, and in town the Africans and West Indians who lived in the area also had few places to go. So I called a meeting and made an appeal: 'The Indians and Chinese have restaurants,

135

so what about us?' 'We have no objection but we have no money.' 'All right' I said, 'I'll do it.' So through my savings I was able to get a licence for the Ethiopian Teashop; it was a building for which I only paid £4 per week and it had a basement, first and second floors; prices in property were very low, because Manchester had receded greatly during the period before the war, and things hadn't picked up again. As there was a lot to be done in the way of knocking down partitions, I challenged my colleagues at the University to come and help me knock the place up. I got Dr. Jones, his brother Ademolo, and a number of Nigerian students. Then I called in a plasterer, and told him the sort of decoration I wanted. Some of our friends also from the Art College, English boys and girls, came and made some lovely murals.

For the heavier investment in crockery, cutlery and other items, I was helped by some of the close Jewish friends I had in the Left. In particular there were two brothers, James Harris who was a jeweller and his brother, a lawyer; they provided me with letters of credit to one of the large mercantile companies, and allowed me to use their names if I needed to raise some capital. There were other solid men like the Quaker, Marsh, who had a soft spot for me. Many of them had come across me through my public meetings on Ethiopia, and they knew me to be quite fluent. Also, however, Manchester itself was rather like an African community. People were human and warm and you never were made to feel a stranger.

After reconstruction, I was able to fit in twenty-two tables, eleven on the ground floor and eleven above. In the basement I installed two toilets, and used another part as a coal room. I also rigged up a primitive fridge. The running of it was also straightforward; I found a Hungarian woman, Mrs. Adler, who was one of the many Jewish refugees in the city. (We met at the internat onal club.) She took over the place from eight in the morning until five, when I came back from the University. I then joined them in the preparations because most of our trade was done in the evenings up to midnight. Originally I had calculated that if I was able to take £10 a day for four days that would bring in £40 between Monday and Friday; then if one was able to take £20 per day over the weekend (the English worker is paid on Friday), it would bring us about £100 a week. Well, this is exactly what happened for about three months, then suddenly a jump, and we skyrocketed to £50 per day. I felt ashamed that I seemed to be becoming a bloated plutocrat overnight; however, it was a godsend from the business angle that I was kicked out of the Co-operative College, for I was able to give myself full-time to the new work. I now proceeded further down Oxford Road four blocks, towards All Saints Cathedral and nearer the University. There I found a tremendous building for £8 per week—four floors of it.

It took me some £3,000 to renovate this, and I called it the Cosmopolitan. What distinguished it were its murals. You see, I had a good friend who was an Austrian Jew (I'd met him by chance in London) and just at the time I needed him, Jean appeared in Manchester. I told him, 'It's not a question of money, but racial prestige. We have to make these white folks know that we are enlightened. I want you to go to town on this.' Well, he did and it took him four months to complete it. He created murals of humanity, showing the contribution of each, whether African, Scots, Welsh or Austrian; he showed the common humanity through depicting the gardens of the world from Japanese style to English. But it wasn't all just decorative. Take the mural on the Poles; one part of the canvas showed the death of Poland in Europe with the cannons and the invasions, and then in the New World we could see the Pole reappearing, but this time what was portrayed was the typical immigrant Pole leading the charge against the blacks. I had him write above this, 'Whither Mankind??' It made a big impact on the Black American soldiers who were pouring into England at this period, and they reacted also to the picture of the big Texan with his hat and his pistols, drawn as a threat to the darkies.

It was of course fortunate that Manchester became a base for many of these black troops once America had entered the war, because when these black boys heard they came like wild men. It now took all my time, and I had to buy 58, Oxford Road which I used as a central base. This is where I did all my 'white-market' operations—I won't say black-market! I made a big item of goats, because at that time they were not rationed, but we also used turkeys and other meats. My job was to keep the two restaurants supplied. We formed a link with chaps from Cyprus (they became fraternal members in our Pan-African Federation later);

137

I tended to use them as managers, and employ a few Indian waiters and Chinese. So it really was Cosmopolitan. We had two Chinese cooks whom I had brought from Cardiff in charge of the Chinese menu which was some thirty dishes, and the Indians made curry dishes.

Soon, however, the two restaurants were not enough, and so I opened another, The Orient, near the University, and this was only curries. Finally, I opened a club. It was difficult to get a drinking licence, and the easiest way was to open a club. I got therefore a beautiful building next to evons College at the University renovated it, and we called it the Forum Club. This again had a good cuisine, and I added the element of music here with performances by the great calypsonians like Lord Kitchener. A number of my African and West Indian colleagues helped with the organization: Jomo Kenyatta, for instance, at one time was in charge of the Cosmopolitan; George helped out with another small place I acquired, called the Belle Etoile. But the crucial thing was planning the menus and the supplies, and once we had organized this, the thing went like clock-work. The bank was quite near, so late at night whoever was in charge of the various centres would come to me. I had a safe key, and everything would be deposited safely. But the more compli-cated money side of it I left to Gaisey—he's on that photograph with Kwame and me [see plate VIII]. He was then doing account-ancy in Manchester, and would return to become a big capitalist in Ghana.

But I required someone then, because at the height of our operations there were sixty-two on the payroll, Cypriots, Chinese and others, and so many different menus to order for. We didn't have many spec fically African dishes, because I reckoned that Jolof rice, say, was really identical to certain kinds of Spanish pilaff. But some of the West Indian boys would tease me over their dish, peas and rice: 'Could I have some peas and rice, Mr. Ras. I'm not insulting you, I know you belong to the nobility with your name, Ras. But it have a different meaning to the way we use it in the West Indies.' To get some of the clients over to the restaurants from where they lived, we organized some of the professional men who had cars, such as Milliard or Martinson, and they'd ferry some of our clientele back and forward.

I think a lot of the success of these ventures could be attributed to the fact that I was no stranger to business. My early orientation in Guyana, the observation I had made of my father in the diamond industry meant that I was prepared to venture where someone with no background would hesitate. I wasn't interested, as I've said, in any hole in the wall operation with a heap of funny girls. One had to be prestigious, and I tried to make these places equal to the best, waiters in tailcoats, carpeted floors, to counter this lurking European suspicion that black people are black because they don't wash and are dirty.[23] So one had set to work to convince that there was no difference between us given an opportunity. You had to combat it even with your university friends who would joke at you during wartime: 'How was the blackout last night?' (referring to drunkenness and the curfew). And you'd answer, 'Come on, don't insult me. A black man doesn't feel the blackout. I can see and you fellows have to eat your carrots!'

But I did not regard these restaurants as mine, nor the takings for that matter. This was what the pan-African thing was all about. I suppose I felt that they made it possible to carry on a whole range of defence operations for blacks at home and abroad, in rather the way that the International Labour Defence (ILD) had been doing in the United States.[24] For instance, one day when we were in the thick of the restaurant business, I picked up the *Sunday Observer*, and read that there had been a mutiny on the River Plate; some one hundred and twenty blacks had revolted and were going to be charged.[25] Looking through the names I could see that the majority were Nigerians and Somalis. Immediately I picked up my telephone and asked my lawyer: 'Do you know anyone in Plymouth?' 'What's up?' 'Haven't you seen the headlines that a number of our boys have been charged with mutiny on the River Plate—and you know what mutiny means during wartime? I want something done.' Well, he got to work right away and rang a lawyer friend of his in Plymouth; he rang me back to say he'd made arrangements, and had told his friend that I'd be coming down right away. As the boys were going into court the next day, Monday, there was not time to lose. I called a few of my henchmen, including one man, Raj Fini, who had a gambling house and was a noted debaucher.[26] I said, 'Raj.' He said, 'Oh, father,

139

I was just trying to get to bed.' I said, 'What, at ten o'clock in the morning?' 'But, father, you know I live by immoral earnings; but what's the matter?' I told him, and ended, 'Raj, we're leaving tonight, and as most of the names are Nigerian, you'll have to come and do the interpreting!' Raj was a notorious character with the police; still he had his value when it came to building up a defence when you didn't have all the facts.

We drove through the night and reached Plymouth at about nine o'clock. Straight to the solicitor, an affable man, Page, linked to the Labour Party and a good friend of Sidney Silverman. He was prepared to go ahead, but warned us, 'It's a rather dangerous wicket because you have the Commodore, and the Judge of the Court of Admiralty is this fellow Wills who's tied up with the cigarette people.' We told him that our plan was to work for a postponement at least for ten days, on the grounds of language problems and the need for interpreters. Soon we had gained access to information and found out that the thing had blown up to a crisis because the ship they'd been on, *The Princessa*, had sprung a leak in the River Plate at the very time that the German battleship was menacing the British merchant marine in the area. These blacks eventually went on strike because it was a hopeless job bailing for sixteen hours nonstop and keeping the steam up. Finally the chief engineer went there with his pistol and drew it. The mutiny followed. It was as simple as that. But we also found out that already a certain amount of tribal or national differences had sprung up within the accused blacks. We were allowed access to them, and immediately pointed out that 'whatever your tribal differences are, you'd better unify!' And fortunately my good Somali friend Ali Mira arrived just afterwards; so that took care of that difficulty. We then told the blacks that there was to be no talking in English; they were to use Creole, Yoruba or Arabic, and our interpreters could then use their talents to make the story hang together. Next we organized a first line of barristers to assist the solicitors. I got Mrs. Herbraun, a famous Jewish woman Q.C. and another man who was the Recorder at Liverpool. Even Pritt and Sir Stafford Cripps offered to take part.

However, the affair got me into trouble with the tax men, for in a few days' time the newspapers splashed the headlines 'Ethiopian Restaurateur Stands Bail for £62,000.' This covered a hundred and eight of the men, and my banks were all ready to produce the money. The thing was that I hadn't paid a penny of income tax during all my time in Manchester, because I felt that in this colonial struggle paying income tax would be a crime. What was one paying income tax for after four hundred years and more of slavery ended with no compensation to the blacks? The headline put the Inland Revenue people on my tail, and in about two years' time they had caught up with me!

But it was a fantastic case. It lasted over fourteen days, and point by point the barristers broke down the thirty-four charges which had been levelled against each mutineer until only three charges were left, and finally everyone was acquitted bar eight or nine fellows who had to serve six months. The Colonial Office people were also rather anxious for an acquittal, because they knew that otherwise these rotten fellows like Makonnen would make it difficult for them, and Lord Haw Haw might get hold of it, and give the news to the colonial world about this travesty of British justice.

This wasn't an isolated case. A few years later, in December 1946, there was an equally dramatic affair in Manchester. It started with a group of about forty West Indian RAF chaps who at that time were based in Manchester, and who on one particular night were having a meal with some white girls in the Cosmopolitan. Well, by about eleven o'clock they had finished eating, and as it was a very cold night—snow on the ground and heavy snow falling—they decided to escort these girls home. Now when they got to Piccadilly in Manchester, between Woolworths and the Grand Hotel, they were attacked by a group of white boys. As I think I said, a Jamaican never retreats; he's a cantankerous fellow and fights to the last. I don't know the whole story, but the result was that one of the white boys had his jugular vein severed. We actually didn't know anything about it until about 5.30 that Monday morning when I was rung up by a European friend, Horace Gill. He was a kind man and had very good relations with the coloured people; in fact I had bought him a taxi to help in taking clients to and from the restaurants. At any rate this man Gill came round to my place—I was staying at the Orient overnight—and said, 'I want to tell you you're in trouble without knowing it: one of our boys got killed last night by one of your boys, and I think the

141

police have got the wrong fellows.'

I thanked him and by seven o'clock I had arranged for things to be done for the day in the restaurants. I rang my solicitor, and told him to hold a watching brief, and warned him that we didn't want the Colonial Office interfering this time, as it had tried to do at Plymouth. It held no consular authority over us; we didn't accept the Colonial Office as our master. We after all knew its history, that it had only been created back in 1838 to lessen the impact of crude imperialism upon our kinsmen, and it had often co-operated with the plantocrats. Now however that we were free men, we didn't look to the Colonial Office to interpret our wants. No, we would defend ourselves.

I discovered that the man they were holding for murder was Beard, a Jamaican; so I decided to call the large Jamaican community in Manchester together—many of them the Bevin boys who had been called across to help Britain out in technical skills when her back was really up against the wall in the early forties. They responded well because I was well-known over the restaurants, and also I had invested a little money in setting up a tailor shop which two Jamaicans had opened. We met; I said, 'What are we going to do? This is no tribal issue; we could easily get some of our European friends to help us, but I think that we should really get a black lawyer to defend this man here. We want to project the image that the black man is capable of carrying on his own defence.' 'Oh, sir, that is easy, sir'—you know how the Jamaican talks—'sir, sir, we have a man called Mr. Manley from Jamaica. The man has never lost a criminal case yet, sir, and if only we had the money . . . ' 'Don't talk about money,' I said. 'It's a question of human life and all of us are involved. And don't forget we have had a number of incidents like this: a West African had his eyes gouged out by a bunch of hoodlums. And God knows where next it may fall. You chaps have come here to help in the war effort—all of you— and this is what you are getting. So don't talk to me of money. We must fight this thing to a man.' It was decided therefore at once that a group of four would get together to prepare a telegram and send it off.

By Tuesday we had received a cable back from Manley accepting. He would send a man across to hold a watching brief along with my lawyer, Rosenthal, until he himself came over. At once

I sent £1,500 for Manley's passage and the rest. Well, he came over about a week later, and there was the most spectacular trial. The man was so methodical. The first person he wanted to see was the meteorologist to know what had been the snowfall on that particular night, and what had been the visibility. Finally when he got to court, he made asses of the police; on the one hand he showed that they really believed all niggers looked alike; yet individual police were claiming that they identified Beard at a distance of forty yards. That night the visibility had of course been less than ten yards. Well, the judge had to stop the case, and admitted publicly that since the days of the great Bannerman he had never seen such a brilliant performance. Also, he was flattered because Manley had been at his own Inn. But it was fantastic. The darkies went wild, and there was prestige galore for the community.[27]

These were possibly the most spectacular two cases, but this defence business was almost a daily concern. A bit later, in 1948, we had forty of our chaps arrested for fighting with the Irish in Liverpool, and there again we had to call in Sidney Silverman and this Jewish woman barrister we had used in Plymouth.[28] All of it was to show that as people of African origin we were determined to stand by each other. This was as important an aspect of pan-Africanism as the formal conference which was held now and then. Often, too, it made for a certain amount of working relationship with people in the LCP, even though we might differ with them over the purely political strategy. Take for instance another result of the black American soldiers in Britain: hundreds of illegitimate children born of English women. This confronted all of us with a problem. We tackled it in two ways. Sir Leary Constantine got some help from his Jewish friends in Leeds, and I gave over £5,000 to found a home for coloured children. We then sent Eddy Duplan, who was working with coloured seamen in Liverpool, on a mission to the United States.[29] It was a very crucial time in America, because the Daughters of the American Revolution were trying to get a law through Congress outlawing coloured children born of American black fathers: 'These black men will be marrying English and Italian women and will be coming into America and lording it over us. So for white prestige's sake we must do something to keep them out. Marrying an American doesn't make the children

American.' This was the sort of line. Fortunately, however, Duplan was able to capitalize on the usual pan-African solidarity, and was able to contact a number of American women with no children who were prepared to adopt some of the ones with us.

It was the same with the blacks who arrived illicitly at the British ports. The immigration people termed them stowaways and put them in jail. But when the word reached Constantine in the LCP or us, we would do our best to get them out. We were prepared to go a bit further than Constantine and perjure ourselves if it helped to get the fellows free. And as the Colonial Office was anxious to avoid any race incidents during the war, it was possible to get away with a lot. Our line was to go down to immigration and say, 'What's this nonsense? This man you've got is from my village; he's come over here to help the war effort, and you're calling him a stowaway when he's a patriot. Watch out or you'll be driving him into Hitler's arms.' So the officer would become apologetic and release the man. For all I know the word may have got around that it was better not to trifle with Padmore or Makonnen, otherwise they'd bring the house down!

A final example of this defence activity involved a different kind of refugee. Sometimes when Padmore was out on one of his sorties to Europe, or when I was up in Denmark or elsewhere, you would come across Jewish women who needed some way of getting out of this hell into Britain. Well, you marry them, and for a couple of months they become Mrs. Padmore or whatever it is, reach England, and from there some Jewish refugee group can manoeuvre her over to America. What did it matter if you were infringing the law? What is the law in a bourgeois state anyway? So, all this was justifiable if it was preventing in some way man's imposition on man.

The place of the black writer was something else that I felt we should tackle in Britain. It was all very well having famous Negro entertainers, but we also needed to project this other more serious side. Of course we had had people like C. L. R. James and Cedric Dover in the 1930s,[30] but such few writers as there were had to enter a field that was predominantly white— white journals, white publishers, and nearly always white men writing about black. All right. But what this meant in even such a radical circle as the Left Book Club series was that your work

144

had to be read by a white man to see if it had any merit. It was reminiscent of the situation in America where the white-controlled magazine, *New Masses*, was always 'discovering' talented black writers, but frequently they fell by the wayside once they began to resent their poetry being assessed by some mediocre Jew boy. The feeling was always that they were being used. Now in England we had begun the process of making ourselves independent with the *International African Opinion:* nobody could suggest it had been produced with Moscow gold or other white funds.

So once I was firmly set up in Manchester, I decided to go about this thing more thoroughly, and set up a publishing house. I registered it as the Pan-African Publishing Co. Ltd., I think the name was, and we had as directors, Padmore, Jomo, Milliard and myself. I had the capital coming from the restaurants, and also I had developed good relations with some of the printers; a number of them used to come and lunch at my places. In particular I knew the director of the printing firm that dealt with Sylvia Pankhurst's *New Times and Ethiopia News*, so there was little to get in the way. I became a bona fide member of the publishers' association, and proceeded to bring out a number of number of pieces that needed publicity. There was a pamphlet by Kenyatta, and a kind of Socratic discussion between Nancy Cunard and George Padmore on the black man's burden, and a manuscript by Eric Williams.[31] I was also asked to look at a manuscript from the South African trade-unionist Kadalie.[32] Apart from these we brought out the monthly periodical *Pan-Africa*. Having one's own press allowed me to keep up with my Ethiopian interest, and I was able to aid Sylvia and her son Richard Pankhurst with the publication of their book on Italian war crimes in Ethiopia.[33] It cost about £75 to produce.

The publishing was associated, however, with a bookshop that I started called the Economist. It carried the books from the press but also I had close contacts with Manchester University students, and through consulting their syllabuses was able to provide for some of their wants. Just at the point when I needed some assistance with the shop, I had a letter from an LSE student, Miss Nichol, who had earlier been involved in helping some West Indian girls. She had just finished her course, and wondered if we had a job for her. So she became the general secretary of

the Economist. We put out a number of feelers to African countries
and offered to send a lot of the Oxford University Press books
out. But it wasn't a race bookshop, either in the sense that it
catered only to blacks—there weren't enough around for this to be
possible—or in the sense that we only sold books about blacks.
However, when there was some particular book on blacks that
I felt needed promoting, we went to town. I gave a big splash to
Kenneth Little's book, *Negroes in Britain*, also to George Padmore's
How Britain Rules Africa, and to Bill (Eric) Williams' book.[34]
Once this place was going you could say that Oxford Road
was my main street; you could go from the Ethiopia, to the
Cosmopolitan, to the Forum, to the Orient, and finally to the
Economist, then down to the university.

George used to rib me about this with his: 'You damn businessman; you'll become an octopus and we'll have to restrain you.'
Probably he reflected on what had happened with the Garvey
affair, when people had started out with wonderful intentions
of working for the race and had ended up being either spend-
thrifts or big bureaucrats. I think he was also concerned because
he had seen the way Zik was operating his publishing company
in Nigeria. Zik was basically a man who had made capitalism
work, like Lord Beaverbrook, and there's no doubt that he
used sweated labour to bring out his *Pilot*. Also he used the same
formula that had made Abbott, the editor of the *Chicago Defender*,
into a millionaire. Abbott had made his pile by selling Negro
injustice; Negroes bought the *Defender* to see how they were
being lynched or kicked out of restaurants. As we weren't
going to this extreme, we didn't expect to make money out of
Pan-Africa; we thought we'd be lucky to pay our way.[35] In
fact it had to be subsidized by my other concerns, just as the
Manchester Guardian received subsidies from a Jewish front
organization, or *The Spectator* for maintaining its tradition of
a high intellectual standard.

Our contacts with white girls were invaluable in all this
literary and promotional activity. Many of them were partial
to our cause, and when I took a manuscript round to them for
cutting on to stencils, they were quite prepared to steal the stencils
and other materials from their offices. Our best helpers were what
you could call the typical English type of devoted girl, from
LSE or like Dinah Stock from Newnham College, Cambridge.

We didn't have to seek them out either. They would hear us addressing meetings at Trafalgar Square or in some of the London halls, and they'd come round and ask if there was anything to be done. Dinah in particular was invaluable because of her contact with Reg Reynolds who was involved with the Peace Group. Unlike a number of these peace-groupers, he saw that this peace movement was just a bubble unless it touched the colonial question. He could see that peace meant maintaining the *status quo* in the Empire.

We recognized naturally that the dedication of some of these girls to our cause was an expression of equal rights for women. One way of rejecting the oppression of men was to associate with blacks. To walk with a Negro into a posh club like the Atheneum was to make this point. But many of them were viciously attacked for this. Nancy Cunard was said by the *Express* to be sipping and sleeping with black men, but she was successful in stinging them for libel.[36] The trouble was, however, that a number of blacks and Indians were determined to associate with white women for a different reason. They felt it was a revolutionary act to get their own back on Europe by seducing white women. I had to speak about this in Hyde Park once, and attack these apparently intelligent students who felt that by getting a bastard child they could solve the problem of imperialism. George had no time for this either. In fact he went almost to the other extreme, and was very cagey about women. You could never say that George was around with the girls.

Looking back on this period, you certainly couldn't say we were living the sort of life that one heard the eighteenth century revolutionaries lived—morbid fellows who were distracted and had never a gay moment as they thought how they might destroy society. We were operating in the midst of a radicalism unmatched in Europe, but it was a gay period, a period of purposefulness. You had the feeling that the truth was being told once and for all. Britain was really in a ferment—seething, in fact, like an African pot. And people wanted to know if the things which we spoke about were really true. So the opportunity which that historic period provided us was rather valuable in the cause to which we were committed.

NOTES TO CHAPTER 9

1 For the general background to blacks in Britain, see K. Little, *Negroes in Britain;* M. Banton, *The Coloured Quarter* (London, 1955); St. Clair Drake, 'The Colour-Bar in Britain: A Study in Social Definitions', *Sociological Review*, December 1955; Sheila Patterson, *Dark Strangers* (London, 1963).

2 Useful detail on Nancy Cunard is supplied in Hooker, *Black Revolutionary*, pp. 27–8. For Bridgeman's contacts with Africans, see Rhodie, 'Gold Coast Aborigines', pp. 391, 393, 401–2.

3 See, however, some interest in the Scottsboro affair in the *Keys* (publication of the League of Coloured People), iii, 4 April—June 1936, p. 63.

4 There is forthcoming a biographical study of this Gold Coast intellectual by J. Ayo Langley in the Oxford Black Biographies series (New York). See also below, p. 275n.

5 Since Fredericks and Bruyning had formed the Negro Progress Convention in 1924, there had been a number of developments; following directly in the Booker Washington tradition; land had been acquired in the Demerara area to build a 'Tuskegee'; however, later in the same year, 1934, Fredericks died. The *Keys* noted in its obituary that he had been 'British Guiana's Booker T. Washington', ii, 2, October–December, 1934, pp. 29, 41; also, ii, 1, 1934 and iii, 1, 1935, p. 10. It is interesting to note that C. L. R. James read a paper on his fellow-Trinidadian, 'The Life of Captain Cipriani', at the First Weekend Conference of the League of Coloured People, 24–27 March 1933.

6 Aggrey's original parable was 'You can play a tune of sorts on the white keys, and you can play a tune of sorts on the black keys, but for harmony you must use both the black and the white keys', E. W. Smith, *Aggrey of Africa* (London, 1929), p. 123. See also, King, 'James E. K. Aggrey', pp. 511–30.

7 The United Africa Company was the result of a merger between the Niger Company and the African and Eastern Trade Corporation in 1929.

8 For WASU, see J. Coleman, *Nigeria: Background to Nationalism* (California, 1958), pp. 204–7. Also the publication *WASU* (Journal of the West African Students of Great Britain) from vol. i, 1926.

9 For the hostel episode, see 'The Truth about Aggrey House', a brief publication of WASU, reproduced in V. B. Thompson, *Africa and Unity*, pp. 335–7. Also, Philip Garigue, 'The West African Students Union', *Africa*, xxii (January 1953), pp. 55–69.

10 See further Ladipo Solanke, 'United West Africa (or Africa) at the Bar of the Family of Nations' (London, 1927).

11 For Vischer's earlier role in Africa, see Sonia Graham, *Government and Mission Education in Northern Nigeria, 1900–19, with Special Reference to the Work of Hanns Vischer* (Ibadan, 1966).

12 See further, Williams, *Inward Hunger*, ch. 4, *passim*.

13 Chris Jones, a Barbadian, had, interestingly enough, first met George Padmore at a mass meeting organized in London for the Scottsboro boys. Jones died in September 1944, and the committee set up to organize relief for his six children and wife consisted of Ethel Mannin, Padmore, Makonnen and Reg Reynolds. See also Jones, 'Britain's Coloured Seamen', *Keys*, v, 1, 1937, pp. 17–18.

14 For mention of Pastor Eckhart's African Churches' Mission of Liverpool, see Padmore, *Pan-Africanism or Communism?* p. 163.

15 Both J. Taylor and E. J. Duplan (also from the Gold Coast) were involved with the Negro Welfare Societies; note the role that Duplan played in the Manchester Pan-African Congress in the session on 'The Colour Problem in Britain', in Padmore (ed.),

History of the Pan-African Congress (Hammersmith Bookshop, London, n.d.), pp. 27-8. For Duplan's later role in Ghana, see W. Scott Thompson, *Ghana's Foreign Policy* (Princeton, 1969), pp. 367-9.

16 On Kenyatta in Storrington, Sussex, see Savage, 'Jomo Kenyatta', pp. 615-32; also G. Delf, *Jomo Kenyatta* (London, 1961), pp. 118-29.

17 For Dr. Cedric Belfield Clarke, see Hooker, *Black Revolutionary*, 40n.

18 Milliard had returned to England after his spell at Panama, and at the onset of the Ethiopian campaign, he had been responsible for organizing in Manchester the International Brotherhood of Ethiopia. His secretary was G. Fiagbenu and treasurer, P.O. Jackson.

19 Lamina Sankoh represented the People's Forum at the Manchester Conference.

20 Some of the background to the co-operative wholesale movement is contained in Harry Laidler, *History of Socialism* (London, 1968), p. 683.

21 Strickland wrote widely on co-operatives; see, for example, his 'The Co-operative Movement in South Africa', *Journal of the African Society*, xxxvi (1937), pp. 461-8.

22 For the complicated manoeuvres of some of these African businessmen in Britain, see Rhodie, 'Gold Coast Aborigines', pp. 389-411.

23 For a black American's impression of Makonnen's restaurants, see Hooker, op. cit., 83n.

24 The ILD had been set up by the Communist Party of North America in 1925 specifically to fight certain types of cases through the courts; its most notorious role was over the Scottsboro Defence.

25 Details of *The Princessa* are in St. Clair Drake's papers.

26 R. Fini was present at the fifth Pan-African Congress, representing a group called the Young African Progressive League, along with E. Brown, G. Nelson and A. Agunsanya.

27 For Manley in England over this case of Gerald Newton Beard, see *Keys*, xvi, Dec. 1946, p. 51, and Jan. 1947, p. 57. Also *The Times* (London), 28 Nov. 1946, p. 2.

28 Makonnen's part in the Liverpool riots of 31 July—3 August 1948 is detailed in *Keys*, xvii, 103, pp. 82-6.

29 For Duplan, see note 15 above.

30 It is interesting to note that Padmore dedicated his book on the history of the Pan-African Congress to Cedric Dover.

31 These titles were Kenyatta, *Kenya: Land of Conflict* and Eric Williams, *The Negro in the Caribbean*, and Cunard and Padmore, *White Man's Duty* (an enlarged version of a book first published by W. H. Allen, London, 1942).

32 This manuscript remained unpublished until 1970; see Clements Kadalie, *My Life and the ICU* (Frank Cass, London, 1970).

33 'Italy's war crimes in Ethiopia', *New Times and Ethiopia News*, n.d.

34 Padmore, *How Britain Rules Africa* (London, 1936); William's book referred to is *Capitalism and Slavery* (Chapel Hill, 1944).

35 *Pan-Africa; a Monthly Journal of African Life, History and Thought* began publication in February 1947. Makonnen mentions in the first number of 1948 that it had lost some £400 over the first year, which was not considered excessive when account was taken of booksellers' reluctance to display the journal.

36 See Hooker, for the background to the Cunard libel, p. 28.

CHAPTER 10

PAN-AFRICANISM AND
THE RISE OF AFRICAN LEADERSHIP

AFRICANS were attracted to go to England for a variety of reasons. Many at the lower level simply felt that if they went there they wouldn't starve; they had seen the life style of the white man abroad, and felt that he must come from a land where there is plenty. Others went to get an education they could not find in Africa. But those who were already politically minded, like Jomo Kenyatta, went to London because they held the belief that there were two Englands—the England of the colonies, the settlers and the plantocrats, and the England of Westminster, the anti-slavery societies, and the rebel movements of the Left. Africans felt this contrast instinctively, and were therefore determined to have one of their men over there in London, at the centre of things; someone who could put our case for us. Most, however, left Africa without a thought of politics in their heads. Kwame Nkrumah did not leave the Gold Coast with a definite message, but merely as a student who was prepared to immerse himself in the trend of things.[1] And certainly the majority of the boys from Sierra Leone left without an idea of politics in their heads. They were the very last people to be thinking of politics, for they had come out of an ordered background, informed by institutions like the Church Missionary Society and their old college at Fourah Bay. If such people were asked about politics, they would dismiss it as a very expensive vocation, and not one for a young scholar with a shirt and two pairs of trousers to be thinking of.

But once you got to England, you were often forced to adopt a different attitude, and you began to understand dimensions you were not aware of back home. For the first time you heard of trade unions, which simply hadn't existed in your country; or if they had been there in an area like Takoradi or Sekondi in the Gold Coast, they had only been there for a very small number of skilled workers. Now, however, you were automatically involved in trade unionism, and you saw that along with it went a whole machinery for dealing with grievances. Even if you were just a seaman from the colonies, you began to see what the occasional delegation of lawyers or chiefs coming from your own country to London were driving at. And as you had been sitting day after day in the pub alongside Englishmen, or Scotsmen, or Welshmen, hearing them discuss the day-to-day problems, you began to take a different attitude towards employment. At a stroke you got removed from a world that talks about the *ju-ju* into one of ideas and movements.

Whether you liked it or not, you would find as a student that your university had socialist, conservative and liberal clubs, and the talk of the common-room was about the serious issues of the day. So that however much you might be a retiring student, events imposed certain conditions on you that couldn't be escaped. And if for instance you were thinking about education one day, and you began to add things up: 'That commission that came to my country when I was a small boy that talked about African education . . . and that occasion when Stafford Cripps said that it will take a thousand years at the rate things are going in South Africa for the average Bantu to get a decent education . . . .' These became real issues. In just the same way you would be forced to think out a thing or two when your girlfriend asked one day: 'Is it true that you carry a badge or a mark of slavery on your body?' It might only have been meant in fun, but when the others clustered round and said 'What's he hiding? Come on, show us it,' you would be forced to think about the role of the African in history.

This sort of thing happened several centuries earlier when the first Africans arrived in Europe. The theory prevailed then as now that they were not really human beings; so they were on trial. However, once they were ensconced in a university like Heidelberg or elsewhere in Germany, they were able to prove their worth, and write articles contesting these assumptions about race inferiority. Such early scholars as Amo and Mauritius in Germany have actually been unearthed recently by certain

Germans to project their country as one that recognized African achievement at a very early date.[2]

Be that as it may, almost every African has had to be a pioneer all over again. When he leaves his country he takes that ancient charge that he is a member of a group on trial, and as an ambassador he must give a good account of himself wherever he goes. The same thing went for West Indians; for the New World darkies also felt that they were accountable to their people, and when things were said of them in a derogatory manner, you would be quick to retort: 'It's not so.' And your ignorance at that moment would drive you to research into the history of your people. This is the sense, then, in which Europe has been an important mother; it has been the melting pot of so many ideas and conflicts, and since the black man has been the object of a great deal of this controversy, he has had to deliberate. This is why many of the students throughout the time that Africans have been going to Europe have felt that they were on trial for the race. 'This black one you've got here with hair like my sheep—what is he?' It wasn't all hostile inquiries, of course, but sympathetic or not, race questions were forced on the African abroad; they became his field, and people soon expected them to know their history. If you came across an African or a West Indian who had no visible signs of interest in his race, it might still be there inside him; he might just be taking the line of least resistance because of money troubles, or a fear that if he opened his mouth in Britain, then the little job he hoped to get as a magistrate back home would slip out of his grasp. He wanted to have a clean slate.

There was a great difference between students from Africa domiciled in Britain and those in the United States. You could say that the politics of England were much more realistic and closer to you. People like the Nigerian student, Mbadiwe, and others in America were out of the current of events[3]; we in England were in the mainstream. We were supplying questions to parliamentarians through our close links to the Labour Party. But for America at that time to be discussing Africa was something far-fetched; it seemed like interfering in the good-neighbourly relations between Britain and the States.

But we felt ourselves to be at the centre of gravity as far as Africa was concerned. Every day there would be some cause of concern from there: some judge who had ladled out a heavy sentence and the case was being appealed in England, some question of land being alienated in East Africa. On any one of these occasions we had the machinery of our organization and access to the press to contest reactionary British justice in Africa. Students might come across from Gambia or the Gold Coast and initially they would join WASU as a social convenience, but when there was an outrage in their country, or when a delegation came over, they suddenly found themselves caught up in politics, and directly affected by the outcome. But the fellows in America could only grouse over the whole matter. And often in the absence of the British journals and papers, they were not sure that they had the facts right; and even if they did get the British journals or some of the West African newspapers, it would be a fortnight at least after the event. The big debate in the House of Commons would be two weeks old. You were a spectator rather than a participant. Especially if you were studying in one of the remote Negro colleges like Tuskegee or Hampton, there would be no chance of obtaining the relevant papers, and you would have to rely on hearing from friends back in West Africa. This is why if you look through some of the student newspapers of these colleges at that time there is not much that would pass for African politics in them.

The temptation on the American scene was to play upon the average American's ignorance of Africa. You would therefore try projecting yourself as a prince or a chieftain—the Nigerians were the worst offenders here. Or you would set up some African institute in New York with the object of starting business links between America and Africa. You would approach American industrialists and businessmen and point out that your land had valuable mineral resources; you were beginning to carve out a little world for yourself. All this was much more difficult in Manchester or London. You couldn't dupe a Manchester businessman with stories about diamonds on your ancestral lands. He could find out in a day from the Colonial Office what the position was, and learn that the Crown had all the mineral rights in your home area.

Certainly some of the African students in America became political. Take Ako Ajei who would later be Minister for External

Affairs in Ghana. He knew perfectly well after he had finished at Lincoln University in America that he was not ready to go to work in the Gold Coast, so he went to England to finish his law and be armed properly. It was the same with Kwame. He felt after his time in Lincoln, that he had better come across to England and get a solid legal qualification. But we pooh poohed the idea in his case.[4] We pointed out to him that if he wanted a profession then being a rebel was as good a one as any. After all it was a full-time profession for John Strachey, Harry Pollit, Padmore and Makonnen, so why not? Had he armed himself with law, then he might still have gone into politics, but he would have followed a different style. It would have been more like the situation of the lawyers we mentioned in the West Indies, still political, but a more constitutional approach. Like many colonial lawyers in West Africa, he might have found himself defending other Africans to the hilt, but doing it partly because in the profession he had taken a kind of Hippocratic oath to do so: 'Your Honour, I would like to present this thing on its merits, and I shall quote appropriately. I have a brief and I must defend this brief with my life.'

Kwame had actually shown his interest in politics in the States, which is how we first got to know about him. C. L. R. James was at that time in North America and had noticed that he was getting involved with left-wing groups.[5] He wrote to me about him. 'I have found an exceptional fellow, and he's written a little pamphlet about colonialism which is just perfect; he's not a liberal. He's one of the boys.' Subsequently he came across in time for the Manchester Conference in 1945 and became involved with the struggle. When one met him, one could see that he would become some kind of leader; he had the mark on him. But it was interesting to see the difference in Ako Ajei and him once they were both back in Ghana and in power. Ako Ajei would argue as a lawyer the legal difficulties of extending to some outsider like myself Ghanaian citizenship, while Kwame would cut through such talk: 'What's all this? We have a job to do. We have created this state, and its citizenship is ours to do what we like with.' This is the kind of difference refusing to join the legal profession made to a rebel.

Azikiwe had been in England before he ever went to America, but he had been in America at a much earlier period. Both

Padmore and I knew him when we were there, and, as I mentioned, he attended the meetings of the Libian Institute in the Harlem YMCA. He was already interested in Africa beyond his own Ibo country and was writing on Liberia in world politics.[6] Consequently, when the time came to go back to Africa, it didn't matter which part he went to, because he saw himself as a spokesman for Africa. Zik was, however, very much out of the ordinary run of students who went to America.

But when you look at the results of those Africans who had been to England, you wouldn't be far wrong in saying that England had been the executioner of its own colonial empire. In the sense that she had allowed these blacks to feel the contrast between freedom in the metropolis and slavery in the colonies. Hence it became the old retort: 'What are you going to do with these boys back on the farm, once they have seen Paree (Paris)?'

Africans were not only compelled to think out the position of their own people, but were forced by the pressures of the times into making alliances across boundaries that would have been unthinkable back home. I was reminded of this the other day when Chancellor Brandt reminisced in Kenya about his meeting with people like Kenyatta in Paris in the late thirties.[7] He was, I think, referring to a meeting of the Rassemblement Coloniale in Paris in 1938 where a number of British blacks met their French colleagues and a group of trade unionists like Brandt.[8] The background to the meeting was the worsening situation in Europe, the Middle East and Africa. We were concerned at the Jewish question, at the way large blocks of land were being sold off by the Grand Mufti of Palestine to the Rothschilds and others. This particularly worried some of our French North African members such as Ben Bella and Bourghiba. What was equally worrying to the other French Africans, both Arab and Senegalese, was what the role of the coloured colonial troops was going to be if, as seemed likely, another war was to break out. Was it going to be the old question of the coloured Frenchmen fighting to save democracy in France and maintain imperialism abroad?

The presence of German Social Democrats in the meeting raised equally important issues. For it was quite apparent to us that German imperial ambitions were on the move[9]; recently there had been attempts to revive German influence in southern

Ghana. There had been infiltration into Nigeria and of course in the Cameroons—which they had once held as a colony—agents were buying up plantations. Some of us were even approached by some of these fascists with offers of help against the British imperialists. But we were in no mood to swop one brand for another. We had had strong links earlier with members of the German Communist Party, in particular with Thaelmann who had died in a German prison, and it was members of that sector who had done so much in their time to live down the stigma of German colonial expansion. By 1938 our only links were with the remnants of these Left movements; so many of the intellectuals had escaped to Guyana, or to Scand navia, and I think Brandt himself had come down from Norway as a refugee.

The conference itself was held in the Latin Quarter of Paris at the agricultural school there, and it was attended by an assortment of blacks and Arabs. There was, for instance, Holman Jameson, a Sierra Leonean student, and C. L. R. James who was working on his book from the archives of the Bibliotheque Nationale.[10] From the French black possessions, there were quite a number: Kouyaté from Sudan was conspicuous, also Houphouët-Boigny and Lamine Gueye from West Africa, Césaire from Martinique, and Damas.[11] But what one noticed in contrast to Britain was a lack of freedom of expression. The French blacks gave the impression of being pursued, which meant that a lot of the serious work of the conference had to be carried on behind closed doors, and even there within tribal groupings. We found it in fact more profitable for blacks to discuss black questions, and Arabs Arab, although there were joint sessions.

Back in England, the Spanish Civil War confronted us with a further set of questions, and some new allies. Nehru played a very significant role here by highlighting the use of colonial troops in the various European empires. He was able to show very clearly the role of certain Indian troops which were fighting on many fronts to defend the British Empire, and pointed to the same role that North African troops were playing on General Franco's side. Nehru himself went to Spain, and a number of our people also went across, and saw at first hand the tragedy of these Spanish mercenaries. When he came back a big meeting was organized—a conference on peace and empire.[12] To us this seemed a very misleading approach; how could you have peace *and* empire after all? We determined therefore to go along and demonstrate our feelings on this subject. Now the communists and the Peace League were behind its organization, and naturally the former had managed to get together a few blacks from one of their little front movements in Britain. We objected strongly to the idea of their representing Africans, and took along our own pan-African delegation.

It was a meeting of about 1,500 people, and was being chaired by Commander Young who had forsaken his Rule Britannia military job to become an important prop in the communist movement. Stafford Cripps was there and members of the Socialist Youth League. So at a certain point I appealed for the right to address the hall. I got to the front of the speaker's dais and let them have it: 'This is a conspiracy against Africa. How can you have peace with empire? What you really want is peace of mind to continue to loot your empire. Naturally we are against this. In fact we want war not peace, because only war will settle the contradictions latent in this empire, and show how false its pretensions are. We are not for peace—we can't have peace; we are at war with you now. Instead of peace, we need to be freed from the pass laws, the confiscation of our lands, from carrying the *kipande* in Kenya, and many other badges of our slavery.'[13] Well, to many of our Indian friends even this seemed a bit extreme. All they had wanted was a broader front to stimulate more interest, and now these darkies had come along and had broken the whole thing up. Indeed many people walked out in disgust after I had led this charge.

The Spanish War in general, however, allowed us to focus on the primacy of the colonial question. We were able to show how Franco's alliance with the King of Morocco involved thousands of North Africans in fighting for fascism. We used this example to warn our Left friends of how far a ruling class would go to maintain its position. Many of them felt there was no possibility of the same thing happening in England; that the English ruling class would never bring colonials to England to fight against a socialist revolution. But our attitude was that the ruling class would do anything to preserve itself. It seemed that everybody was just using the colonials for their own ends.

For instance, the French popular-front government under Leon Blum was eagerly pushing the unemployed blacks and Arabs in Paris to join up and fight against Franco, and it was hard to assess the motive uppermost.[14] Was it a clearing of blacks out of France, just as at an earlier period England had got rid of its black poor?[15] Or was it a fight for democracy? There was the same thing with some of the American troops in the Spanish campaign. There the Communist Party of America had signed up a lot of the more advanced left-thinking blacks in Harlem and Chicago and formed them into an Abe Lincoln Brigade to fight against Franco.[16] But it was the old story of blacks fighting for somebody else's cause; in this case because it suited the Russian line at that time. Our feeling was simply that if there was any fighting to be done, and if there were to be any marshalls and commissars, then we should be the ones with the baton in our hand.

It was all the more necessary for us to take a tough line on communist manoeuvres at this time, because they had just recently had an important acquisition to their ranks. This was Max Yergan who had served for many years in the YMCA movement in South Africa[17]; it wasn't so strange, as I knew myself, to move from YMCA radicalism into left-wing politics, and now he was touring round Europe making contacts for his organization, the Council on African Affairs. He formally inaugurated the council in the early forties, along with Paul Robeson, but already in the pre-war period Max had been touring Europe, working among the student element. This put us in a terrible mess, because we knew very well that whoever got signed up by Yergan would then simply become part of the Russian axis, and would proceed to move according to whatever the line from Moscow was. We were particularly concerned to prevent the many South Africans from being used to this end. But I think the only man they did partly manage to use for a time was our old friend Marco Hlubi, a Zulu, who worked as a dancer in the Negro Theatre Company at the old Unity Theatre near King's Cross.[18] Yergan and the communists behind him preferred to make advances towards indigenous Africans like Kenyatta or straight black Americans or West Indians; I dare say they didn't know what to make of Makonnen, 'this man of dubious origin. He is with the King of Kings in

158

Ethiopia one moment, and is just a bourgeois nationalist. He and Padmore are just generals without an army, they have no base and must depend on their pens.'

None of this should suggest that we were vehemently anti-Russian, or anti-communist. Our attitude was this. 'If you are interested in communism, then buy the book! Just as Lenin originally bought the book of this German Jew, Marx. Buy the book. Don't join the club! The Bible is there to buy if you want to know about Jesus. You don't have to join the Catholics.' It was not our intention to stop Africans from reading literature on Marxism. On the contrary. But whatever we did we must not give these communist boys, British, Russian or French, the chance to strengthen their position by joining up. Because in a way they were there under false pretences. Harry Pollitt, the British CP leader, with due respect to him now he's dead, actually wanted a communist empire, and he was not in politics to break up the British Empire any more than Churchill.[19] For him, being a good communist did not mean that he wanted to destroy all these good English values. So in his eyes we blacks with our nationalistic talk were a threat to the *status quo*. The real point was that if we were interested in communism we would apply it without having British or Russian commissars telling us how to make communism work. So we warned our students and other friends to keep out of this sort of entanglement. With the majority of Englishmen, we said, if you scratch them, regardless of their complexion, you'll find a Tory underneath.

However, a number of our closest associates in the pan-African movement had gained a perspective on Russia by travelling there at various times in the thirties. Padmore had been there frequently and had been responsible for bringing others. Wallace-Johnson and Kouyaté knew it well. And Kenyatta and I had travelled there also. Indeed Kenyatta used to tell an amusing story of the Russian woman who embraced him and said: 'At long last I am able to see Pushkin, and I am prepared to die now for having had this privilege'.[20]

We have to remember that the Ethiopian issue did not subside once the Emperor had left the country, and it had fallen into Italian hands. The groups around Sylvia Pankhurst and ourselves kept the pressure up right through the Ethiopian war, and we needed to because in the period before the Second World War broke out there were many manoeuvrings between Italy and Britain. The aim was to keep the former out of Germany's clutches by coming to some agreement with her and with Haile Selassie over Ethiopia. Britain had actually suggested that Ethiopia should cede so much of her territory outright to the Italians, and the British would compensate by adding to Ethiopia some of the desert land north of Isiolo in Kenya. It was an attempt to appease both Italy and Ethiopia, but it came down to sacrificing Ethiopian sovereignty, and I'm sorry to say that a number of the stalwart supporters of Ethiopia in the early period were actually prepared to back this manoeuvre.

These Ethiopia meetings gave us a chance to speak on broader issues, or make some point on Africa in general.[21] There was, for instance, in 1938 a meeting called between the Abyssinian Society and the League of Coloured People. Princess Tsehai, the Emperor's daughter, was attending, and also this fellow Mbanefo, who later became a judge and played a prominent part on the side of Biafra. Donald Cameron, successively the governor of Nigeria and Tanganyika, was a main speaker. Well, he did a most unusual thing, for few Englishmen will go to such an extreme in public. Mbanefo had been on his feet attacking the British record in Nigeria, and had been speaking about the famous Aba riots, when Cameron interrupted him. 'You, Mbanefo, naked boy belonging to the Ibo community, you dare to get up here and speak in such a manner about Britain!' Well, it was too much for me and Padmore. We turned on the League of Coloured People and its chairman Harold Moody, and publicly denounced the whole proceedings. 'What have you organized this meeting for, Moody? To reflect on black people by bringing men like this old colonialist Cameron along? These old people dying but still holding on to the empire doggedly. This is a reflection on our manhood. How dare you, Moody, who receives so much of your money from missionaries and the Colonial Office, use your apparatus to denigrate and defame African people?' This effectively broke up the meeting, and I subsequently felt that I should apologize to Princess Tsehai. Still, it had been too important to let such a thing slip past.

The prevailing feeling in these last few months before the war was that we should insist on seeing the colonial world as a whole. So if there was to be a commission sent out to investigate

160

trade union conditions in Trinidad as happened in 1938, we were determined to submit a manifesto on trade unionism amongst blacks that did not restrict itself to one small fragment, but showed what was happening in West Africa as much as in the West Indies. It was naturally considered off the point by Sir Arthur Pugh's commission[22]; nevertheless we circulated it to the trade union movements in Guyana, Trinidad, Jamaica, and to cells in West Africa and North America. The same grasp of the wider issues was what brought us into close touch with other coloured groups in London. We had, for instance, a healthy *rapprochement* with the most radical caucus of the Sinhalese students, and there was also a little group around the Burmese students attached to the London School of Economics. This was very active, and we found it profitable to co-operate in a number of spheres with them too.

When we turn to consider the social and intellectual life of some of these Africans who would later return to lead their countries into independence, we can say that they were very much men of their times. Corduroy was the predominant fashion for everyday work, but if you were one of those going to the garden party at Buckingham Palace you would dress more appropriately. A number of us, including Kenyatta, wore beards, but this was less for fashion but as a pledge that we would continue this form of appearance until Ethiopia was free again. There was little to set us apart from the general student body with the exception of Kenyatta. What was unusual in his case was his giant topaz ring that he wore on one of his fingers. It stood out almost an inch, and commanded a great deal of interest amongst people.

Another foible was for an African student to identify with a particular English manner. This happened I think to Jaja Wachuku, who after his time at Dublin's Trinity College felt the weight of his learning.[23] 'I am equal in learning to Zik. I belong to the debating club in Trinity, and I have the gold medal for debating named after Connolly, the great Irish patriot.' In this sort of way he would identify with various aspects of British life, and already one saw him with his hand sticking out from his waistcoat imagining himself a Disraeli or Lord Palmerston. When he came across to Manchester or London for his holidays, we would be having our little caucus, discussing the future of our people, and he would break in with his 'Mr. Chaaarman, sir, may I . . . .' All of the airs already. Just like the boys who were attending some of the Inns of Court. Many of these did not have the deep background of a Danquah at Oxford, and they often read only a part of the course. They might have been long-serving railway clerks or District Commissioners in West Africa, and now they wanted to qualify as fast as possible, by reading the catechism and cramming for their finals.

In between the Danquahs at the scholarly level and these lawyers, you had a Kenyatta who was simply concerned to get certain things known about his people. He had arrived at this through his professor at the London University Department of Anthropology, Malinowski. While he had been attending there, Kenyatta had been putting together a series of essays on the social life and customs of his Kikuyu tribe, and he wanted these published. We had first thought that we would get one of our own boys to give some sequence to these loose essays, but when that did not transpire, I took them to a mutual friend of ours, Dinah Stock, a specialist in English literature. She agreed and it only took her about three weeks to complete the job. It was relatively easy then to find a publisher, who was prepared readily to pay Jomo a sum that was larger than anything he had received for work done since he left Kenya.[24]

In the book he was able to deal amongst much else with one matter that had been outraging a certain sector of prudish society in England since 1929. This was female circumcision. He was able to demonstrate its social and psychological importance in the Kikuyu society, rather than being seen as yet another instance of African barbarity.[25] He was also able to make known to the British public the terrible conditions which obtained in his country, and it gave him an opportunity to develop in the English people a more balanced mind towards some of the contradictions in African society.

But a man like Kenyatta was much more obviously marked for leadership than many of the others in England at that time. There was a fascination about him that led people like Baroness Blixen to invite him to Denmark; other friends in Germany and France had him over to stay there. Something natural in the man which singled him out in a crowd. So he was a man sought out by many Africans, some probably lousy law students who simply wanted to talk to a seasoned revolutionary. He was also the close friend of Paul Robeson and was of some help to him over that film *Sanders of the River* where Robeson took a leading role.[26]

Now one place where Africans like Kenyatta, Nkrumah or Wallace-Johnson could be seen as professional rebels was at the fifth Pan-African Congress in Manchester. This was obviously an important occasion for projecting some of the African leadership upon a wider audience, but its importance can be over-stressed. Unlike the earlier congresses of DuBois it was not an isolated event, but just a natural outgrowth of a ferment of pan-African activity. It had been preceded in the 1930s and war years by innumerable conferences which had brought together West Africans, West Indians and North American blacks, and it was to be followed in the later forties by a large variety of similar contacts. In the pre-Manchester period, this pan-African activity had centred round the IASB; shortly before the conference it was decided to initiate a more explicitly political organization with the Pan-African Federation. It was this federation that launched the Manchester Congress.

There was no question where this should be held. We had all the conveniences in Manchester. Fortunately for my people I had succeeded in establishing myself as a businessman at this place. This was important for the English community which lived on nothing else but business round there, and it made for easy access to certain people in the town. I knew the Lord Mayor, and also Harold Laski's brother who held an important position in the Labour Party. I was a member of the party myself, and had connections with Bolt, who was the local secretary. All this made it relatively easy to get halls booked for the congress, and simplified the question of hotel accommodation. There had always been a problem with certain hotels in Britain not taking in black people graciously,[27] but in this case it didn't arise as I had a number of houses where people could be put up. With the restaurants also operating there was no difficulty in feeding the delegates. Indeed I opened the Orient just before the conference to experiment in catering for this group.

The timing of the conference was fixed at a historic moment, to coincide with the World Conference of Trade Unions in

Paris, and we had advance information that a number of the colonial delegates to that conference would be anxious to come to the pan-African gathering.[28] It therefore saved our organization a great deal of money in that some of the delegates were in Europe already. Also by this time Manchester had become quite a point of contact with the coloured proletariat in Britain, and we had made a name for ourselves in fighting various areas of discrimination. It's possible therefore to see the conference as not only concerned with international issues, but as a protest against increasing discrimination in Britain. One felt it particularly bitterly with the Bevin Boys who had come across from the West Indies during the war.[29] 'Here these boys have come to defend the whole damned empire—the very thing we'd like to destroy. You British haven't got the courtesy or the humanity to treat them decently. Also you don't realize how you are thwarting our development in the West Indies by bringing these people over. Their skills took half a century to accumulate, but they'll be lost to the islands because these men will stay in Britain because of the inducements.' It was the same thing in the other areas of discrimination that I mentioned earlier: unwanted coloured children, wives whose husbands' ships did not return from the war, innocent soldiers being whipped by crowds of recalcitrant whites in Bolton or Manchester.[30] In fact for me Manchester had taken on a quite different type of activity than the speech-making at Hyde Park that had been so much part of our daily fare in our London base.

Looking at our conference and residence in Manchester, you could say that we coloured people had a right there, because of the age-old connections between cotton, slavery and the building up of cities in England. We also felt that in a way we were remaking history by coming to stir up that other side of Manchester, its fierce anti-slavery streak. Equally, I sometimes saw myself like Engels whose father had made a lot of money in Manchester and was able to support Marx in his great undertaking. I felt we were almost mimicking history. So Manchester gave us an important opportunity to express and expose the contradictions, the fallacies and the pretensions that were at the very centre of the empire. But on this home front, by the time of the conference, we had built up a network of stategic committees for the welfare and defence of coloured people, and on the central committee we had people like Mrs. Braddock and Sidney Silverman.

Then there was the international side of the conference. It was important to make the link with North America, for regardless of how America may try to disguise black progress, there were already a large number of highly trained scientists and agriculturists there. Some of us hoped that Africa's backwardness would be able to accommodate some of these sons. Within the American context they might be prevented from using their scientific knowledge to the full. Instead let them put it to the use of Africa. It was the same idea that had gone out from Russia after the revolution, the call for enlightened people who may have left Russia three generations back to come to the aid of the country. All this made it vital to call DuBois across from America to the conference; we were aware of his historic ties with the early pan-African congresses, and it seemed important to strive for some continuity in this fifth gathering.

It was also a tactical move to invite DuBois at this time. It stressed the role he was still playing in pan-African affairs even though he was becoming a suspect person to many Americans. However, he was given a passport and allowed to attend. He came over, we outlined our policies and programmes and he performed an excellent job as chairman of a number of plenary sessions.[31]

The blacks living in Britain were strongly represented through their various organizations, from Duplan's welfare movements to Dr. Peter Milliard.[32] From Africa there were people like the young writer Peter Abrahams, Fadipe from Nigeria, Wallace-Johnson from Sierra Leone, and many other names. But major roles were assigned to Kenyatta who had now been in England some fifteen years, and to Nkrumah who had himself just arrived from America. So it was lively for a week; we discussed the imponderables, our plight and the role of the few African intellectuals that existed. We talked about how independence is never given: that it has to be taken. But how were we, such a small group, to meet this situation? We didn't worry about the paucity of numbers; there was plenty of evidence from Russia and elsewhere that a small committed group could soon win support from the people.

A number of influences impinged on our thinking at this time.

Undoubtedly what was going on in Palestine with the Jews was an important experience for us members of this other diaspora. For here was another people who had lived for so long and in such large numbers away from Palestine, and yet they had been able to register their claim. The spirit of pan-Africanism was the same kind of awakening, awareness of origins, the certainty about the link back to Africa. There should no longer for the blacks in the New World be this fear of not knowing who you are, no longer a story of the Negro being like Topsy, who just grew, belonging nowhere. So the Jewish experience was formidable. We felt the particularity of the Africans, our Africanness, just like Jewishness. And later we wondered when we saw a handful of Jews in the Haganah movement gaining independence militarily for Palestine, whether we could do the same.

There was very little French African participation in the conference, partly because of language differences, but mainly stemming from the structure of black association with metropolitan politics in France which was very different from English-speaking blacks. Some of the former were deputies in the French parliament, and quite openly were attached to the Communist Party. So there was the feeling possibly that they had nothing to learn about politics. 'What can this group of English boys teach you when they've never even sat in parliament?' It was the same at the level of trade unionism in West Africa itself; despite the proximity of Ivory Coast and Gold Coast there was no fraternization; Wallace-Johnson's group did not work in conjunction with Houphouët-Boigny, and Sekou Touré did not work hand in hand with Sierra Leone, or a man like Garba Jahumpa in the Gambia. Relations between these French and British traditions was to be one of the toughest obstacles once independence had come to West Africa, as we shall see.

It looks at first sight as if the English-speaking blacks attending the conference were a completely unhomogeneous lot, but this is only at the superficial level. The great mistake that is too often made when dealing with the African or the Negro is to assume that capitalism has removed the black educated group from its historical moorings in the mass of the people. Perhaps you can talk about this class cleavage in parts of the West Indies with those fellows who brought back European women, and separated themselves from the larger group. They would be apt to disregard their traditional relationships at home, their grandparents, and live in abodes which were almost barred to the poorer members of their families. This was like some of the English aristocratic families who would think of their poorer relatives: 'I recognize them all right, and if somebody is dead, I'll send a cheque to assist; but I don't want them around me.' But with the generality of Africans or American Negroes, there was always something to remind you that you couldn't escape from your group. 'Black boy, you are trying to be a white man. Watch it.' Or in the colonial service it was always possible for an upstart colonialist to kick a black lawyer or some other outstanding member of the community. So despite the appearance of dissimilarity, there was that ever-present consciousness.

At that point the people that we may call leaders were tied very closely to their communities. If they went off to London or to Manchester, they had to give an account of their stewardship when they returned: 'You go to this conference in London which they call this thing the African Pan, what is it all about?' So he had to explain: 'Uncle, the thing is this, you remember those black boys who have left here and who you used to collect money for school fees for. Well, those stories that all the money went on drink are not true; we have built an organization there which strengthens our position here. We can do very little here in Africa, but over there some of those fellows of ours can take our case to parliament.' So the message of activity abroad was continually being brought back to the source. The old men would be able to speak to other people, so, for instance in Ghana when George Padmore went to live there in 1957, they knew about him: 'This man, we know him a long time; this boy was fighting our battles; we saw his articles in our own papers.' They would come out all over if he was visiting parts of the country, or if there was some big durbar, to thank him for the good work he'd done. 'Our pickin (our child), yes, he no lazy. He know he belonged here and make our story known.' It was the same here in Kenya when people would say sometimes after I had come here, 'Ho, Makonnen, the man who Jomo used to tell us about. Welcome.'

It is wrong therefore to make a rigid or mechanistic approach to the people attending the conference. This is in fact one of the myths of Marxism, that classes in their separate and distinct forms are a better way of analysing a population than taking an amorphous cross-section.

Now one important thing that came out of the Manchester meeting was the declaration made there which resolved that the struggle was not to be found in Europe for the majority of us. The old idea that you could do more work for liberation outside Africa was being laid aside. And here we were only taking a lead from the Indians and other colonials whom we saw making a tremendous impact upon their people in the homelands. Manchester was a recognition that the time had come: we are no longer devoid of the knowledge that we belong somewhere. We must make our own freedom, assert our freedom in the land which we have been defending all along. So to be in Britain is a counter-revolutionary act. It wasn't only the young African leadership going back to Africa, but it was also people from the West Indies and North America. I saw them myself once I had reached Ghana. I saw in a way that our dreams had come true; that these distant sons of Africa were coming back with tears of joy from the diaspora. 'We have come back to the motherland, and I'm an old man.' Delegates to Ghana from St. Lucia and St. Kitts would say, 'At long last, eh? My grandfather used to tell me about our family being Congo men. Here I am.'

Kwame went back not long after Manchester, but the man I knew most about as he set off back was Kenyatta. The return had been planned for several months, and he had revealed to me some of his plans for education once he had reached Kenya. He was taking a large number of books with him, because he was determined to build up the tiny number of educated Africans in Kenya. Who was there after all? Don't forget that countries like Kenya were very hesitant to give these darkies passports to go for higher education abroad. They much preferred to let them go to a place like Lovedale in South Africa where they would not be confronted with a different style of race relations.[33] This is where Eliud Mathu went, and Charles Njonjo (the present Attorney General), and Mungai Njoroge (the Foreign Minister).

But at the time that Jomo went back there were only a handful of people who had any sort of higher education. His idea therefore was to help direct the school which had been set up by Mbiyu

Koinange after his return from North America—Kenya Teachers' College.[34]

But a word about the day Mzee Jomo left England. We travelled together from Manchester to Storrington where he had been during the war. Then, after completing packing we got the train from London to Plymouth. It was a difficult moment realizing that we would now be separated after fifteen years. We looked at each other unable to speak, but walked over towards the ship. There we had the first reminder of what lay ahead in the attitude of some of the white settlers travelling by the same ship. By their remarks to us, they had obviously forgotten that they had not yet reached the Indian Ocean. But we were then too heavy in our burden even to retort. I left him after embracing, well realizing the hell he was returning to.

A few years later when Jomo's arrest was imminent, I was surprised one morning to find three of the well-mannered boys from the MI 5 waiting for me. Courteously, as no one but the English are capable of being, they said, 'We are here to find out to what extent you have been in touch with Kenyatta.' 'Well, we are always in touch spiritually. You know, we have what is known as the sum-sum which allows us to know what the other is feeling even though we are about 5,000 miles distant.' Shortly, they returned with a search warrant to see if there was any correspondence that would guide them. I told them there was no need to search, that the only document to be found was the original copy of his book, *Facing Mount Kenya*. 'As for other correspondence, we never used writing for this, but preferred the bush drum.' I could anticipate that once the trial of Kenyatta was under way, the newspapers would belabour the fact that his brother runs restaurants in Manchester. So to avoid the obvious, I disappeared from the scene and was in Liverpool for ten days reading the papers and listening to all the crimes that they had dared to suggest my brother was guilty of in Kenya. It was not easy because most of the things said were far-fetched— all this stuff about plotting the murder of women and children.[35] So it went on, and it was difficult to come to the defence of him, for what paper would listen to a story from me when some of the most outstanding liberals had decided he was a leader to death and destruction?

Another of the group who had returned was James. Like others he recognized that he had a base, he had people. It was no longer like St. Paul writing from, say, Cyprus to the Corinthians; it was a question now of: 'Brothers, I'm here; I have answered the call from Macedonia, and I'm here in the flesh.' James had written all his articles in Britain, and had become known to the intellectuals in life and letters but now suddenly the emphasis was: 'Go to the masses, go to the people and learn a new lesson. Don't talk down to them. Go there and together let a thousand flowers blossom.' So he began to work there to strengthen the party locally. Eric Williams started to do the same, opening his school in Trinidad, and with that and the popular press he began reaching a wider audience than was able to read the various books he had written.[36] It made one reflect with thanks that the British system was not the same as the French; if it had been, many of these fellows would have been caught by it, and remained in London as deputies representing their various constituencies. They would have become possibly like some of the French blacks with their houses in Paris, and the occasional visit back to their constituency in Martinique or wherever. Here, therefore, in the British world was a historic process of decentralization, moving out from London to declare war on the empire; no longer worried about the stamp of approval in London, but determined to show that the system at the outpost of that empire was shady.

This then was the general process, and we worked hard to point out to people that we didn't want them hanging on in England. However, there was another side to it. Take the Bevin boys in England, some of whom had got their European wives. Now they supported the proposition that Jamaica and other places should be independent, but did this mean that they had to pack up and leave England? 'We have had a tie with you English for four hundred years. Much of that time we have worked without wages. Now you have given us our independence, but you haven't given us a kopek. Well, how are we going to be truly independent, man? This is the place—England— where you have kept all the gold, all the culture. This is where all the art galleries are with their pictures of the great colonialists done in oil. Everything is here. And I'm to go back to my empty house just like the days of slavery. You think I'm a foolish man to leave this place like that. I've got as much right here as I've got in Jamaica.'

What this kind of attitude raises is the whole concept of the Commonwealth. Britain had been determined, after the American colonies won their independence, to establish a different way of parting. As good friends. Now that the question of the non-white Commonwealth came up, you could see two schools operating in Britain. The more extreme line was: 'To hell with this Commonwealth; it's all humbug. We must be free as in the heyday of capitalism to conquer markets and set our stamp here and there. What's all this about moral obligations to coloured people in Britain. This is all damn sentiment. Let them stand on their own feet.' The more moderate view was: 'We have been trying on and off in Britain to preach the humanity of man to man. Are we suddenly to say that we are dogs or lions, and should devour each other? What were all those hopes and aspirations about turning swords into ploughshares? So trying to kick black people out is a terrible and loathsome thing. Disengagement from the colonies shouldn't mean the disintegration of all human values.'

Many of the West Indians saw their staying on in Britain in just this sort of moral way. 'I'm too old, sir. I saved all the substance of my youth to come here. I found winter is not like it is in the tropics. You want me to go back to the West Indies. You didn't say after emancipation that each nigger is entitled to fifty dollars and a mule; instead that we were all equal. Then when the call went out during the war for skilled men to come across, I answered. I've given my skill these last fifteen years, and built my little house. If I'd been back in the West Indies I'd never have achieved this. There I was getting five shillings a day, here thirty shillings. Do you mean to say that I haven't got a right to live for all this?'

To those of us who had read our *Negroes in Britain*, we were able to give some of these recent attempts to get the blacks out of Britain their true perspective. Back at the end of the eighteenth century there had been a similar drive to clean up London and other cities. There had been all these ex-slaves then; so the idea had been to gather them all up, marry them off to white prostitutes, and then ship them away to Africa. So we used some of these historical glimpses to point out to some of the British blacks when they arrived, 'Whatever you do here, arm yourself to return to your own country; you never know when the British will administer another shock to remind you that you don't belong here. So try to prevent yourself and your children being completely cut off.'

Many West Africans would do this—stay with their wives in London and send the children back to thegrand mother so they would not later be looked at as some strange creatures. But sometimes when you found a Ghanaian man going back to Ghana at the time of independence, he would be involved in the same thing as the West Indian. He arrived to find very few jobs and no blueprint to produce more.[37] After his ten or fifteen years in England, a short time in Ghana might make him think again, especially as his extended family began to close in on him; they had invested in his education. Now where was the pay-off? So he begins to think, 'Don't mind the racial discrimination in England; I can find my place more easily in that community than with all these relatives hanging on me; I'll write a letter to that white girl who didn't even know I was leaving. "Whatever you do, darling, forgive me. Send me some passage money, and I can come and join you".' Or he might use other excuses, anything to justify his running back. 'Kwame Nkrumah is a usurper, calling himself Osagyefo and God, sir. I have left that place and come back to Britain, God help me.' In this sort of way they would become counter-revolutionaries. They had thought in the euphoria of independence that they were really with this new freedom movement, but they began to realize that they were only passengers on that ship, and that they didn't understand at all the nautical laws or where the ship was really going. So it produced a reaction: 'I'm just a passenger in this independence business; I came along originally because I thought it would be a reflection on me if I showed no interest. But now after all, God made me a human being first, and it was only an accident of geography that I was born in this place they're calling Ghana now. Powell may be trying to divide us, but I was brought up a good Anglican to believe we are all one. So he's just the same as this thief Nkrumah and this blackguard Makonnen. But now I'm here, sir, I'll fight tomorrow for the defence of the British Museum.'

There's nothing particularly African about this reaction. You

172

got exactly the same thing with the Jews for instance in Germany after the Second World War. 'It is true that Hitler has killed so many, but what am I going to do in that place Palestine? I'll share some of the wealth I'm making here and thus put one little foot in Palestine, but this other anchor I'll drop right here in Germany.' It's a human phenomenon. Here in Kenya some of the whites have decided to stay on, explaining that they never held with all the white settlers did. They are now determined to be Kenyans, and ask if this is not their right. Of course it creates great contradictions for the Kikuyu rebel who had been promising his people that all the whites would go. It now looks as if he has failed to carry his revolution through to its logical conclusion. It seems as if he is giving some whites the chance to take over power again.

It was so complex, this double loyalty. Africans whose fathers had sent money to help the pan-African movement would come up to Manchester and drink hard to celebrate Ghanaian independence, but had no intention of ever going back to Ghana. So also the famous Calypsonian in London, Lord Kitchener from the West Indies, would do his famous pieces (What a day . . . in 1957 when Ghana etc.).[38] Over in India it was the same thing during their independence period ten years earlier. The few Europeans and Eurasians who stayed on in India did so because they knew no other place for their home; they might have certain misgivings, but after all the Eurasians felt they had contributed something to the liberalization of caste ideas just by being in India. So even if some of them slipped out to England at independence, they would find their way back. 'I'm better off there because I know my way in India and who I am.'

To end with my own position; it was rather different. I now had no ties with Guyana. But my being in Manchester was just an accident of history. As I have said I only went there because of the Milliard connection when the war broke out. Rather than work in some war factory, I would simply contrive to remain independent by lecturing here and there and doing a little publishing. I never dreamt that I would accumulate property the way it happened. And because it had all come about so suddenly, I was prepared to drop it just like that when I moved to Ghana in 1957. I hadn't come to England to stay, any more than I saw myself becoming a YMCA secretary in Texas for

173

any length of time. When I had set off for Denmark I had intended to do my thesis in the Agricultural College on abortion in cattle, but my friends there and in England had suggested that I should concentrate on no research which was not of immediate bearing on our cause. Thereafter all my travelling to Russia and other places was to get knowledge to prepare me for working in the West Indies or Africa. Wherever I was, it was necessary to qualify so as to justify my claim to speak, but there was never any question of marrying and settling down in, say, Manchester. Those I had been advising would have turned on me for going back on all I had been saying about loyalties. I was in transit, whether in Manchester or in Ghana. Nor did it mean that once I had reached even Ghana I should stop fighting. I hadn't built up a reputation for fighting foolishness in England to let it pass in Ghana. If they didn't recognize me as a black man in Ghana, or if people went in for clannishness there, it was as necessary to combat this as it had been in England. I was there in Ghana to awaken people's consciences on certain issues, but it was only another staging post. I used to say there, 'I am at your beck and call. If you want me to go to Central Africa, or to go to Nyerere or Obote to take the message, then let me go. That's my job. It's an endless process. If you're serving in the people's army, you must be prepared to move as necessary.' So here now I am in Kenya as I was once in Manchester. I had many friends there, because one was a centre. In Kenya I don't know the inside of more than two or three African homes— I know Mathu's, Koinange's and I see Jomo's fleetingly. But I have no roots. In other words, I am where I was. From the very beginning my preoccupation has been to share my knowledge with people and to carry the revolution to what I may say is its logical conclusion. Now we have our independence. We must ask what are we going to do with it. We must keep projecting certain things which symbolize the ideal beyond this present. And so the chain becomes endless. This is how it is, and none of the revolutionaries that I have known about have had a different life than just that.

NOTES TO CHAPTER 10

1 Nkrumah gives as his reason for going to the States a desire to emulate his teacher, James Aggrey, who had had his education there; *Autobiography* (Edinburgh, 1957), p. 15.

2 See for instance an Africa-oriented diary produced by the Federal Republic for 1971, which has a section on St. Mauritius and Anton Wilhelm Amo; the cathedral of Magdeburg was under the former's protection, while the latter was a professor at the University of Berlin in the first half of the eighteenth century.

3 For Mbadiwe and other African students in North America, see H. M. Bond, 'Forming African Youth', in J. A. Davis (ed.), *Africa Seen by American Negroes* (Dijon, 1958). See also on the effect of America on Africa, J. Coleman, *Nigeria*, pp. 243–8.

4 Nkrumah, *Autobiography*, p. 51. Evidence for what may be considered Nkrumah's first 'tactical action' can be seen in the glowing letters sent by him to the educational director of the Phelps-Stokes Fund, Thomas Jesse Jones. Jones held the highest hopes that Nkrumah would turn out a non-political African, and Nkrumah, verbally at least, gave him every encouragement: ' . . . I can assure you that I will never disappoint you in the hope that you have in me. Were it not for the fact that great men are generally the children of the circumstances of their day, I would emphatically promise you that it is my pet ambition to carry on where my teacher and inspirer Dr. Kweggyir Aggrey left off. My interest in you and Dr. Aggrey is profound and immeasurable . . . . Yes, Dr. Jones, I have been seriously studying your books. It is not a question of casual reading, I am digesting every thought with the aim of making my philosophy of education part and parcel of me . . . . The day is fast approaching when a memorial statue of you will be standing in some coastal town in Africa.' Nkrumah to Jones, 29 January 1941, Phelps-Stokes Fund, New York. See also, F. Nkrumah, 'Education and Nationalism', *Educational Outlook*, November 1943 (Philadelphia).

5 Nkrumah, op. cit., p. 44.

6 B. N. Azikiwe, *Liberia in World Politics* (London, 1934).

7 See *Daily Nation* (Nairobi), 16 Jan. 1971, p. 24.

8 This may have been the 1938 meeting of European socialist parties in Paris referred to in Hooker, *Black Revolutionary*, p. 56. Rassemblement Coloniale is mentioned briefly in Padmore, *Pan-Africanism or Communism?* p. 335.

9 There were a number of occasions when blacks in Britain were protesting against giving Germany a place in the sun; e.g. the Negro Welfare Association protest of April 1937; and Wallace–Johnson writing on behalf of the West African Youth League and the IASB on 15 January 1938 to the *New Times and Ethiopia News*. The British section of the IASB made the point in the *New Times* of 30 April 1938 that it was not only Germany that wants colonies in Africa but also small powers like Poland.

10 James, *The Black Jacobins* (London, 1938).

11 For details of the many French blacks from the West Indies and West Africa involved in Pan-Negro organizations, see J. Ayo Langley, 'Pan-Africanism in Paris, 1924–36', *Journal of Modern African Studies*, vii, 1 (1969), pp. 69–94.

12 This meeting must have been held shortly after Nehru returned from Spain in Ju n 1938; see F. Moraes, *J. Nehru* (Asia Publications, 1956), pp. 270–2.

13 For illustration of the metal container (*kipande*) worn by all adult Kenya Africans during the 1920s, see H. Thuku, *Autobiography* (Nairobi, 1970), plates iv and v.

14 It is interesting to note that Garan Kouyaté who with George Padmore had been strongly anti-colonialist in the early thirties was by the outbreak of the Second World War exhorting the blacks of French West Africa to fight loyally for 'our "Mère Patrie".'

'Brothers and sisters of French West Africa, you who desire the well-being, the liberty and the fraternity of all peoples under peace, we must tighten our ranks around France and always remain with France and be at her service . . . . ' *New Times*, 21 October 1939.

15 For the campaign to rid London of its black poor at the end of the eighteenth century, see C. Fyfe, *A History of Sierra Leone* (Oxford, 1962), pp. 14–17.

16 A number of blacks from the New World and Africa were intimately involved with the Spanish Civil War, including Paul Robeson, Nicholas Guillen (the latter the Cuban poet and journalist), Langston Hughes, and Nyabongo from Uganda.

17 Padmore has an interesting sketch of Yergan's activity after his break with the YMCA in South Africa; *Pan-Africanism or Communism?* pp. 315–17.

18 This is the same Hlubi who turned up at the Fifth Pan-African Congress representing South Africa along with Peter Abrahams.

19 cf. Pollitt's denial that the Communist Party was 'aiming at the destruction of Britain and the British Empire' in Padmore, *Pan-Africanism or Communism?* p. 363.

20 Kenyatta went twice to Russia—in 1929 and in 1932–3. One of Peter the Great's favourite slaves was Hannibal, reputedly an Ethiopian. Hannibal married a court lady one of whose daughters married a Pushkin. Although Pushkin was considered a white man by many Russians, he was proud of his Negro ancestry and was at one time going to write a biography called *Arap Pyetra Vyelikovo* (the Negro of Peter the Great); I owe this information to Xan Smiley.

21 Makonnen is mentioned as being one of the principal speakers in a number of the Ethiopian protest meetings reported by the *New Times*—for instance the issues of 29 May 1937, 15 June 1939, 27 July 1946.

22 For the Pugh Commission, see Hooker, op. cit., pp. 53–4.

23 Wachuku represented the Association of African Descent, Dublin, at the Fifth Pan-African Congress, and was later to be Federal Foreign Minister of Nigeria.

24 Kenyatta, *Facing Mount Kenya* (London, 1938).

25 Kenyatta, op. cit., ch. 6.

26 It is interesting that Marcus Garvey strongly objected to films like *Sanders of the River* on the grounds that they 'libel and slander the Negro race', *New Times*, 17 October 1936.

27 For the famous case where Leary Constantine was refused admission to a London Hotel in 1944, see *Constantine* v. *Imperial Hotels*, K. B. Div., 28 June 1944, *Times Law Reports*, 4 August 1944.

28 For the connection between the World Federation of Trade Unions Conference and the Manchester Conference, see Padmore, *Pan-Africanism or Communism?* pp. 154–5.

29 See A. H. Richmond, *Colour Prejudice in Britain: A Study of West Indian Workers in Liverpool, 1941–51* (London, 1954).

30 For Makonnen's comments on discrimination within the wider setting, see his 'The Greek for "Colour Bar" ', *Pan-Africa* (Manchester), June 1947, pp. 22–6.

31 At the Manchester Conference, Makonnen was the rapporteur at the 17 October session on 'Ethiopia and the Black Republics', chaired by W. E. B. DuBois; see G. Padmore (ed), *History of the Pan-African Congress* (London, n.d.), p. 44. Makonnen presented DuBois with a cigarette box at the end of the final session.

32 For Peter Milliard's role in the conference and his standing in Manchester since he arrived there in 1923, see Padmore, *Pan-Africanism or Communism?* pp. 160–1. Duplan's

speech at the session on 'The Colour Problem in Britain' is reported in Padmore, *History*, pp. 27-8.

33 For examples of passport blocking of East African students seeking higher education, see King, *Pan-Africanism and Education*, pp. 71-2.

34 For Koinange, see below, pp. 200-1.

35 Few of the lawyers who had anything to do with the Kenyatta trial believed him guilty and Reg Reynolds, travelling through Kenya at this time commented: 'And those of us who knew him (even people like myself, who did not greatly care for him) never believed that he was remotely implicated with Mau Mau', *Beware of Africans* (London, 1955), pp. 164-5.

36 Williams's adult education campaign is described in his autobiography, *Inward Hunger; the Education of a Prime Minister* (London, 1969), pp. 113-17.

37 For an East African example of a man who intended returning to independent Kenya but stayed on in London, see R. Mugo Gatheru, *Child of Two Worlds* (Anchor Books, 1965).

38 Other examples of Kitchener's calypsos are contained in Shiela Patterson, *Dark Strangers* (London, 1963), pp. 209, 341.

CHAPTER 11

PAN-AFRICANISM IN PRACTICE

IN my own case and that of some of my colleagues, there was something like a ten-year interval between the Manchester Conference and moving into the African scene. In the meantime we used our publicity skills in England to spotlight every significant move in Africa. We concentrated on the leadership there, keeping them informed with dispatches of what was happening in the circles of the Labour Party, and giving the widest coverage to events in Africa. If you look back to the articles and papers of the time, you will see that our method was to swell incidents out of proportion; if there was just an ordinary strike in the Gold Coast, we would publicize the fact that the whole country was in flames. We had built up a certain organization in the Pan-African Federation,[1] and had a range of contacts in the parliamentary Labour Party; so in this lull period between the war and independence in Africa, we kept our fingers on every grouping of importance in Africa, and as far as it was possible facilitated anything they wanted done in Britain.

There was no question of disbanding our organization once Manchester had passed. It would have been suicidal to forsake the cause just at the moment when we had really joined battle with the enemy. The previous ten or twenty years had been probing attacks, just making the enemy aware of our presence; but now we had our fingers at his throat. The trouble was that other forces had come into the arena apparently on our side, and these were trying to become the spokesmen for Africa. I am referring here to Brockway's Movement for Colonial Freedom. Now when I saw Africans hiving off to work under this umbrella movement, I felt it was a disaster. The whole point of our creating first the IASB and then the federation was to break with the age-old tradition of blacks depending on white organizations. As has been seen, we would tolerate white people who offered some skill or money, but never let them interfere in guiding the affairs of our institutions. Reflecting on black history, one could see so clearly that this had been one of the mistakes in the National Association for the Advancement of Coloured People, or in the LCP, and we weren't going to repeat it. Ours was a strictly black organization. I was not going to take another group of white people who would want us to say later that if it had not been for them, we would never have gained our independence. Not that we had a general grievance against Brockway; in fact he had been consistent in talking about the rights of man, and in saying that he would not fight an imperialist war. It was just that the power and platform provided by his Independent Labour Party (ILP) was a potential danger to us.

At a certain point I felt that George Padmore was really seeing too much of the ILP office, and writing consistently for their paper, the *New Leader*.[2] To me this was almost as treasonable as working for the British Communist Party. And personally I took some pride in knowing that Brockway probably did not even know my face; I couldn't even tell you where the ILP office was except that it was somewhere around the Fleet Street area. This sounds like chauvinism, and as if I was carrying my defence of blackness too far. But I had no intention of weakening my own personality or altering the approach to black politics that I was creating. I knew all the terminology of collaboration— Toadyism, Uncle Tomism, lackeyism; all these could be used to describe blacks who worked in with whites in varying degrees. But I wanted to be a purist, in the revolutionary sense, and in the sense of racial self sufficiency. So the more a Wallace-Johnson or George Padmore wrote for this ILP paper, the more I felt we were damaging our case to speak for ourselves. I had to take George up on this: 'Look, George, there were moments when you were rather feeble. You probably recognized that the resources of some of the ILP-ers were greater than our resources in the early period. But now we have resources. Haven't we established a conference on our own, brought our brothers from far and wide to it? How can you continue to feel that Brockway is so important in our struggle?' He would say that he was doing it because it was good publicity. 'But', I would answer, 'the age of publicity is past, we are now at grips with the enemy. There is a battle on now, and we can't let our own forces just peter out, or rely on Brockway for succour. Otherwise we shall be back to the age of Frederick Douglass, and discover that the great anti-slavery champions were part and parcel of the plantocracy.'[3]

I don't know how this feeling of having to get a big white man to help you came about. There was certainly a tradition in West Africa of paying lawyers and court assessors big sums to do your work for you. And for many of these West Africans, if they wanted to get somebody to intercede for them in England, they preferred a white member of parliament to a man like me: 'Who is this damn Makonnen anyway? He sounds like a prince or a Ras, but he probably has no power. It'll be better to get a prestigious Brockway, a man who is loathed by the English upper classes.' This was the trouble with a lot of the Africans who hung about Brockway's place. To me it seems a bit like the mentality of the typical house slave of the American plantation, passing on titbits of news to the master as he picks up the dishes: 'I don't know what is happening to these plantation niggers, sir, but they sure are planning something, and I don't like what I hear.' Too many Africans passing on information to the big white man. You saw it quite clearly when Mary Attlee, the former Prime Minister's sister, came back from South Africa after forty or so years of being a missionary[4]; a number of Africans—some Kenyans included—made much of her, and would use her as a front. It was part of this old idea that if you want something in the newspapers you'd better get a white person to send it; I objected therefore to their placing too much confidence in some friends in high places. Scatter your risks was my policy; don't put all your eggs in one basket.

What was antagonizing was the idea that some of these people had grown great at the expense of our own leadership. The danger of this reliance was shown up starkly over the Mau Mau rebellion in Kenya. Once Brockway, the great spokesman, had decided that this was a treasonable and an abominable affair, it was very hard to convince the English public otherwise. He began to ask what independence was going to be in the face of these Mau Mau atrocities—this savagery of Africans destroying white men and women, cutting them up while they slept.

In fact he was laying down what was legitimate and what was not. And instead of taking the line that the savagery of white colonialism in Kenya begot the Mau Mau uprising, he preferred to suggest that it was an unfortunate reversion of the African to his latent barbarity.[5] Others of our white associates took a similar line, which always to my mind showed up the inherent dualism of the liberal element; one moment they would be praising you for suffering peacefully, putting up with so much oppression and nobly bearing it, and the next they'd be shocked if the worm turned: 'Why this fearful hostility, taking a *panga* (knife) and cutting up innocent women and children as they slept?' This is what made it so refreshing to come across an Ethel Mannin whose immediate reaction to the Mau Mau killings might rather be: 'To hell with these settlers. Let the blood flow. Give 'em more!' One needed this kind of hard core, the uncompromising element—people who saw the priorities like Sylvia Pankhurst and would shed no tears. Sometimes in this area I felt that even George Padmore was too much of a humanist. To my mind he wasn't sufficiently prepared to distinguish between the various Africans around our group; he didn't test out who was really committed to the revolution. I suppose he felt that we couldn't begin deciding which of us was more rebel than the others, putting all our followers under the microscope. I was all for taking no prisoners myself.

Some members of the Fabian Bureau had this approach, mostly the earlier members. I mean, a man like Horrabin, the geographer, was a pearl. And there were some other genuine men, absolutely uncompromising over colonialism such as Pritt and Postgate. They had the answers because they were steeped in Jacobinism and the French Revolution. These varying brands of radicalism were much more marked within the Labour Party proper, and especially when it came to power after the Second World War. We had put so much trust in some of them, but once they were in office one felt: 'These traitors, that's what they are. The old Ramsay Macdonald is still lurking in Labour's cupboards. Scratch a Macdonald or some of these other socialist fellows, and what do you find? A Tory.' You couldn't indict the whole lot, for there were some genuine people; but these various volte-faces left you rather confused. You began to evolve a theory about these contradictory British; that one will split your head open, while the next will sew you up. Alternately, if the confusion became too great, you felt trapped and asserted that the only good Englishman was a dead one.

The other thing was that despite the obvious divisions within British politics, some of these Labour fellows still felt that the Africans in any country should present a united front. If we had all been under oppressive rule, then this should have forced us together; they didn't believe it proper for Africans to have splinter groups. Of course, in suggesting this, they were simply failing to recognize that we in our divisions were living by the same principle as the English—the right to agree or disagree in politics. Take the Gold Coast. Some of the English MPs— even the Labour ones—couldn't tolerate our leading a movement that was hostile to the chiefs and traditionalists. And it was on those occasions that we were grateful for the clear-headed critique of Jimmy Maxton, the Scottish ILP-er. He would say: 'What's all this about putting all Africans into a united front with the chiefs? Who are we coming to believe in? The supposed natural rulers of Africa? But these Tories in Britain have exactly the same claim, that they are natural rulers, destined to rule; and that going to Eton and Winchester has given them the licence. Yet nobody suggests that the ILP and the Tories get into a united front.'

It was with these sorts of attitudes towards the English political scene that we began to draw the various African groups in Britain into our Federation, and to lay down guidelines for the numerous delegations that were coming over to London at this time. A few cardinal principles of our method were shown up when we tackled the problem of the Somalis in the seaport towns of England.[6] Somalis had gradually come to Britain because of the British sea route to India through the Suez Canal. Over the years the shippers had come to realize that it was much more costly to employ Indian than Somali seamen, especially as one Somali could do the work of two or three Indians. Just like some of the West Africans, therefore, these Somali seamen began to settle in towns like South Shields, Hull, Grimsby, Liverpool, Cardiff and Manchester. Their habits and food preferences were different naturally from the locals, so, being a very co-operative people, they soon turned to opening their little boarding houses and restaurants. Soon there was Habdi and Husseini House in some of these parts. Now although these Somalis were all Muslims, they were often regarded as inferior by the Adenis and Egyptians who were more able to bring pressure to bear on the shippers to employ their own people. Quite suddenly we were brought into this Arab-Somali dispute when things flared up in South Shields. News came that the Somalis were being victimized by the Arabs. On investigation I found that the Mayor of South Shields, Gompertz, was a Jew, but that paradoxically the local Arab population were using him to restrict the Somalis from getting licences. The Somalis were constantly alleged to be dealing in hashish in these restaurants, and having little girls there for pleasure. The police were raiding the various houses, and one after the other they were being closed down.[7]

I went there myself, found that the local MP was a Labour fellow, and discussed this victimization with the Mayor. The thing then took on national dimensions, because we brought Mrs. Bessie Braddock into it. Questions were asked in parliament, and the contribution of the Somalis to the war effort was pointed out. Riding on this new wave of sympathy, we were able to intercede successfully for them to be allowed to open further restaurants in Merseyside, Grimsby and Newcastle. All of this naturally made them strong members of our Pan-African Federation.

Now my tactics in all this were quite clear; to push the Somalis into recognizing that their future lay with the African world and not with the Middle East. It would not be easy, for a lot of them regarded Africans as quite different from themselves. There was also the complication that the Somalis—some of them— had played the role of *askaris* for the Italians during the conquest of Ethiopia in 1935-6. My aim was therefore to try to show the Somalis that their interest lay in friendship with the Ethiopians, and one had therefore to interpret this Somali mercenary campaign against Ethiopia in a new light. One did not take the line that the Somalis were traitors, of course, but that imperialism had set brother African to fight against brother. But one had to make the point about imperialism absolutely plain, for there was already some evidence in the early 1940s that the Somalis were interested in certain parts of Ethiopia and Kenya. I had to argue sometimes on these lines: 'We have to educate you people on this question of imperialism because you yourselves are making certain claims to parts of my country (they all believed I was an Ethiopian).[8] Decide for yourselves whether you are going to be good Africans, or whether you are going to be invaders. If you settle to be Africans, then you cannot have one foot over in Jeddah or Mecca, and one foot in Africa. You can't be African and have your policies dictated from outside. So decide. And on this question of your claiming Ethiopia, let me remind you of one thing. You Muslims bury or burn your dead in a certain way, whereas we Ethiopian Christians observe a classical form of burial with particular tombstones. Now the fact is that you can find these tombstones and monoliths right down in present-day Somali country; so don't you fellows start any trouble, because if it comes to history, my ancestors were there before you people.'

It was a considerable task to put this conviction across in the mid-forties, because don't forget this was when Bevin in Britain was encouraging a 'Greater Somalia' concept amongst the various Somali groupings in the Horn. His strategy was this: the Emperor had by now returned to Ethiopia, but there was still a British military presence there. It was always possible to show that the British should stay on indefinitely if you could point to a Somali threat around Ethiopian borders. Also we must remember that Bevin shared with C. L. R. James the notion that the Emperor was a feudal reactionary, and that these fine Somalis should not be placed under such an antiquarian rule. Bevin was undoubtedly quite sincere over this last point, but he had support for this policy from many of the old reactionary British colonels and administrators who felt: 'By God, give me a Somali any time. You can't find a better chap than those Somali Camel Corps anywhere.' So Bevin was playing a dual policy of weakening the Ethiopians and preserving his nomadic Somali.[9]

We were able to influence Somali policy over these issues by our close contacts with individuals in Britain. There was, for instance, Abdi Farah, an old Somali who had been living in England for a very long time. I knew him back in the thirties when he was conspicuous as a businessman with a number of houses. His sons went to a college in England and went back as pioneer teachers to Somalia. They were not actually Muslims, because Farah had married an English woman; so they were able to do some important work in some of the early mission schools in the homeland. In fact I gave the sons a typewriter when they went off to Hargeisha to begin their work. There was another man, Ali Mira, who I knew well, and as I mentioned earlier, he played an important part in that mutiny case down at Plymouth. Then there was Ali Noor. He was a good business-man too and well established in the Cardiff area. He also made his way in Hull when the black American soldiers were stationed there; he had two restaurants there which were very popular. Now it was through these kinds of links that Kenyatta and I worked to bring the Somali into our Federation. Jomo as a Kenyan was as concerned as I, because there had been a very vigorous presence of Somali pushing right down through the Northern Frontier District to Isiolo and northern Kikuyu country. We therefore helped create an English arm of the Somali Youth League which felt the way we did about Kenya, Ethiopia and Somali relations.[10]

Because of our connections with various MPs and with groups in America, we were able to be of some use to the different Somali leaders who came over from time to time. Mohamed Jama, one of the organizers of the Somali Youth League, came across, and together with Ali Mira we had discussions in Salford about tactics. Then Abdulalli Issa (who would later be the Somali Foreign Minister) came over at a very critical time. He sought our help to get him over to the United Nations where he hoped to plead the case that a mandate over his part of Somaliland should not be handed back to the Italians. We managed to procure a passport for him, and explained to him very clearly our position on Somalia-Ethiopia relations: 'You and the Ethiopians have to live together in the area; so it is better for you to understand the realities of the Somali position. If you are going to try to play the role of an outsider, we shall treat you with as much contempt as the Englishmen. Now, when you get to America, you will find brothers in men like Walter White and Roy Wilkins of the NAACP; they will give you money for your stay, and we shall pay them back through Ralph Bunche.' He got there eventually and received red carpet treatment from our brothers. Then at the UN he pleaded along with Ethiopia the point that the Italians be not given back sovereignty over his territory.[11] His mission did not succeed in the narrow sense, nor did we expect to sway the British delegation through one

185

solitary man. Our role was as vocal men without a country ourselves to facilitate the connections between the various peoples of Africa.

We had similar useful contacts with the Sudanese. The Anglo-Egyptian Sudan had always had rather a special position in British eyes; so there were consequently a number of Sudanese students in London whom we knew. One of the best known of these was Osman, who would later be Sudan's ambassador to the Soviet Union. He was one of those who in the thirties literally lived in Hyde Park at Speakers' Corner. This is the way we first got to know him. But once our association had deepened, we were called upon by some of the young Sudanese to contribute articles to some of their papers. George in particular wrote a number of pieces for the *Sudan Star*. But for both of us it was a rather similar position to the one concerning the Somali. We felt that Sudan should look to Africa and not north to the Middle East. And certainly it should not allow itself to become a southern extension of Egypt. I had personally gathered these ideas at first hand, when Lawrence Taezaz, secretary of the Ethiopian legation, had gone over to Sudan during the occupation of Ethiopia. His task had been to maintain contact with some of the guerrilla movements there, but he had come across in addition some of the leadership of the Sudanese, such as the Mahdi's son. Later, therefore, in London and Manchester we were able to renew contact with these people when delegations came over. George, who was pretty constantly in London, would phone me up that a delegation had arrived and that they were expected in Manchester shortly. When they came up I met them and showed them around. They were members of the Umma Party which was very progressive, and very opposed to Egyptian domination of the Nile Valley. Abdalla Khalil Bey was present, and this noted poet-cum-politician of the Left, Mahjoub.[12] I took them over to the *Manchester Guardian* offices, because the *Guardian* had been playing for a long time an important role in informing the British public of the development of the Sudan struggle. I also used the opportunity to point out the need for accord between Ethiopia and Sudan, and the danger of Northern Nigeria regarding the Sudan as part of her frontier. I warned them against the designs of these reactionary Fulani boys from Nigeria who already had a presence in Sudan. But more practically we were able to help the delegation in getting a botanist they wanted to take back for work in the development of the cotton industry around Gezira. Fortunately Padmore was in a position to produce a very able Jamaican scientist, and they took him back with them to the Sudan.

In other discussions we brought up some further delicate issues. There was this talk of how other Africans making their way through Sudan or Mecca for the *haj* were sometimes caught and enslaved. Then there was the position of some of the small Ibo communities which had migrated from Eastern Nigeria and were to be found labouring in various parts of the Sudan— often for absentee landlords. Finally there was the critical difficulty of the Southern Sudan. In all of these cases there was the suggestion by the British that these groups would be denied the rights of self-determination in the event of independence. Our tactics were therefore to urge our Sudanese brothers to act with all speed, but to counter the adverse British propaganda over treatment of the people of the Southern Sudan. 'Look,' we would say, 'tell the British, "Africans will be able to settle their own internal problems.[13] So don't draw red herrings over our path. This is just a typical part of the British outlook— always bringing problems about African incompetence in government. Remember, you've been there for sixty years, and you haven't settled a damn thing. How do you expect that overnight we can settle everything? It's a huge human problem".' So to these and to later delegations we would stress the primacy of Sudan being free, independent and unfettered with Egyptian influence, and at the same time urge them to avoid practising on their own southlands the very policy they were preventing the Egyptians from working upon themselves.

Our connections with central and southern Africa were much less firm. So little was known about the growth of an indigenous leadership. Still there were a number of critical points of contact. The first of these concerned Bechuanaland, and its ruler Tsekedi Khama. I was a student in America at the time, but it left a deep impression on a number of us when Tsekedi was deposed. It arose from a certain white man who had gone to live amongst Khama's people. This man had been accepted by the African community and in the eyes of whites had 'gone native'. He was entitled like other Bamang'wato to practise polygamy if he so de-

sired, but when he began to disturb the tribal practices and introduce strong drinks, he was called before the Khama's council and
asked to give an account of himself. As a result certain punishment
was assigned to him. At this point white racial pride was insulted
at the idea that a black might mete out punishment to a white,
the troops were called in, and Khama was deposed.[14] Well,
what sort of racial sell-out was this, we wondered? These three
places, Swaziland, Bechuanaland and Basutoland were meant
to be protectorates, designed to show the difference between the
ways blacks were treated in the South Africa of the Boers and the
protectorates of the British. As students we hadn't been able to
do much about this earlier case, but when Khama's nephew went
one worse, we were able to act. The uncle had tried to beat a
white man, but the nephew, Seretse, had actually married a white
woman. In doing so he was going right against the idea that there
was a fundamental difference between white and black, and was
thus considered to be a danger to the peace and good government of the country. In this way the bitterness which had been
engendered over the uncle in 1933 flared out with the treatment of
Seretse in 1948.[15] But in the latter case we were able to project
the continuity of the same racial policy to the British public.

The other issue that came out of South Africa and had so much
impact upon us in England was what happened to the Industrial
and Commercial Union of Clements Kadalie. This was the first
and most successful unionization of blacks in Africa; there
were hundreds and thousands of members in South Africa who
swore by this organization, for it had been able to do a wonderful
job in getting collective agreements for the miners. They then sent
out this Scottish trade-unionist, Ballinger, in order to investigate.
He decided quite quickly that the structure of the movement was
not in keeping with what prevailed in the West, and disturbed
the whole union.[16] The next move was for Herzog and Smuts
to form a united front and declare the break-up of all such
militant trade union movements amongst blacks. They would
no longer tolerate collective bargaining. For me the whole
sordid episode was simply another example of the danger of
introducing white advisers into black organizations.

We had close contacts with policies in Kenya through Jomo,
and after he had left, with Koinange, and already the younger
generation of Kenyans was beginning to appear on the scene

with Tom Mboya, Awori and Njonjo. From Tanganyika, there was Nyerere, then studying at Edinburgh University. People like Margery Perham used to regard him as one of the rising stars, a sort of African counterpart of the brilliant West Indian economist, Arthur Lewis. Nyerere's articles used to appear regularly in the *Manchester Guardian*, and generally he was seen as a sober and able spokesman for his people. However, when the Kabaka of Buganda was also summarily exiled in the early fifties, he became very vocal.

From West Africa one of the problems that we tried to deal with in the Federation was the clannishness of some of the groups from the Coast. The Kru-men from along the West African coast were an example of the better side of clannishness. Wherever they settled in England they organized little cells of co-operation.[17] So that if a Kru-man passed away, the whole local group would come and put money in the box for his burial. You know, many European women looked upon them as better providers than their own men, because the Kru-man was always at sea, doing the hard work, and making sure that the money was set aside to educate his children. In many parts of the English Midlands, the children of these early Kru-men have done very well, and you could hear the old fathers putting their beliefs in pidgin English: 'Bobo, as for me, me no know book, but I go see that the pickin learn book.' One could say therefore that there was a greater degree of respectability in some of these Kru homes than in other West African groups. Some of these, however, tried to bring over to their life in England the prejudices they had held about the Kru people back in West Africa. So sometimes you would find a Gold Coast man speaking his Akan language, but carrying with him round the world his little prejudices: 'Oh, a Kru-man! He's a man who handle *kaka*, a man who looks after my faeces in my country. Tsha. Am I to come here and try to live near him?' This is where we would try to intervene and set the record straight on the Kru-man's achievement and the need for a larger harmony. 'The Kru-man is very important here in England; he may not know book, but this man has prestige in the community. He pays his bills, he doesn't beat his wife, he doesn't live on immoral earnings. He wears a Homburg hat and a decent coat, and he doesn't go and gamble his money away. So don't start this funny business with your little Gold Coast prejudices, saying that this man is your scavenger. It won't work here.'

The same thing would occur between the Gold Coast man and the Nigerian; plenty of little tribal tales to distinguish the one group from the other. You would overhear the Gold Coast man saying: 'This Nigerian, you know, he can eat a cat. Your cats are not safe, you know. All these nice English pets around—he'll chop them, sir. Also, sir, they are not clean, their house is full of palm oil. After all we Gold Coast men have a record of being the greatest consumers of soap in the world, you know.' So here it was again with people always splitting up into the smallest particles and forgetting the wider humanity. The hope was that we could get such groups to sink their narrowness in some broader cause. But it was never easy. Sometimes it was just doggedness that kept you at the task, because it has been far from a pleasant journey these last thirty-eight years.

But if one did feel despair at the obstacles to pan-Africanism, it was at least cheering to reflect that class-consciousness had not yet eroded a certain basic solidarity. You would see it so clearly in some of these respectable delegations coming over through the Colonial Office or the British Council to attend some conference in Surrey or in a London suburb. As soon as they could, they broke away from the routine and came to King's Cross or Poplar in the East End: 'Man, I want a bit of that country food and to see my people'. They couldn't take the artificiality of it for long, and would slip away from the Colonial Office rooms to some dive in Soho which is manned by this Nigerian Babalola Wilkie or some of the other boys. It doesn't matter how big the man, whether he is a milord in high places, he has this yearning for his own people's company: 'Man, I want to go to Soho to meet the boys, or to Cardiff. Where is Makonnen's Forum Club? Where is Jimmy Taylor's Shangri-la?'

As a group we were not tied to relations within the African groups. We were also forced to come to grips with the Indians, because in so many parts of the black world, you find the Indians and the Africans living in the same country. The former were almost a pan-African problem, since they cropped up in East Africa, South and Central, as well as in Guyana, Trinidad and other parts of the West Indies. Again it was fortunate that we had been able in London to have discussions with some of

190

the future leadership of India. Nehru we knew well. Then there were those other idealists such as Professor N. G. Ranga;[18] he was part of the Gandhi movement to give land back to the peasants, and had shared a common experience in prison and the ashiam. He was a trusted emissary, a member of the Legislative Council, and he had very early on been acquainted with Jomo. The two of us met through Dinah Stock, and he embraced me as a brother. We had immediate accord because he was livid about the behaviour of certain Indian groups at the outposts of the empire. We kept the flame burning for several years, and he was finally instrumental in passing that great bill through the independent Indian Parliament; it declared that mother India would not be responsible for those Indians of the diaspora.[19] They would renounce them, and would refuse to let them use the name of India for furthering imperialism. So it was when Nehru and Ranga had got this bill through that you could observe the Indian communities of East Africa and Nigeria beginning to tremble. It was the start of a number of gestures towards Africans, the first of which was the offering of scholarships to study in India. Even in Nigeria, the small Indian Muslim community began to do this, although it was more pronounced in Kenya. So for this crucial struggle, we could not have had better allies and champions than Gandhi, Nehru, Nehru's sister, and my very close friend Krishna Menon. When Menon eventually went to represent India at the UN, we knew he took with him the right and the lawyer's brief to defend not only India, but also some of those African communities where Indians were playing too dominant a role.

Consequently, we were greatly perturbed at the divisive role played by the future leaders of Pakistan, men like Jinnah. This meant that from now on your Indian communities abroad would be split between India and Pakistan, and there was the further division that so many of them owed their loyalty to the Aga Khan. To me he seemed to have little concern with India, spending his time spinning with the kings and horse-racing. It was also disturbing that the South Africans seemed to be prepared to grant special privileges to the Aga Khan's Ismaili sect at the expense of the larger Indian population. It looked as if the Ismaili were quite prepared to sell out the other Indians.[20]

At this point we became more closely involved with this

191

South African/Indian conflict through the activities of the Rev. Michael Scott. With his Jesuitical concept of justice, he had begun a process of winning the whites, the Indians and the Africans into a united front. He had also become deeply involved in the Herero victimization within the South West Africa mandated territory. And it was with all these questions on his mind that he came through England in 1948 to try to make his way to the United Nations.[21] When he was in England a meeting was called by the Indian League; Krishna Menon called me to attend, and there were others, such as Sam Morris, secretary of the LCP, present. We met and in this *tête-à-tête* Michael was describing what the situation was and how difficult it was going to be for him without a passport or visa for America. Out of the blue, I broke in, 'Look I'm not being a chauvinist, but as far as I'm concerned the Indians have got sufficient luminaries to represent their case. I am suggesting as secretary general of the Pan-African Federation that Rev. Scott drop the Indian question and go on to New York to present the Herero or African case pure and simple. If he does, there will be no difficulty about getting him a passport.' Well, this was a bit of a surprise, and Padmore looked across at me as though I was carrying the thing a bit too far; but I carried on. 'I have a plan, gentlemen. There is a powerful caucus around the NAACP with Wilkins, and more generally in America around Mrs. Roosevelt there has grown up a kind of united front against fascism. I think we can bring pressure to bear on selected points and a visa will be forthcoming.' We closed the meeting shortly and during lunch I gave £25 to send off fifty cables to leading blacks and whites in America, stating that Scott had been appointed to represent the Herero case in the UN but that his passport had been denied. Simultaneously we made use of Ralph Bunche in the American Embassy in London. The result was that a passport was forthcoming, and he went off to the UN. In addition we sent an SOS to the NAACP instructing them to make money available to him during his stay, and that they would be reimbursed. His presentation of the South African case at the UN was sensational, and naturally it reflected well upon our organization; it could be seen that it was not just a little conspiratorial group, but that it was really solid and involved.

The reason I had tried to restrict Scott was plain. The Indian factor would be an entanglement because there was no single Indian position. As I have suggested the Ismaili and other Muslim elements linked to Pakistan were manouevring to come to terms with the South African government. A few of these Muslim Indians in South Africa were extremely wealthy, were married to European women, and it looked as if it would just confuse the issue to have Scott present an Indian case along with the African.

My anxieties about presenting the Indian case along with the African were sharpened by what was happening in Guyana. Here the Indian leader Jagan was apparently a close associate of the black leader Forbes Burnham.[22] But Burnham at that stage did not sufficiently realize the unevenness of the alliance—the great wealth and business power that the Indians exercised. Both men were communists, but like other communists in East and South Africa they were tied to the party line, prisoners of the movement. Also the union at the leadership level did not reflect the great difference between the Indian and African communities in Guyana; the ordinary Africans could not understand what Burnham was up to in this tactical alliance with the Indian, and they told him so quite openly: 'After all this Burnham has joined this coolie man (Indian) to oppress me; it was the Indian who came quietly to my village selling me everything, lending me money to send my sons to school. I even mortgaged my land and my family house to him, and I keep on having to pay interest back to him on these loans. So all the properties have come into their hands. Yet now you say we are united. How can this be so? How can the lion and the lamb be united unless we first take all the lion's teeth out? Secondly there's his caste system: how can you be united if you can't marry into his camp? He sees to it from the time that his children are born that they have husbands or wives allotted to them and he lives in a totally different world. So how come all this talk about our being one society?' To me it was all further proof of the thesis that alliances cannot be constructed out of the foreign policy of the Russian communists; instead it should have been a question of separately we march, together we strike.

In all this nascent nationalist activity that we have considered it would be profitable to investigate the intellectual source. I should think that with many of the fellows we've mentioned and with many others we never met, the impact of George's book, *How Britain Rules Africa*, was crucial. It came out in 1936, but the ideas expressed in the title continued to guide many of us for years afterwards. To Africans who did not want to be confused either by the communist missionaries or the Christian ones, here was the message; here was the anatomy of our misery laid bare. Naturally there were other texts, such as Buell's *Native Problem in Africa*, and Lord Hailey's ponderous tomes on African administration, but George's book had the real impact. It gripped these African lawyers who might have been hiding behind their statutory conventions, and incited them to see the black problem as it was. I know the reaction from Africa, because letters came in from students we didn't know saying that up till their reading of this thing, they had been in darkness; but now they had a Magna Carta. Even now in the 1970s when George is long dead, and many studies have been made on pan-Africanism, I still feel the impact of that book upon us. It was part of our spiritual campaign.

NOTES TO CHAPTER 11

1 According to Padmore the birth of the Pan-African Federation was in 1944.

2 For Padmore's closeness to the ILP, see Hooker, *Black Revolutionary*, pp. 50, 52–3.

3 The way that the black abolitionist, Douglass, had his political priorities circumscribed by Lloyd Garrison is well told in Philip Foner, *Frederick Douglass* (New York, 1964). Eric Williams has outlined the hypocrisy of some of the anti-slavery movements of Britain in *Capitalism and Slavery*, pp. 183–8.

4 See, for instance, M. Attlee, 'The Coloured People in South Africa' in *Journal of the African Society*, 46 (1947), pp. 148–51.

5 Brockway wrote in his *African Journeys* (London, 1955), 'It cannot be denied that many of the practices of Mau Mau represent a reversion to a primitive barbaric mentality; this has shocked, perhaps most deeply, those of us who have co-operated in the political advance of Kenya Africans' p. 169.

6 As early as 1937, a Somali Association of Great Britain had come to the attention of the *Keys*, v, 1 (July–Sept. 1937), p. 18; there was also by the mid-forties a United Somali Party of Cardiff, and an English branch of the Somali Youth League.

7 The general background to this incident is contained in an article, 'Colour Persecution on Tyneside', *Pan-Africa*, i, 2 (1947), pp. 24–30, where it is reported that the Pan-African Federation had sent a representative in August 1946 to investigate police victimization of coloured cafe owners.

8 Makonnen's own position on the Ogaden and Reserved Areas under British military administration in 1946 was that they should be returned to Ethiopia to whose ancient empire they had originally belonged; see *New Times*, 29 June 1946, and 20 April 1945.

On the latter occasion, Makonnen was introduced as a 'a native of Tigrai Province, Ethiopia'. For a statement of the Ethiopian case, see Sylvia Pankhurst, *British Policy in Eastern Ethiopia: The Ogaden and the Reserved Area* (Woodford Green, n.d.).

9 For Ethiopian-Somali diplomatic moves at this time, see C. Hoskyns, *Case Studies in African Diplomacy*: 2: *Ethiopia-Somalia-Kenya Dispute* (Nairobi, 1969) and pp. 9–10 for Bevin's proposals.

10 The Somali Youth Club (later League) was created in Somaliland in May 1943; see I. M. Lewis, *A Modern History of Somaliland* (London, 1965), p. 121.

11 Issa was the Somali Youth League representative at the United Nations from 1949 to 1952.

12 Makonnen's good friend, Reg Reynolds, has recorded some interesting conversations with Khalil Bey and Mahjoub in *Beware of Africans*, pp. 77–83.

13 This was a typical attitude of Makonnen on many African problems; cf. his feelings about the Somali-Ethiopia dispute of 1945: 'If we Ethiopians have any differences between ourselves about methods of administration, it is for us to settle those differences between ourselves. We consider that it is our right. The Scotch or the Welsh may have differences with the English, but you do not want any foreign power to come between you', *New Times*, 28 June 1945.

14 See Padmore's account of the affair in *How Britain Rules Africa*, pp. 135–8.

15 J. Halpern, *South Africa's Hostages* (Penguin, 1965), pp. 274–7 contains a discussion of the Seretse conflict.

16 Kadalie discusses Ballinger himself in *My Life and the ICU* (London, 1970), pp. 177–81.

17 Kru organization in Britain is discussed by M. Banton, *The Coloured Quarter* (London, 1955), pp. 217–18.

18 Ranga wrote a number of times for Makonnen's journal, *Pan-Africa;* see N. G. Ranga, 'Full Independence', i, 4 (April 1947), pp. 2–10.

19 In a foreign policy debate of 15 September 1953 Nehru stated: 'This House knows very well that all along, for these many years, we have been laying the greatest stress on something which is rather unique . . . . We have gone out of our way to tell our own people in Africa . . . that they can expect no help from us, no protection from us, if they seek any special rights in Africa which are not in the interests of Africa', quoted in V. McKay, *Africa and World Politics* (New York, 1963), pp. 175–6.

20 There were also a number of rich Hindus in South Africa who were opposed to Afro-Asian solidarity in the Non- European Unity Movement; see Padmore, *Pan-Africanism or Communism?* pp. 358–9.

21 Scott's mission is described in detail in Ruth First, *South West Africa* (Penguin, 1963), pp. 182–200.

22 The Indo-African conflict in Guyana is covered in P. Newman, *British Guiana* (London, 1964); cf. also, Cheddi Jagan, *The West on Trial* (New York, 1967 edition).

CHAPTER 12

THE POLITICS OF EDUCATION:
ENGLAND, KENYA AND GHANA

O ne thing that exercised us greatly before we came back to Africa was the state of education in various parts of the continent. In West Africa there was at least a consciousness of the needs amongst the colonial governments of Sierra Leone, Nigeria and Ghana, but no such feeling existed in some of the East African countries or in South Africa. A place like Kenya took South Africa as its model, and feeling that they should be guided by the South African experience, allocated only a ridiculous amount of money for African education. The rest of it went to the Asian and white populations. So what little African education there was lay in missionary hands. They, too, really hadn't the means, but they assumed a moral control of African development, and in their own way proved to be a brake on African education. You see, some were well intentioned, and some were frankly cranks who had taken on their shoulders the whole of the white man's burden. This kind of person couldn't tolerate any African who felt he was now ready to assume some responsibility in the mission or school; he was treated as an upstart. Reaction to this kind of treatment had already appeared in Kenya with the independent African church movement, and some of these churches were striving to provide schools also[1]; but our main feeling was that the backwardness of mass education in Africa was as crucial as any of the other political disabilities. You might make adults walk around with their pass-cards and *kipandes*, but to keep thousands of little children out of school was much more criminal.

This was where our experience in England came in. For a number of us had really spent a lot of our time in adult education;

196

we had been part-time lecturers for years, and had had first-hand knowledge of the various forms of workers and adult education in Britain. There were two main trends in English adult education, and one of these looked very relevant for adaptation in Africa. There was the Workers' Educational Association (WEA) first of all; this seemed to us more of a bourgeois, middle-class affair where once you had twelve people interested in studying Shakespeare, a lecturer would be at your beck and call. Rather a highbrow educational system. Then there was the National Council of Labour Colleges (NCLC) —the really hardcore Keir Hardie-type of class education. This was much more what we were looking for, and both Jomo and I had seen something of their operations in Scotland. The approach was strictly Marxian, and a lot of miners and other Scottish workers were brought in so that you would get a more enlightened trade union leadership.

We shared, too, in the wider outlook towards education of the English intellectuals themselves. There was almost an army of Oxford and Cambridge graduates in the thirties and early war years who were prepared to work in adult education. Popular education was in the air, and many of our political friends combined their politics with teaching and extending the popular consciousness. The world was on the move, and people wanted to be taught about the Spanish Civil War, Ethiopia, the co-operative movement in other countries and a multitude of other subjects. I had caught the spirit particularly when I was lecturing in the Co-operative College in Manchester, and Jomo had done the same through his time in the Quaker Selly Oak College in Birmingham and his lecturing in Kent during the war.[2]

The agricultural element was also crucial. Some of us had this agricultural preoccupation from America, where every state had a state university with a heavy agricultural and scientific emphasis. Even the Booker Washington tradition we felt should not be despised, if it could be adapted to help in African agricultural development. We in the West Indies also had the Royal College of Agriculture in Trinidad, and I continued to keep abreast of developments there through its monthly journal even when I was in England. But one was also aware of the importance of agriculture because of the Russian experiment.

197

Being steeped in Russia, one had been following the development of the co-operative farms and the elimination of the kulak element. And even in England, there were agricultural experiments that were worth noting; down in the Wye College in Kent, old-style gentleman farmers were going for crash courses to learn new approaches. Fortunately a few of our boys were also turning up there, but the majority were still desperately hanging on to their law. Or if they were interested in education, they were determined to go back home and make education pay—go and set up schools like shops, and make money out of the magic of the pen. There were not enough counterparts in Africa of the Oxford Greats man going off to lose himself in miners' education in Scotland.

Some of the Jews too were blazing a trail. They could see what was threatening in Europe, and had begun buying up farms in England, deliberately to train the refugees to take on a new agricultural life in Israel. I saw the parallel for the hundreds of thousands of Ethiopian refugees from Italian rule who were sitting doing nothing in the camps in the Sudan or in northern Kenya.[3] So I prepared a letterhead 'Education Foundation for Ethiopian Youths' and prepared over three hundred letters to institutions in India, America, Ceylon and elsewhere—but principally to the American Negro boarding colleges of the United States. I explained in it the tragedy of these thousands of young men, and also the formula that the Italians seemed to be applying of wiping out the intellectuals. Indeed, in that massacre of educated Ethiopians in Addis Ababa, some of my own friends like Yohannes and Makonnen Haile from my American days were killed.[4] If Jewish families in America were able to adopt some of their European kindred, then surely the black American could do the same for Ethiopians.

I was taken aback by the response. Out of the 200 odd letters that went to America, some 80 per cent responded favourably; immediately I set off for the Ethiopian Legation in London, to my friends Taezaz, Teklehiwot and of course Emanuel Abraham, and I laid the matter before them for urgent consideration. Then I went on to my good friends Sir Sidney and Lady Barton to get their support, because of their close connection earlier to Addis Ababa[5]; instead they began to point out the obstacles—that King Emanuel of Italy was *de facto* ruler now of

Ethiopia, and it would be difficult for the British government to assist a major operation behind his back. I said, 'What has this got to do with it? Our Emperor should still be able to issue passports for study in America, because none of us have accepted the conquest by Italy. The battle continues. Have you forgotten the conquest of Europe by Napoleon and the similar united front of exiles in Britain? It's the same with the Emperor. He may not be in Ethiopia, but the struggle goes on.' At this point I saw that people like the Bartons would be ready to show a deep sense of charity, and would dispatch any amount of old clothes to refugee camps, but they would not consider dealing with the problem in a radical manner.

What we wanted was to insure the continuance of an educated class of young men and women, so that even if the Italian Empire lasted for a thousand years there would be a group of dedicated people who would be able to hand on the fire in their hearts to their children. I even approached the Japanese Embassy in London (this was about 1937), and suggested that some of their ships trading in East Africa might be able to pick up some of the refugees and help them on their way to America. But we kept coming up against this business of passports. The Emperor was not prepared to stick out for this one as he was strictly a guest in England, and did not see the wider implications of this international aid.

In all this unofficial activity, I simply assumed the Ethiopian outlook, and took it to its logical conclusion. These were things I saw needed doing. Perhaps if I had actually been a son of the Ethiopian soil, I might not have carried the thing so far, because of the tradition in that country of checking everything with the Emperor first. As it was, I was embodied with the spirit of the West and felt it an affront not to push the venture as far as it would go. However, being so distant from the actual refugees, it was impossible to do what was so easy with the West African stowaways and others who wanted to get to Britain or America. So the difficulty with passports effectively killed the quest.

At this same period, just before the war, we were also working on another educational front. Jomo and I had both been exposed also to the International People's College in Elsinore, and it seemed that its style, and that of the socialist college I had visited in Austria, would make a good model for a similar venture in

199

Kenya. So marrying the spirit of these and the NCLC, we projected a people's college in Kenya, and got a number of our leading supporters in the Labour Party involved. What also seemed to make it feasible was that the Royal African Society had just gone through a reorganization, and from its large libraries it was disposing of some of its triplicate volumes by selling them to the public. I bought some 2,000 volumes, many of them absolutely critical works for an understanding of Africa. They were to provide a basis for the college, and were despatched to Mombasa when Jomo finally returned to Kenya.

As soon as one decided to return in the educational field to Africa the difficulties began. In West Africa, there were quite a large number of frustrated BAs and MAs who found that despite their qualifications they could not penetrate the citadels of the missionaries. This happened to my friend, William Ofori Atta, the son of the noted Gold Coast chief.[6] He found the usual reaction, and decided therefore to start an independent school in the Cape Coast region. In fact he was one of the architects of Ghana's huge self-help movement in schooling which overnight produced hundreds of these independent schools. In East Africa, one of our student friends had already gone back in the mid-thirties—Kalibala—and we knew well enough what he had suffered at the hand of the missionaries[7]; they had simply dismissed him in the usual way: 'You Africans, you spend ten years getting a big book education, but you don't know a thing'. Then Peter Koinange, the son of the old chief Koinange, had been preparing to return in the late thirties. He, too, had had enough of the missionaries during his time in America, and he knew along with us that many of them had no real cultural background to impart to the Africans.[8] Often enough they were lower middle class English or Scots who were moved by their pietist beliefs to serve in Africa. Nevertheless, they were always ready to scrutinize Africans for their ability as teachers and other roles.

Koinange had had to undergo the same screening when he was with us in England. It was pointed out to him by the Colonial Office that he couldn't expect to come back and serve properly in Kenya if he only had American educational experience; so he was steered into a course of English teacher training, where they managed to fail him. This was of course part of a more general British disregard for American education, but there was an

200

additional scrutiny of Africans from America; the idea was that individual Africans would really have to be tested by the Colonial Office people to make sure; you had to go through a fine sieve. And this was particularly so as the number of Africans with good American qualifications began to knock at the door, and demand decent positions in Africa. It made you feel a stepchild in your own land.

These busybodies pointed out to Koinange that he would have to continue his studies to come up to scratch, but he overruled this and returned, telling us: 'My brothers, as soon as I go I will avoid these people as much as possible and with my father's influence set out to create a school outside their control.' This happened in due course in 1939, and a nucleus was created in the Kenya Teachers' College at Githunguri which Jomo would be able to build up further when he also returned after the war.

But at that point just before the war, it had all been falling into the sort of pattern we had been planning. Our close friend Ralph Bunche had paid an important visit to Kenya in the late thirties, and it began to look as if pan-Africanism could really come to the assistance of Kenya in a big way.[9] Much earlier there had been Garvey sending out his various groups to serve in Africa, but now we had the great advantage of having in Koinange and Kenyatta sons of the soil, and around them the people's college concept could be constructed. It all began to synchronize. Nor in our naïvity did we really anticipate any opposition to such an educational programme designed by Africans for Africans. Kenyatta might be regarded as an agitator by some, but he was also well known as a teacher and the author of this book on the Kikuyu. Indeed, publishers had followed up his success with that volume by asking him to write a series of African children's stories. They were going to be published by Blackwell's of Oxford. So there was quite a lot in our favour to show that we were not simply bent on destruction, but had a serious purpose.

Initially we were correct, and the government did not interfere significantly with Koinange's teachers' college, even though it was independent, nor with Kenyatta teaching there after he returned. Whether they would have allowed blacks of the diaspora like myself into Kenya to associate with the school is another question. But we were never able to put it to the test, because war broke out in Europe, and by the time it ended, my immediate priorities had changed. In the interval, we had built a movement in Manchester; we had money, and we had the opportunity for a time to work on a world front. We had constructed close working alliances with white liberals and revolutionaries. What would have happened if we too had come out to Kenya can only be speculation. In Kenya at any rate, Koinange's and Kenyatta's educational plans were swiftly terminated in the early fifties when all these independent schools were banned by the government.[10]

The focus naturally swung from East Africa to Ghana in the mid-fifties. This time, with Ghana's independence, it was an African country rather than an individual that was on trial. I had arrived in Ghana myself in 1957, and felt this was a critical time for Ghana to demonstrate that her people were not going to fall behind the world proletariat in its standard of education. If it did, there would be always the threat of reconquest.

One thing was immediately clear: that there was going to be a struggle between the old classical concept of education and the new more relevant forms for Africa. This was symbolized in the contrast between the old style University College at Legon and the Kwame Nkrumah Institute of Science and Technology at Kumasi.[11] At the former there were all these fellows—both black and white—who had all the old fixed ideas about being dons. It was an élitist ideology of feeling that 'now we're in the saddle here, we'll ride hard to keep this horde of commoners from lowering standards'. On the African side, you had the old Oxford men who saw themselves as the cream, the men of tradition; they might even look down on London University on the grounds that they were Oxford men after all. Most important, their degrees would not be tarnished by any hint of practicality. Pure learning. I felt about them: 'You, with your false conceit about knowledge, what were your degrees anyway? You didn't want to deal with the day-to-day problems confronting your people; instead you got tied up in anthropological confusion . . . you are no more than *ju-ju* men, and you are not coming forward with new philosophies of life which will help liberate the masses from religion and from colonial rule.'

Even if you had taken a science degree at your Oxford college, you didn't come back to Ghana and set about starting, say, a brewery business, or exploiting the possibilities of palm wine. You went into the civil service where your talent in science was lost. With them, if Kwame tried to promote some fresh academic blood, there would be a swift reaction. They would burst out with: 'Who is this upstart, this Nzima boy, this goldsmith's son (Kwame)? He is not a part of the old Oxford brigade; he is one of these damned American-educated types. Look at these strange people—these Makonnens and Padmores— he has dug up and brought into our Ghana. We don't even know their ancestry.'

Although they were hostile to Kwame, they were quick enough to agree with him when he tried to promote the idea of a separate national university for Ghana. Back in England all the talk of people like Creech Jones was of a single university for West Africa,[12] but Kwame with his American background was fighting for a plurality of institutions. So naturally these academic conservatives were in favour. Like the professionals who backed Garveyism, they saw that there would be more jobs for them in a system of national universities; they would go on: 'We are a proud people, we Ghanaians. We're supplying almost half of the world's cocoa needs. We have some £200 million in a reserve, so we can afford to push forward fast with our own institutions. And yet you in Britain are trying to lump us in one university along with these backward Nigerians and other savage peoples. You have no decency, no respect. So don't come here with your commissions trying to confuse us with figures.'

But one university or several, what these people liked was the same: the candles burning on the 'High Table' as the dons conversed. They also felt that they must continue to observe the best of British standards by having an English presence. 'The British know what is best for us, and they will send us this man, Balme, for our principal, one of their best sons, a man who is a great Greek scholar.'[13]

None of this was in keeping with Ghana's needs at all. This was going back a thousand years to the medieval concept of the cloister of scholars, whereas Kwame had made it quite clear that what it had taken Britain a thousand years to change, Ghana must try to change in one generation or two. For me this meant keeping abreast of the times.

Again the American perspective and the Russian one were influential. But the conservative types were holding doggedly on to the English tradition and did not seem to realize that there were two Englands. You did not have to go to America to discover a different concept of university from the Oxford model. It was right there in England before your eyes. You had a man like Dr. Lindsay of Balliol (he was almost like a father to me) who was sent out from Oxford to create a new style of university, in the Potteries and elsewhere, which would not be modelled on Oxford. And these red-brick universities were able to surpass the old ones in many ways. But these Ghanaian conservatives did not notice any of the revolutionary progress in education in England. They did not see the significance of the Education Act at the end of the Second World War, and were consequently trying to continue with a concept of education in Ghana which the Labour Party and other forces had actually been wiping out in England. Had they been aware of these modern trends in education there would have been no conflict between the Kumasi and the Legon ideas. As it was, Kwame had to try to break out.

We first of all tried to bring some of the Israeli experience at their Technion into the Kumasi Institute. I was a member of the first commission that went to Israel, and this led to a tremendous educational alliance in the widest sense. The Black Star shipping company was born from this, and a new organization instead of the old colonial Public Works Department. With the Weizmann Institute in Israel, too, we were able to see further examples of an institution that turned out scientists to work in crucial areas of the country's technology. This was what we thought was required in Kumasi, and this was one of the reasons why we appointed a new principal—someone British of Jewish origin—at that institution. Even though the old Achimota College had turned out a few boys in the early days who would prove useful in technical fields, we were acutely aware of the shortage of trained engineers. For far too long Africans had not taken this subject up abroad, since they saw no opportunities for practising it on their return.

At the lower level of education there was also a substantial move forward. A Ghana Educational Trust was set up to aid in the development of secondary schools. It seemed to me that the idea of a trust was a good one in England where a few of the big boys who had made their millions could be prevailed upon, but I couldn't see the relevance of the term in Ghana. After all, there are no rich black men of this order; so the money for the trust had to be taken from the Cocoa Marketing Board funds.[14] Once the fund of so many million pounds had been set up, then regionalism began to play its part, with each Minister and MP claiming the need for a Ghana Education Trust school in his area; there was a tendency therefore for the trust to become a bit of a racket, because once the money was allocated to a particular area, it could be used to build up individual contractors, the MP, or whoever else was involved. It did have the effect, however, of giving the educationally backward northern territories quite a number of new secondary schools. But the idea of a trust school did not seem to me to be a very revolutionary concept.

As these schools were being founded it became apparent that there was a great need for teachers. So a teachers' college was created in the Cape Coast region, where it was intended that teachers would be rigorously trained to be professionals in their outlook—a teachers' university almost, where trainee teachers could be made aware that they were specialized people involved with modern affairs. There was a tactical side to the creation of this college also; it was the idea that if the old conservatives at Legon proved too stubborn, the college could be used as an alternative regional university. In the meantime, we looked out for fine people to man the place, and found in Kwame's brother-in-law a principal. He was said to be a well-known Egyptian educationalist.

At another level entirely, the Ideological Institute at Winneba was founded to train cadres; young people who would be custodians of the revolution. It would provide, we hoped, the commissars, the people who would be placed in every ministry. They would have to keep an eye on things, and make sure that once we had taken over this government from the British we didn't settle down to sleep on the job. But its inauguration was not particularly carefully thought out. Although there were tough-line professors available from abroad, who had had wide experience, some of the young Ghanaian cadres thought they were their equal, and overnight it was necessary to appoint to key posts men of little experience. Admittedly Kodwo Addison had played some part in the early trade union activity around Takoradi, but such background was not very useful to him in his post as principal. At least you would have thought it important for such a man to make a tour of some of the established, new-style educational institutions in various parts of the world, but the pressure against this was too great. And his students were a mixed bag. They were not university level, but colonial drop-outs; boys who had been active on the party platforms; the trade union organizers; boys who might feel that had it not been for colonialism they might have been doctors or lawyers by now. They were the party stalwarts, who were getting some pay-off. They might have been some of the fellows who had been hired to subvert the activities of the Opposition, but whatever it was, now they could get a little compensation. Ideally they were to be the watchdogs of the people's education, like some of the people in Nyerere's Tanzania today; but the thing was not organized properly. Everything was undertaken too quickly, and before you had finished one thing you had started another. Apparently we had not learned enough of the British method of having a commission of inquiry, you await their report and debate the pros and cons before you move. Instead, there was a great deal of in-fighting, and if someone came and told you a lie about another man's conduct, you would push that fellow out and put one of your trusted friends in his place.

There was a good deal of fragmentation in the training efforts as well. In another centre, you had John Tettegah with his trade union training school; he would be training his cadres to be loyal to himself. The farmers, too, had a kind of training under the eye of their leader, Appiah Danquah. He was the man who had the task of pacifying the farmers when the Party wanted to take some more money off the cocoa price. He would call these big meetings and explain to them how they had so many free textbooks for their children now, and would they agree therefore to lessening a load of cocoa by so many shillings. But if you analyse it, he was training up his cadres too, to be loyal to him and to work against the Department of Agriculture. This seemed criminal, trying to undermine a body that is central in any country of the world. It would be rather like the notion of trying to provide health services without a ministry of health, if a few doctors came along and said: 'Don't worry about public health; just give us money to establish a few clinics here and there, and we'll see everything is all right'.

And then there was the education provided at the African Affairs Centre to the freedom fighters who were coming from all over the continent. My feeling was that we had to provide a training as well as a refuge. We would be fools to let the communists train such people. Equally we would be fools to let Nasser with his particular bias train them. So I set about it. Immediately, I remembered that the two thousand volumes originally sent out to Kenya were still tied up at the docks in Mombasa; so I had the state send for them, pay the freight of several hundred pounds, and this collection then became the nucleus of what was called the George Padmore Memorial Library. With this opportunity, I felt something should be done, and I organized therefore a number of specialized lectures for these hardened freedom fighters three times a week at the Centre. I explained to them the nature of British, French and other imperialists, and used Padmore's books and Kwame's little book on colonialism.[15]

All in all you had this fragmentation of effort. These various fellows all had their own battlefields. Appiah Danquah with his farmers' army, John Tettegah with his workers' army, Addison with his ideological college, and Makonnen. 'You don't have to worry too much about Makonnen; he's an international pan-Africanist, and he can only create a loyalty amongst the international brethren.'

When you compare the principals we had and those to be found at Brookwood, the co-operative colleges in England and other places, you are struck by the contrast. These Ghanaians seemed to have a different attitude towards personal power. A Ghanaian cannot get away from being a big man; the institution of the chieftaincy seems to be deep inside him. The overall mood was of a constant search in the corridors of power, and it was summed up in the phrase you heard all around you; 'power sweet'. Even if you are a commoner and you look out and see a man, some chief, being carried on his palanquin, the people are clapping, and you think to yourself: 'Power sweet. How can I translate myself into that palanquin some day?'

207

Now you can't have this feeling if you are trying to train up disciplined revolutionaries, because the boys are all plotting how they may become the successors to the ones they're overthrowing. They praise Osagyefo (Kwame), but they'd like to be Osagyefo. Nothing fragments a regime more than when there are so many contestants for every position.

It also meant that you were inevitably the object of envy and intrigue if you held a number of positions and were not a Ghanaian. I was qualified to do many jobs, so there was no love lost. You could see it operating quite clearly in the machinations of a man like Barden, who was making inroads in my organization, with a view to taking it over. Just as he had done when he had been a stenographer to George Padmore. While he was meant to be merely working under George in that Committee on African Affairs he was actually understudying him. He was taking copies of letters that George was preparing for Kwame or other leaders and would use these copies to ingratiate himself with those who wanted to be in the know.[16] I had a Ghanaian secretary too—in fact my older brother from Manchester days, Eddy Duplan. He was from the Nzima people like Kwame, and even with him I could sense this resentment against the outsider with power. He would think: 'That Mak's got too much power; he can even damn Kwame over the phone—just ring up and say, "Mr. President, you don't understand; you can't take certain things for granted. Will you let me drop round and explain?"' This would make Duplan say to others, 'You see, that Makonnen treats Kwame as if he's a boy.'

After George was gone you could see the same tendency working through the Bureau of African Affairs. Welbeck was the chairman, John Tettegah was there, but also outsiders like Mbiyu Koinange and myself were included. My idea had been that the heads of each representative body of Africans from outside should find a place on the committee. But what happened was much nearer the Russian model of centralizing everything. After all Ghana was spending the money for African liberation; so they felt the positions should be theirs. Again, therefore, no outstanding theoretician was placed as secretary of the Bureau; we got given this man Barden. He was just a police boy who had managed to worm his way into Kwame's favour, and now wanted to try his hand at playing the intelligence game right across Africa. Once he was there, the opportunity was lost of using the Bureau as a truly pan-African instrument of policy-making. Equally, it was difficult to ensure that Barden did not begin to train people in some unorthodox ways. Solid workers' education did not stand much chance with him in the saddle.

NOTES TO CHAPTER 12

1 A recent account of the independent Kikuyu church and school movement is contained in J. Anderson, *The Struggle for the School* (London, 1970), pp. 115–22.

2 At present there is no adequate biographical account of Kenyatta; however, J. Murray-Brown is shortly completing a book that should have much new material on Kenyatta in Britain.

3 A number of blacks in Britain were deeply committed to the cause of the Ethiopian refugees; at a meeting in London during March 1937, 'Ato Maconnen [sic] spoke of the exiles from Ethiopia who had taken refuge in Madagascar, the Anglo-Egyptian Sudan, French and British Somaliland, Kenya, Uganda and Aden. Among them were many helpless women and children. They were stretching out their hands to the English people and would be pleased to hear from him that that meeting had been convened for their sake . . . . ' (*New Times*, 13 March 1937); Kenyatta received news from Ethiopian refugees at this same period, and Nyabongo (who was also involved in the Negro People's Committee to aid Spanish refugees) had visited Ethiopian refugee groups in Kenya, Aden, Jibuti and elsewhere during 1939.

4 Christopher Clapham has recently drastically revised the estimates of Ethiopians liquidated by the Italians; see *Haile Selassie's Government* (London, 1969), pp. 19–21.

5 Barton had been the exceedingly influential British ambassador in Addis Ababa immediately before and during the Italian invasion.

6 Ofori Atta was at one time Minister for Justice in Nkrumah's government, and was Ghana's Foreign Minister during the Busia government.

7 On Kalibala's controversies with the missionaries in Uganda, see King, *Pan-Africanism and Education*, pp. 240–3.

8 After his time in America, Koinange spent a year at St. John's College, Cambridge and another in the London University Institute of Education. Koinange did in fact make some very close friendships with his white teachers in the United States, and even when he was the official representative of Kenya African Union in London during 1953, was still in warm correspondence with Rev. Chazeaud from his Hampton Institute days in the early 1930s. See Koinange to Chazeaud, 14 June 1953, Hampton archives. Also, his booklet, *The People of Kenya Speak for Themselves*.

9 One of the results of Bunche's visit was his 'The Land Equation in Kenya Colony', *Journal of Negro History*, xxiv, 1 (January 1939), pp. 33–43. There is an interesting photograph of Bunche, Kenyatta and Koinange sitting together when Bunche revisited Kenya shortly after Kenyatta's own return there; see H. Thuku, *Autobiography*, plate xviii.

10 According to Koinange he was at one time in charge of 400 African independent schools with 62,000 students, of which the government closed 150 at the Emergency.

11 For the debate over standards and curricula in African universities, see E. Ashby, *Universities: British, Indian, African* (London, 1966), pp. 236–49.

209

12 Creech Jones served on the Elliot Commission: *Report of the Commission on Higher Education in West Africa, 1944–5* (Cmd. 6655), and was one of the minority who proposed that there should only be a single West African university college.

13 David Balme's view of the African university is set out in Ashby, op. cit., p. 241.

14 For the Educational Trust Schools, started off with a £2.5 million grant from the Cocoa Marketing Board, see P. J. Foster, *Education and Social Change in Ghana* (Chicago, 1965), pp. 193–4.

15 Nkrumah, *Towards Colonial Freedom* (London, 1962 edition).

16 Something of Barden's political manoeuvring can be found in W. S. Thompson, *Ghana's Foreign Policy, 1957–66* (Princeton, 1969), pp. 221–4.

CHAPTER 13

FREEDOM-FIGHTING AND
THE AFRICAN AFFAIRS CENTRE

NONE of the activity around the African Affairs Centre can be understood without putting it in the context of Ghana as the vanguard of the African revolution. For this reason there had to be an ideological message worked out to show what this whole thing was about. This had been true of the American Revolution and also of the French. Our concern was that Ghana should have something to instil in our kinsmen in other lands. They should receive from our example the feeling that now they had a duty to perform; they were not any longer to wait meekly for independence to be handed to them on a silver platter, but to work for it with an awakened conscience. We were in a great tradition, and we mustn't be caught without an ideology to support our freedom. At all costs we should not repeat the tragedy of Liberia. Would to God that the pilgrim fathers of Liberia had had some political philosophy! As it was they had been slaves in America, and on their release and pilgrimage to Liberia they became determined to be like their old masters. They went to Africa not to build anything solid, but to aggrandize themselves; they formed themselves into a tight little Americo-Liberian group, and proceeded to treat the native Africans of Liberia in the same way they had been treated by their own masters in the Southern States.[1] 'Man, these Africans are very lazy, you know. You've got to beat them.'

One could see already in the early fifties that the African revolution might not be able to live up to some of our expectations. Unlike some of the great European revolutionaries who were selfless, there was a different attitude in parts of Africa. It's an unpleasant historical fact but it must be stated nevertheless.

Most of my African colleagues in the various revolutionary movements have always had a sense that the revolution must pay off. It was a profession like other professions, but it must pay dividends. Traditionally the dividends of a revolutionary in Europe have been winning over sections of the masses, or gaining a seat on a revolutionary platform. That has been sufficient. But many of my colleagues did not hesitate to associate revolution with acquiring property. Being a big man was part of proving yourself a revolutionary. So there was a considerable degree of opportunism evident in the movement. The white man was the whipping boy, and anti-colonialism became a substitute for real ideology.

Now if we in Ghana were going to provide any lead, it was essential that there should be facilities whereby visiting revolutionaries or freedom fighters could be accommodated and made useful to themselves and to the development of an African ideology. There had to be structures, and this was a desperate need, because from the time of independence in 1957 there had been groups of stragglers from various countries to be found in Ghana. But they were living like kings, taking a bottle of whisky here and there, and charging it to the government.

Kwame and George saw therefore that it was high time this whole thing was institutionalized, and as I had been involved with this sort of thing in Manchester, they thought I'd be in a better position to deal with it. I was considered a seasoned veteran, and it was assumed I'd get on with the job without any programme being laid down. It shouldn't be too different from some of the things I'd been doing in African welfare work in Manchester, Liverpool and other places.

I got the actual buildings that formed the nucleus of the Centre through my own initiative. They were down near the airport and had been built for staff at the time when Tema harbour was being constructed. Fortunately the Americans had fumigated the whole area and cleared it of mosquitoes during the war; so it was quite an attractive spot. In fact, I managed to get my hands on it just in time, because the Ministry of the Interior were also after it. However, I got the keys and simply took the place over. Immediately, I opened a credit at the bank and got £2,000 worth of barbed wire, and succeeded in fencing

212

in not only the original forty acres, but as much again. I mentioned to Kojo Botsio, who was then Minister of State, how things were going, and he said: 'Keep it going, Mak. You know how these things are done; so don't let anyone get in your way.' The next thing was to form a committee of progressive-minded people to manage the affairs of the centre, and particularly to put the thing on a working basis before the All African People's Conference of 1958.

Actually the imminence of the conference, and the lack of hotel accommodation put me in a very strong position to get things done. It allowed me also to take over some twenty-five chalets which had been used in the pre-independence period for trasning secretaries. They were furnished and were in town, Accra, but the Centre needed furnishing fast if we were to put up all the guests who were due to arrive shortly. Our committee was going to be given an appropriation to deal with all the costs but I said: 'I don't want money, I just want the right to credit these things, and the government will pay the bills.' To be an outsider as I was, and to be handling money like an insider would have been a rather delicate question. So I got permission to credit so many hundred sheets, pillow cases and utensils. For the heavier construction work I called in the Public Works Department. They broke down various partitions, and made one of the buildings into a regular mess hall which could hold one hundred people. Meanwhile in the town compound, there was a larger hall which was commodious enough for two hundred. This I got modernized overnight by using the same people. A field kitchen was established and for the time of the conference I enlisted some of the brigade girls to man it. They prepared food and I taught them how to wait on guests.

Gradually over the years, I was able to add to the facilities out at the Centre with brick buildings. And as the grant for the running of the Centre was not large, one had to use what influence one could to get things done. I would approach some contractor who was making a lot of profit from the government, and blackmail him into giving me concrete and building materials free of charge; they would always hope that if they had done me a favour out at the Centre, then when some lucrative contract with the government was in balance, things might tip in their favour. Another fellow was quite ready to let me have 10,000 blocks and tiles. So by the time my five years of management came to an end, they had perhaps gained an institution that was three times more valuable than when I took it over. This was even more true of the chalet area in Accra. It had demonstrated the need very clearly for more than the single Ambassador Hotel then in the city. So eventually with the co-operation of Solel Boneh, this Israeli company which was in partnership with the government, we were able to build the Star Hotel on the same site. It soon became one of the gay spots in Ghana and because I had an open-air theatre included in the complex and there was a good restaurant, people came and the band played nightly.

But these two places had originally come into their own during the December 1958 All African People's Conference, and you could see a similar pattern emerging when there were other top-level meetings of Africans.[2] There were really two types of meetings; there were the official ones at the conference hall where the heads of states would be talking in general terms about the future of Africa; and that's where the foreign reporters would be. Then there were the unofficial meetings at the Centre or at the chalets where you'd find the trade union element mixing with the ideological groups from various countries. They kept off the high-level generalizations about African freedom, and dealt with the practical questions of liberation. But what I noticed quite early in these unofficial meetings was that the Egyptian delegation preferred to eat at the Centre. The Egyptians had already made some contact with the liberation movements in Kenya and Uganda, but this was their first chance to meet some of the freedom fighters from other parts of Africa.[3] It seemed to me that they were making a determined bid for the loyalty of some of these men. So being a jealous man, I didn't see why I should allow them to bore from within our organization. They were not going to be allowed to use the conference for their own ends if I could help it. I called the members of our committee together: 'Look, we've spent all this money bringing these various delegations to Ghana, so we don't want the damn Egyptians using the opportunity to spread their influence with their cells, Muslim Brotherhoods and God knows what else.' I was accused, of course, of being too chauvinistic, but it was the same old message I had been preaching in Britain—that

214

the African revolution must be controlled primarily by Africans and not by interested parties who had one foot in Africa and another in the Middle East. Indeed, there was plenty of evidence in Ghana's recent history of the danger of these divided loyalties; the Muslim group had banded together with Busia's opposition party.[4] So when Dr. Gallal, Nasser's roving emissary, began to propose scholarships for Ghanaian Muslims to go to Cairo, we were able to move against him. After all, we were trying to pull the old Gold Coast into a united Ghana; so there was no place for this type of cultural or religious self-determination.

Now the All African People's Conference was clearly a crucial landmark, since this was the first occasion on African soil that African groups were going to come together to resolve their problems. Some people, as I shall explain, had to be contacted for them to come, but many were drawn by their desire to participate in the atmosphere of independent Ghana. They just came. People came from Malawi by the Congo route and from all over. We would be rung up by the police at the frontier and told that some fellows had arrived; they would have no passports, and they would say simply: 'We've got no documents, because this is our country; this is our land. What's all this about needing a passport?' It was overwhelming, and it meant that we needed enlightened policemen on the frontiers who would know not to enforce the regulations too strictly. The message of independence had gone out; the call had gone to near and far, and the various groups had just set out to come to 'Rome'.[5]

When they arrived they had to be looked after at once, given clothes and a place to sleep. As there was nowhere else to go, everybody tended to turn up at the African Affairs Centre. Some would arrive who hadn't even passed through the police's hands, so the police would trust our committee to keep them in touch with who was who. It was easy enough naturally for some of the West Africans to find their way unaided. But a number of the southern Africa delegations had to be aided. Our couriers had to go to places like Lesotho and Zambia to help with passports, and we had to trust to the good services and contacts of men like Father Huddleston to get others out.

For our contacts with Angola and Congo we also had to rely on some of our friends. The link man here was the Israeli ambassador in Ghana, Avriel.[6] He and I were very good friends, and just before the conference in 1958, I approached him and said: 'Now we are in a jam; we are preparing for this All African People's Conference, but we are short of people from certain countries like the Congo and Angola.' 'Oh,' he said, 'we have quite a number of Jews in those countries; some of them have acquired great wealth; one has been in the business of exporting African sculpture even, but they know a lot of the Africans who are significant.' Well, he left right away to visit Dr. Schweitzer's place at Lambarene, and on to the Congo. Soon enough I was hearing in dispatches from him what he'd found. He put us on to Lumumba who then came up to our conference, and told us also about Kasavubu and others. But, most interesting, he mentioned that there were quite a sizeable number of Ghanaians who had been working in the Congo for a generation or more. Some were working for the big French and Belgian companies, and in the tradition of all these big companies like the United Africa, they tended to use Sierra Leoneans, Nigerians and Ghanaians far beyond their own countries. One of them was actually attached to the American Embassy as a book-keeper, and this chap had married one of Kasavubu's nieces. Well, this was quite a goldmine. But instead of keeping it in the dark, my friend in the Bureau of African Affairs, Jimmy Markham, was careless enough to put this Congo-Ghanaian's name amongst the list of delegates in the conference brochure. Overnight, the Belgians had this man arrested for complicity, and from then on Ghanaians in the Congo were looked on as marked men.

When Avriel got back he was also able to draw to our attention some of the groupings in Angola, and the movements of Holden Roberto in particular.[7] So in all this, our feelings about the relationship between the Jewish government and our pan-African affair were confirmed. This was an alliance that was not built on any shifting sand, but drew on solid New World experience—the support of Jewish lawyers for Negro causes. Don't forget, too, that in part recompense, Liberia had been the first country to propose the acceptance of the Israeli state by the United Nations. Often, too, the men Israel sent to Africa were not old-style career diplomats, but men who had been seasoned by their own independence struggle. Avriel was one of these. In fact he was of the men who had sunk that ship in

216

Haifa harbour in order to focus world opinion on their plight. The feeling that Israel and Ghana had both fought their way to independence of the British in ten years made us something like comrades-in-arms. Hence our early commission to Israel that I mentioned. And when I was there I visited Avriel's own kibbutz for a week.

Relations with the groups that came up for the All African People's Conference did not end with the conference. Often enough individuals or whole delegations stayed on in Ghana, and usually at the centre. Holden Roberto, leader of the Union of Angolan Peoples, was one of the men who stayed on and off in Ghana for a year from 1958.

Like many of these exiled nationalists he travelled around a bit too much, going to the Congo and then up to Algeria, and then settling in Ghana again. He became an inseparable friend of Barden, but seemed to me also to be trying to be loyal to too many masters. I made something of a fool of myself over this one, because I went to Kwame and said I felt that Holden should be arrested. I had picked up some unfavourable information about him which I had begun to piece together; Roberto was not staying at the Centre, but at a colleague's house with one of the girl-friends that Barden had planted on him. Now this girl's brother was a good friend of mine and had begun to feed back to me what was happening. Apparently, Barden was helping himself to a lot of money that was meant to go to Roberto; also from my friends in the post office I had learnt that Holden had a number of American millionaire friends (I had these letters photographed). Geoffrey Bing, on the legal side of things, had also mentioned to me that Holden had an Algerian passport. I wondered therefore what kind of loyalties this man might have. They would certainly not be confined to Ghana, if he was concurrently doing business with both America and North Africa. In fact by the time Holden left Ghana for good, all this had led Welbeck and me to agree that he should be arrested because we didn't know whose revolution he was backing. But for some reason Kwame felt that we should keep our hands off him. I don't know why, for there seemed to be enough evidence that his activities were contrary to our pan-African ideals.

Another piece in this jigsaw puzzle was the group of some sixty Angolan students who arrived in Ghana via France. Up to

217

the time they arrived they had all been studying in Portugal, and it may have been part of Kwame's tactics to establish some sort of links with Portugal through them. Padmore may have been influential, too, for he set off for Portugal just before he died. He had a last drink of sherry with me, and said: 'Imagine me going to see Salazar.' I didn't even know he was ill. After he'd been in Portugal a few days, I had a card from him saying he was returning. Well, he did return that same Sunday, but it was his dead body. So I was never able to tell whether something of the foundation for getting these Angolan students to Ghana had been laid by him.[8]

What happened was the whole group left Portugal and invaded the Ghanaian Embassy in Paris. When they reached Ghana I had to accommodate them, and fortunately found a little hotel for the purpose, about six or so miles from Accra. It had belonged to a lady I knew well, who was related to Kwame, but I took it over, settled them in, and began to fix up various schools for them. Some were prepared to go to the Congo, but did not want to work for Roberto. Others I managed to get places for in Yugoslavia to continue their medical studies. And as there were a number of girl students also, I helped some to get married. At that time I didn't know any of the interior conflicts within the Angolan movement, but I tried as far as possible to keep the group out of Barden's clutches.

When there were clear splits in the various liberation movements from a single country it was the policy to work for a united front. This was the case with the two South African groups—the Pan-African Congress (PAC) and the African National Congress (ANC). It was known that there were two bodies, but the idea was that Ghana should try to bring them together in unity and strength. Often with them, and in the case of other groups, they would close their ranks automatically in a foreign country. A kind of defence mechanism operated, and they would say to each other: 'Look, bobo, we are in somebody's country; so tho' we may fight and kill each other outside, don't open up to these people or it will weaken our structure.' At any rate we had to tread pretty delicately. I called it the law of accommodation, the attempt to absorb these various groups without acting as an imperialist and dictating how they should act.

So the attitude of Kwame, and my concern also, was that at all costs these various liberation groups should be kept in one country. You didn't want one group running off to Nasser in the UAR and getting support from him, or another going to Nigeria. Nor did you want them confusing the people of Ghana with their splits. Instead let them present their case to the Central Committee as a united party representing South Africa, and Ghana would give them offices and support. This was all very well in theory, but in practice Barden, with his ex-policeman mentality, was running hither and thither, detecting critical differences between the parties, and giving his support to the PAC.[9] I knew a number of the PAC people very well such as Rabaroca and Mulutsi, and one could see that they, as a young party, did not have the entangling alliance with the communists that had characterized so many of the ANC boys.

Also from central Southern Africa, we had Banda, Kenneth Kaunda, Joshuah Nkomo and Harry Nkumbula. I put Kaunda in chalet number three and as mine was number four, we saw each other every day. We used to sit in a little recess between our two chalets and I came to know a great deal about what was then Northern and Southern Rhodesia—the role of the labour movement and this train-driver, Welensky. And Nkumbula I had known from his London days; but I didn't know Nkomo in the same way; his politics seemed much less clear than Kaunda's. In fact, Nkomo got in my way by refusing to stay at the African Affairs Centre and demanding that he should have a big car all to himself when he was going to the conference. Possibly he behaved like this because both India and Egypt had given him money, and he felt he should move in style.

What disturbed relations with a lot of these exiles and freedom fighters was that Barden was playing a double game more often than not. You would go along in the dark until some aspect of it came out. For instance, I used to feel I knew the Chinese Ambassador quite well, and another of the chaps at their embassy had been a good friend from the London days. I would go round there for a meal and to drink some Chinese rice wine. Everything seemed above board until I put my finger on what was happening. A friend of mine who had a big family house out about ten or fifteen miles from Accra told me: 'I don't know what is wrong

219

with this fellow Barden, but he is delaying my money.' 'Money for what?' I asked him.

'Well, he runs my big house where he has got some Chinese fellows training some of our people.' At once then I saw that there were worlds within worlds. It always amazed me that Barden was allowed to get away with all his schemes; it must have been partly because Kwame, who had seen no military combat himself, got carried away by this policeman adventurer with his guerrilla training and Chinese instructors. The trouble was that many of the ordinary Ghanaians did not distinguish between Barden and the fellows like myself down at the Centre. They assumed that the Centre was where all these bad fellows hung out; and this explains why at Kwame's overthrow they felt that a whole brigade of guards with machine guns would be necessary to surround the African Affairs Centre. It had got a name for itself.

It was very difficult to move against Barden, because he had also made a united front with Addison who was head of the Ideological College. Together they tried to make sure there was no undue interference from non-Ghanaians like myself.[10] In fact you could see an example of their hostility to true pan-African co-operation when the first *Black Star* liner arrived in Takoradi. One had naturally wanted Ghanaian sailors to be conspicuous, and I had made a point of telling the Israeli backers of the line to come to Ghana via Manchester, hoping they would be able to pick up some Ghanaian crew through my contacts. They couldn't get many, however, and had to make up the complement with Nigerians and others. Still, when the ship arrived, Addison was there on the quay urging the Ghanaians to protest against these foreign African seamen, and saying that they should be thrown out. I was there too, and this was more than I could take: I drew the people together from the ship and said: 'Most of you seamen know who I am: I was with you in Cardiff, Merseyside and other places. Take no notice of people who are trying to disturb the unity between Nigeria, Sierra Leone and Ghana. We envisage a *Black Star* line that will be manned by Africans regardless of a particular group.'

The atmosphere of intrigue surrounded many of the events in which Barden was involved. He wormed his way into the affairs of the Centre so much that at a certain point I was merely a glorified restaurateur. Once, for instance, Mbiyu Koinange arrived, but the first thing I heard of it was from the newspapers. He came with Odinga and for the first time I met this man and discussed affairs in Kenya with him. Well, as soon as Odinga began to show interest and say that 'we should borrow this Makonnen for a spell, since he is so knowledgeable about Kenya', I noticed Barden and Duplan saying something in Akan. Immediately Barden whisked Odinga off, and Duplan warned me that Barden would now proceed to try to turn Odinga against me, and also divide Odinga from Koinange. It would be the same old theme of 'Makonnen is somebody of dubious origin. Don't trust yourself with these foreign Africans.' Sure enough, Barden whisked Odinga off for a quick session with Osagyefo—I had my own man at the gate, so it was quite easy to tell who went in to see Kwame. But what was one to do when there were such wheels within wheels?

My own feelings about East Africa had developed out of a long acquaintance with Mbiyu (for a long time he, too, had shared one of these chalets with me.) Ghana had decided just before Kenya's independence to give large sums of money to help with the creation of a press.[11] It seemed a perfect opportunity for a fresh start in Africa. So I cabled directly to London and got the constitution of Reynolds Press—this famous co-operative enterprise. I was treating East Africa as a unity and trusting that Tanganyika, Zanzibar, Uganda and Kenya could all be brought in. If you wanted to give away £20,000 to create a press, then don't give it to a single country like Kenya; give it in a way that enforces co-operation with a model constitution, and you'll be doing something to reduce the balkanization of Africa. But it was a lost cause; even Ghana's own press, the Guinea Press, was not the faintest bit co-operative. It was just another of those corporations where the top fellows were handling vast sums of money.

I only realized the extent of some of this when later on I was called in and gazetted as head of the Guinea Press. This was partly to help get it out of the red, because it was felt that Makonnen with his various publishing ventures in London and Manchester knew all the ropes. I was also quite close to the various operations of the Guinea Press because one of the sons of the Orgle family, who had lived with me in Manchester, was the printer there. His father had been something of a pioneer with his *Vox Populi* in Ghana, and on the strength of the family name, I had helped the son with his tuition expenses in England. Well, when I took over, it was easy to see where some of the money was going. They had twenty delivery cars, for instance, and a fleet of lorries. I was all for reducing this to two buses and a few motor bicycles, and relying much more on the railways. But working out a budget was nearly impossible. I didn't know at the time I was meant to be in charge that a good deal of money from the press was being ferreted out to back some London publication in the future. You kept having the feeling in some sectors of Ghanaian life that the chaps were out to rob, to take even a farthing from an angel's bottom. And naturally enough after the coup, when the various leaders were up for trial, it was assumed that my hands were not clean either. 'What about the £60,000 that went out to London?' they asked me in court. 'You're one of these socialist boys— one of the Socialist Six in Ghana.¹² What's your part in this loss of money?' 'Look,' I said, 'whatever you're trying to prove, you won't be able to show that Makonnen was desperate to hold on to money. At least I feel I'm an angel when it comes to money.' I told them that if they wanted to check more accurately on how money was spent, they'd do better talking to a man like Ayeh-Kumi, one of Kwame's economic advisers who followed Arthur Lewis. Ayeh-Kumi loved money more than dear life, and he and his committee were very suspicious of me, and would say, 'Oh, you're not like George Padmore; you are too nosy.' I would reply, 'I am not in the revolution just to be seen. George may have wanted to let you fellows be, but my job is to see you fellows executed. That's all. Quite clear-cut.' So if they looked into it, they would find that when the huge contracts were being handed out for the construction of the Guinea Press building, it was Ayeh-Kumi who agreed to supply the steel and the bags of cement. Then there were the enormous sums that went to buy the capital machinery. So the fellows involved in this and other companies were in it for the looting. They had a simple conviction, that if there were going to be any capitalist millionaires around, then they might as well be Ghanaian ones. Some of them had acted in a helpful way with sums of money when the party was just being founded, and they saw to it that once the party was in power, they got their reward.

They weren't even good capitalists, as you could see when some of them were sent around to buy property for Ghana embassies abroad. No capitalist would have paid out what they did. In fact some of us thought that we should have delayed opening any embassy abroad until such time as African states came together in some way, and they could have common diplomatic premises abroad. But Ghana's dignity came first. So we paid out something like £100,000 in Israel for property that was only worth £60,000; in Washington we paid perhaps half a million for something worth £200,000; and in West Germany and Paris it was the same story. Then, of course, once other states began to open embassies in Ghana, it was felt necessary to reciprocate. However, in the early period these isolated Ghana embassies abroad did act in a kind of pan-African way, because a lot of Senegal or Ivory Coast students would flock there if there was any dispute to be settled.

In fact, on the money side of things, I had to be very careful. I was only given sh. 5/- per day to feed each of the men at the centre. So I had to cater with great care, perhaps driving out into the country once a week to buy so many tons of yams or plantains; and when there were less men at the Centre than there was money allocated, I would translate the remainder into new or better buildings. But it was also necessary to make sure that the men at the Centre had something to do. So there was therefore the series of lectures at the Centre that I have already mentioned. Then I got hold of two Benz buses, and every morning at eight-thirty or nine o'clock, they would be taken into the city of Accra. Some would go to the language groups being held in the George Padmore Library to improve their English. All of them were free to move where they wanted. If their inclination was towards trade union affairs they would go to John Tettegah; others would go to the party headquarters and see Welbeck; and the more literary fellows would make for the library. There was no directing them to do certain things, because I was anxious that we should not follow the way so many of our boys had been regimented in Moscow. By all means give the fellows certain guidelines, but remember that they are often representing whole countries that are far away. Content yourself therefore with exposing them to some of your own ideas. This was how I saw our general activity, but of course internationally we were thought to be drilling all these refugees daily and indoctrinating them to plot the overthrow of their own African governments.

I went further than this with a certain group of political refugees, some of the elements in the Union des Populations du Cameroun (UPC). There was a large group of them at the centre, and I felt that instead of feuding there, it might be profitable for this particular group to put some of our ideological discussions into practice.[13] Not far out of Accra, near MacCarthy's Hill, where the water is distributed to the city, I found a brigade camp with huts that could hold about two hundred people. It was in a well-watered valley, and I thought that I should be able to teach a bit of animal husbandry and poultry-keeping in the style of the Israeli kibbutz. I approached Ntumazah, one of the exiled leaders after Félix Moumié's death, and he and others agreed that something constructive could be done. Their womenfolk, too, were of the right calibre; they were tough, and a number of them had been to China and other places. So when I had extracted the promise of some machines from the German Democratic Republic, I saw it would be possible to go in for some co-operative dressmaking. They could also have tilled the soil, and thus saved us some of the expense of looking after them at the Centre. It was particularly necessary to get the women and children some employment, because from time to time, it was found essential to get the men refugees out of the country. If, for instance, there was to be an OAU conference in Ghana, and President Ahidjo of Cameroun was requiring the refugees from his country to be extradited from the host country, you would go to people like Ntumazah and say: 'Look, go and take some fresh air in Sekou Touré's country or Cairo, and when this thing has blown over, you can come back again.' Then, when the foreign reporters came round to Makonnen and asked him where these UPC refugees and freedom fighters were, he would say: 'Refugees? What refugees?'

NOTES TO CHAPTER 13

1 For an early account of Americo-Liberian attitudes to Africans in Liberia, see R. L. Buell, *A Century of Survival, 1847–1947* (Philadelphia, 1947), pp. 7–19.

2 Some of the declarations of the All African People's Conference are usefully brought together in V. B. Thompson, *Africa and Unity*, pp. 350–8; see also C. Legum, *Pan-Africanism*, pp. 42–4, and W. S. Thompson, *Ghana's Foreign Policy*, pp. 58–67.

3 Cairo's contribution in harbouring African refugees, and disseminating anti-colonial propaganda is assessed in V. B. Thompson, op. cit., pp. 72–4.

4 The Moslem Association Party's links with Busia's National Liberation Movement are described in Austin, *Politics in Ghana* (London, 1964), pp. 231–2 and 378.

5 A typical reaction is Nathan Shamuyarira in *Crisis in Rhodesia* (Nairobi, 1967), p. 52: 'The example of this small country on the West Coast fired the imagination of Africans everywhere on the continent. It was partly that their leaders sounded a trumpet call to the rest of Africa which was still under colonialism. But it was more that the Ghanaians were just like the rest of us, but free.'

6 Avriel's diplomatic achievement in newly independent Ghana is further documented in W. S. Thompson, op. cit., pp. 48–51.

7 The most valuable account of the various Angolan nationalist groupings at this time is John Marcum, *The Angolan Revolution* (Cambridge, Massachussets, 1969); for Ghana's treatment of Roberto, see W. S. Thompson, pp. 223–5.

8 An account of Padmore's last years in Ghana still needs to be undertaken; Hooker's biography of him is at this point very sketchy.

9 It is suggested in W. S. Thompson that certain of the South African refugee groups were able to run circles round Barden, op. cit., pp. 222–3.

10 See, for instance, Padmore's difficulty as an outsider in Ghana; Hooker, *Black Revolutionary*, pp. 132–3. See also below, pp. 255, 259.

11 Odinga mentions his discussions with Nkrumah about setting up an independent African press in Kenya, *Not yet Uhuru* (London, 1967), p. 166.

12 For the 'Socialist Six', see below, p. 245.

13 Some of the factionalism amongst the Camerounian refugees is mentioned in W. S. Thompson, op. cit., p. 186.

CHAPTER 14

OBSTACLES TO AFRICAN UNITY:
THE TOGO EXPERIENCE

THIS Togoland question was one of the problems to arise after independence and spotlighted a number of points that would be of central concern to the issue of African unity. The main thing was that the Ewe people were divided between Togoland and Ghana. The Ewe-speaking people of the old British Togoland had been joined up with Ghana in 1956 under a United Nations plebiscite, and people naturally wondered in what direction the Ewe speakers in French Togo would move once they had also achieved independence. There were some good reasons for believing that things would work out amicably.

First of all under the colonial era, there had been no very rigid interpretation of the border between the British and French.[1] The very African policeman who was guarding the French side of the frontier might be the cousin of the policeman on the British. Also the border was easy to cross, either directly, or by going round the north by Upper Volta or taking a boat across the salient down at the sea. So there was this family relationship, and a feeling that you shouldn't cause people to suffer by some artificial solution. In fact, I was involved in this Togo business much earlier when I was in Geneva during the thirties representing the Anti-Slavery Society. People were making representations about the degree of slavery in Ethiopia, and I had been trying to put the record straight by showing that some of the French policy in Togoland was as iniquitous as anything happening in Ethiopia. I said then: 'I am a Togolese. I am from Togoland, and some of my family live in the Gold Coast and some in French Togoland. My cocoa farm is on the

British side but my house is on the French. But the French are no better than slave-masters; when they tax you, they insist that you pay in kind, i.e., in cocoa. So you have to bring your taxes illicitly over the border in the form of cocoa. It's a terrible system.' But despite this French interference relations remained good between the Ewe sections.

Scholars have stressed how discontented even the former British Togoland was at being added on to Ghana. I think it's probably more accurate to say that relations were surprisingly good considering how recently British Togoland was recruited to Ghana. It would be useful to remember that the Opposition and the separatist Ashanti element were doing all in their power to stir up discontent in Eweland. Realizing the potential dangers was what made Kwame try to change the traditional attitude towards both the Togoland and the northern people. The Northerners in particular had been regarded as backward types only fit for domestic service and other menial jobs. So Kwame put a large number of these Ghana Educational Trust schools in the Northern Region, and also introduced roads, re-afforestation and other services.

Discontent also amongst the Ewe was lessened because a number of leading Ghanaians at this time were of Ewe origin. For instance, Gbedemah, the Minister of Finance, had Ewe antecedents, so had Van Laer, and this fellow Chapman too, who had first been a history master at the Achimota College and went on to gain a great deal of respect in the United Nations Organization. Some of the oldest and best known Ghanaian families had Ewe ancestry. They were talented and articulate. You had a man like Dr. Armattoe, who claimed distinction as an atomic physicist, and who I had invited over to the Manchester Congress of 1945.[2] Even the editor of the *Evening News*, Eric Heyman, was an Ewe and so was the brilliant ear, nose, and throat surgeon, Dr. Seth Kojo. He, too, I had known in the Manchester days, and he had reviewed a number of books for *Pan-Africa*. He was very good on art subjects or when dealing with any of this indirect-rule-cum-anthropology stuff that Margery Perham and others turned out. The point is, with such luminaries, you could attack easily and put down the Togolese who made a noise about the status of Ewes in Ghana: 'What are you fellows over in Togo barking about? Do you enjoy the same privileges as those of us in the British sector? Where did some of you have to come to get your early schooling? You had to come to the Gold Coast, because the French didn't offer you any. So what is all this nonsense?'

You would find little pockets or outcrops of Ewe people all over Ghana. They were very hard workers indeed, and they turn up in the remotest places, working on cocoa farms and sharecropping. Many of them were involved naturally in contrabanding cocoa over the French side, because the cocoa price was always higher there after the war, but if they had wanted to they could have made things much rougher for Ghana than they did. They had a strong humanist strain in them.

This was the situation when Togo independence was approaching. A number of the Togolese leaders like Grunitsky and Meatchi were campaigning that Togo, when it left its mandate status, should be attached to France.³ They were the old guard 'yes' men of the French in Indo-China (Meatchi was a soldier), and at the voting time they looked like French props trying to coerce their people into voting 'yes' to stay with the mother country. At the same time there were other more militant Togolese, some of whom had actually deserted and fought with the Vietcong in the Far East, and there was another militant movement called Juvento which could not make its mind up to unite with Ghana or to keep all the Ewe out of Ghana. So if you went up to the Northern Region, you would meet some of the members of this movement shouting for unity with Togo while others were for joining the CPP.

The other very important element in Togo as in Ghana were the women traders. They know all the ins and outs of how French perfume and silks could make their way into Ghana, and their loyalty was to Sylvanus Olympio, because he had been a merchant all his life. This was the trouble with Olympio's politics from our point of view; that he was never able to get away from the mentality of a trader or hustler. Always chasing after a few shillings. He had imbibed this from his years as a faithful servant of the United Africa Company, and may well have made a lot of his money by managing some of their stores in Ghana and Togoland. Once these companies had marked you out as a good boy, it was not unusual for them to send you to England or France to familiarize you with the selection of popular brands, or make decisions on what symbols would most appeal to the masses. So Olympio was obviously considered a versatile businessman, and he came across to England either through the company's help or through one of his successful relatives. At any rate I ran across him in London where he was doing some work at the London School of Economics.

He became the leader of Togo, and successfully managed to have Togo go its own way, and throw itself in with the French again. Ghana may have given some money to some factions in Togoland for their campaign against voting 'yes', but I can't be sure. Gbedemah would be able to tell. In spite of the decision, Togo somewhat suffered at the hands of the French. They refused the country money for the development of roads and services, and the contrast between French capital flowing into Ivory Coast and the lack of it in Togo was very marked. Again, one would have thought this would have helped Olympio to turn to Kwame and wipe out the old colonial boundaries between the two countries.

I think in expecting this to happen all of us greatly underestimated the human factor. We simply looked at the traditional links amongst the peoples at the borders, and felt there would be no problem. During the colonial period it was typical of Padmore as of everybody else to pin everything on the white man and assume that once the whites had disappeared, then Africans could return to being Africans. After all, they had been exploited by the same slave trade, and some of the most infamous slave-trade routes had come through this area from Nigeria across the top of Ghana to Salaga. The same, too, with these African colonial armies. Whether it was Hausa soldiers or Bambara, it was felt that they were just agents of the white man and did not really believe that they were soldiers of the French or British interests. And yet with independence, these soldiers became a new tribe. The corporals and officers were obsessed with these little magic sticks in their hands, and this magic called a rifle. And it turned out that they really believed in all this stuff about their code of values which were quite different to those of archaic tribal communities from which they had been recruited. In a word, we were bad psychologists. It was really ridiculous of us to expect that because the French, Germans and British had taught the Africans to feel distinct, these things would come to an end automatically.

We shall probably have to re-examine the French education system to see how this came about—this alienation of a people from their own selves.[4] It had happened in other pockets of the French Empire where the indigenous people had had a culture, written language and philosophy going back several thousand years. Even today in parts of Indo-China there are people who hold on doggedly to French Catholicism and all the values of the French culture. And it was proportionately easier in Africa, where the people were made to feel that they had no history to speak of, and no cultural contribution, to make them feel that it was necessary to embrace French culture and thought in order to be taken as real men. And after independence, the French did not have to exert themselves to keep Togo and Ghana from getting together. The work had been done already. The élite had become more French than the Frenchmen themselves, and the French were even able to reduce aid to the Togolese without any danger of driving them into unity with Ghana.

But this cultural adaptation also kept Togo divided within itself. Take a man like Olympio. He was one of the people whose ancestors had come back from Brazil after slavery—like those we mentioned in Lagos.[5] So you would get hostility towards them for being so French and being outsiders. If for instance you stirred up an ordinary Ewe man he would break out with: 'This Olympio is some slave pickin, and most of these mulattos are slave people. What are all these funny names? Grunitsky—his father is a Pole. They are not African people, they are all slaves.' This could reach frightening dimensions, and yet there was a little truth in it; the French élite did marry amongst itself. For instance, Olympio was related to Grunitsky though his wife, while other leaders like Meatchi and Kpodar would be looked at as real black men—better Africans—despite all their French culture. It was a morass.

When looking at the difficulty of bringing the two countries together, all this has to be taken into consideration. And then the personal factors have to be added. Olympio's passion was to make money, and being a merchant adventurer, he could see that he might well be submerged if he joined with Ghana. So he would organize his little state like Monaco in the eighteenth century tradition of nationalism, and then he and his family could continue to be the big men and make all the money they wanted.

So we simplified the question of colonial boundaries out of all proportion. For a time it just did not occur to us that the balkanization of Africa could persist in the face of our pan-Africanism. And this led to a tendency to admit to Ghana political refugees who were out of power in their newly independent states. Kwame was therefore not necessarily power-drunk or wanting to be the King of Africa when he admitted all these various elements. His concept of unity was closely allied with the need to start from scratch. In fact this desire for a fresh start meant that he actually helped to destroy certain pre-existing colonial forms of African unity, such as those for scientific research and pestology amongst the French and British West African countries. It was something of a mechanistic concept he applied, destroying the evidences of colonialism in order to re-create. And always militating against your plans for wider sympathies was the legacy of the state handed on by colonialism. This was much harder to destroy. When it came to finding jobs for your own people, you found out about boundaries, and the idea of an alien became as important as considerations of African brotherhood. The employment situation almost made necessary the artificial concept of the stranger, the alien, the boundary.

At any rate the result of Kwame's philosophy—if we can call it philosophy—was that Olympio's opponents began to arrive in Ghana, just as a number of our opposition members began to make for Lomé. It brought us people like Meatchi and Grunitsky. And I think the tragedy of our policy was that we took too much for granted when someone applied for a visa to enter Ghana. If he happened to have been a trade unionist, we dignified him as a Marxist; if he was an ordinary nationalist who had failed to get into office, we called him an anti-colonialist. It was a terrible thesis, and provided cover to a number of people who were barefaced opportunists. And even if they were not in any sense ideological comrades when they arrived, there was always the optimism that we would be able to form cadres out of this material—men formed in our own image. They attended our Ideological College, and we believed they might return to their countries some day and put into practice what they

231

had learnt. Ghana always felt that it must try to train like-minded Africans, particularly for those territories it had common borders.

It was considered in government circles that I had good credentials for liaising with the Togolese who came to our country. First of all, I had known Olympio's nephew, Sylvanus Amegashie, for a long time. He had come to Manchester in the old days along with one of his Ghanaian friends, John Wilson. And when I arrived in Accra in 1957, I stayed with the Wilson household for almost two years. I had a room to myself and was well looked after. So I saw a great deal of Wilson and Amegashie. In fact we were inseparable. The Amegashie branch of the Olympio family had been living in Ghana for a long time, and even one of Olympio's sons was working for an oil company there. Then when these exiles came, I saw a lot of Dr. Simon Kpodar, one of the medical men who had differed with Olympio, and also I knew Meatchi well, and Grunitsky. Well, I didn't take these fellows too seriously, because they were obviously deceptive. I mean, they were Frenchmen first, then Togolese, then Ewes. However, as I was the sort of dean of pan-Africanism, it was my job to do the best I could with this material.

I discussed with them some of the critical questions of Togo-Ghana relations; how Ghana could help set up a factory to process the phosphate in their country, which would aid the agriculture of both of us. We talked of the need to create a co-operative shop on our frontiers, so that all the items which were then being smuggled across to each other's country could be sold in the open. At that time many fishermen, and Togolese across the border, were getting rich by smuggling liquor backwards and forwards in their fishing boats. This was all thoroughly gone over. Of course I don't know how much opportunism there was in their attitude; they might have felt that the way to get to Osagyefo was through me, and so they might side with my ideas without believing them at all.

We also discussed the wider strategies in the area. It seemed that the Americans were pouring arms into Dahomey. Our contacts with the Sawaba Party exiles from Niger who used to come to us through Dahomey confirmed extensive unloading of arms from American planes. Then there were also definite moves afoot for some sort of unity amongst the Benin States—Nigeria, Dahomey, and Togo. And to the western side of Ghana, it was obvious that Olympio was trying to develop closer ties with Houphouët-Boigny and Sekou Touré. It looked pretty much as if it was an attempt to contain Ghana.

Because I had these close links with the various Togolese elements, I was at one point mooted for the post of ambassador to Togo. It was made when I was visiting Guinea once, but I didn't set much store by it.[6] The suggestion came from Ayeh-Kumi, this multi-millionaire, and was probably only designed to get me out of the way. I did think then that I was well informed as to what was going on in Togo-Ghana relations, but I later learnt from my old associate Duplan (who was eventually appointed ambassador to Togo) the extent of the intrigue that Barden was involved in. I was in the dark about much of this during the period of Olympio's rule. However, shortly before his assassination in January 1963, a few glimmers appeared. As I say, Amegashie and I were on good terms, and he used to joke with me, from his French background, about 'this peasant boy', Nkrumah. One day, however, he came to me and said in all seriousness: 'I hear you and your fellows are trying to destroy my uncle, Olympio.' I said, 'Don't be a fool.' Now, after Amegashie left me that Saturday afternoon, I was going to make for Tema, when Kwame called me. He wanted me to do something for him. As the Amegashie conversation was fresh in my mind, I said to Kwame: 'If our relations with Togo are bad, and you want to make informal contact with Olympio, why don't you make use of his nephew. He lives here in town, and quite frequently goes to visit his uncle.' Kwame asked who the nephew was, and I said, 'Oh, don't you know him? He's the principal of your school of business administration down at Achimota.' Now all this was said in complete innocence; I had merely been thinking that such informal contact would be valuable since there were no diplomatic channels.

No sooner had I left than Kwame pressed his button and called in Michael Dei-Anang, the head of the African Affairs Secretariat, and asked him: 'Who is this Amegashie that this foolish Makonnen has just told me about? Go and bring him!' Now, I don't know what he said to Amegashie, but two days later the whole of Accra was in an uproar against me. Amegashie had told people that he had nearly been detained and that I had been in some way responsible. So again I was projected as a dangerous man.[7] Fantastic nonsense. Still, it was believed, and just three weeks later Olympio was assassinated. I was in a terrible position, and Amegashie switched immediately from being my friend to being out for my blood. As his best friend was Harlley, the police chief, he was able to ruin my reputation even more when there was the coup against Nkrumah. It didn't make any difference that I had married one of Harlley's nieces; the whole little clan of them was convinced that I was in some way responsible for the Amegashie and Olympio affairs.

But what this illustrates most is the atmosphere of intrigue that was central to the politics of Ghana. There was the feeling that you had to keep the pot boiling. You have to keep pushing the pieces around, or putting the cat among the pigeons and getting some feathers, even though you say at the same time: 'That's a terrible cat going around eating other people's chickens.' Don't forget, too, that this time was the era of the CIA, and people in Ghana and elsewhere in Africa were jittery. All of this set up ideal conditions for a man like Barden to ascend the ladder. He and the other factions were always responsible for leakages of vital information, because they had their men placed here and there as stenographers or copy typists. In addition there were several kinds of intelligence men, each group keeping a careful watch on who was seeing Osagyefo and in whose company. It meant that very frequently Kwame would not circulate Cabinet minutes or confidential papers, but would decide things in the presence of one man like the Attorney-General, Bing, and then act upon it.

There was therefore a Machiavellian feel to government. Literally. *The Prince* would be there on Kwame's office table, and he was versed in it like the Bible. It meant that he played one group off against another. If he was sending a commission to the Foreign Ministers' Conference in Addis, or to Senegal where an agenda was being prepared, I would be sent to keep some of the dangerous men from the Nigerian delegation in check; it was thought with my purist theoretical background I could do this, but at the same time, the other boys in our delegation would be reporting to Kwame that 'Makonnen was distorting the whole thing when he reported back to you'. So I would be sent along if only to deal with any upstarts who might begin to pull their knowledge of ideology or philosophy, and try to put the Ghana delegation at a disadvantage.

Kwame's tactics were very clear at the time when the Egyptians were becoming more important to Ghana through the Casablanca connection. On one day Kojo Botsio, Ako Ajei and I were sent on a delegation to Israel; the day after we left, Kwame sent a delegation to Egypt. And we didn't hear that this was going to happen until we were in Israel. So it was very awkward being in Israel and the news coming in of the Ghanaians reaching certain agreements with the Egyptian government. But Kwame had also organized it so that these two delegations should arrive back in Ghana within the same hour, and then go along to report their findings to Kwame together. So we had to sit and hear Krobo Edusei of the Egyptian delegation telling Kwame about Egypt, and loud-mouthing about how Israel was just a wilderness of stone. Then it would be our turn, and Kojo Botsio would say what a profitable time we had spent, and how hard-working the Jews were. It was a burlesque, and doubtless Kwame was laughing to himself.

It was certainly no good for continuous development. I mean, one week our trade with Egypt would be nil, and in less than six months, it would have sky-rocketed.[8] Overnight the Egyptian presence became formidable; Koranic schools got backing and students were sent off to Cairo. As I have said before it seemed treasonable. We had seen what role the Muslims had been playing with Busia in his National Liberation Movement. We had broken the back of that resistance, but here you were giving the thing a chance to revive again. It meant also that if you tried to keep to your old belief that the alliance with Israel was a valuable one, then people would report you. This began to happen even in these meetings we used to hold once a week in the National Association of Socialist Students Organizations (NASSO).[9]

I had found lovely premises for this movement, just opposite where Kwame used to live in the early days of the Party. I had rented it for £1,200 and we were able to lease out parts of it for £2,000. These meetings were intended to be open forums, where as equals you could take up any problems, and treat them without axe-grinding, but they began to have 'yes' men attending them, who as soon as they heard you ran back to Kwame with the latest. It became difficult therefore to discuss this sudden switch openly. And this was partly because the tactical change had brought the Lebanese business section into favour once more; it was the beginning of the era of the 10 per cent contracts awarded to Lebanese through the good offices of the Party, with the contractors agreeing to pay so much to the Party in return.

All our commitments to Israel were put in a quandary; and yet when you destroyed some of these links of reconstruction with Israel, what were you going to put in their place? Nasser was not in a position to give you any immediate help. In fact he was seeking aid himself from Russia for his dam, his sugar plantations and the reorganization of land tenure. Egypt was a beggar, and Cairo was full of beggars, but if you went to Israel you could not help making the comparison. Apart from full employment, the organization of kibbutz life was, I thought, nearer to certain socialist ideals than much you could find in Egypt. Also our Jewish advisers had been invaluable. On many occasions they had given Ghana advice which had allowed us to get certain advantages over other African countries. They were old hands at the money game, and were able to advise on questions like the creation of a central bank, or how to stimulate an investment climate, or work out an investment guide for Ghana. But suddenly to turn and put your faith in this Buddha, this cunning Nasser! You could not explain it without accepting that Kwame was a ballet dancer, and loved this sort of intrigue.

To us from the outside, from the relatively open societies of the West, it was impossible to cope unless we admitted that we were working in a different medium. The open society has no secrets; it may profess to have, but they come out. This is what I had come from. My concept of the socialist world was an open world, where you fight openly for the right of a free press, and the right of collective bargaining. You legalize the Communist Party so that there are no conspiratorial groups in the body-politic. You set out and fight for your programmes. Ghana was at times more of a closed than an open society, and there was often no correspondence between the statements of the Party and its actions.

NOTES TO CHAPTER 14

1 For Togo background, see Dennis Austin, 'The Uncertain Frontier: Ghana-Togo', in *Journal of Modern African Studies*, 1, 2 (June 1963).

2 See Padmore, *Pan-Africanism or Communism?* p. 163; Legum, *Pan-Africanism*, p. 31.

3 For further detail on the Togo parties at this period, see Coleman, *Togoland* (1956).

4 A recent revisionist account of French assimilation policies is Remi Clignet, 'Inadequacies of the Notion of Assimilation in African Education', *Journal of Modern African Studies*, 8, 3 (1970), pp. 425–44.

5 A useful summary of the return of these Afro-Brazilians to West Africa is R. D. Ralston, 'The Return of Brazilian Freedmen to West Africa in the 18th and 19th Centuries', in *Canadian Journal of African Studies*, 3, 3 (1970), pp. 577–92.

6 Eventually it was not Makonnen but his old Pan-African colleague Duplan from the Manchester days who became Togo's first ambassador; see W. S. Thompson, p. 367.

7 There is interesting material on this incident in Thompson, op. cit., p. 237, n. 146.

8 See Thompson, op. cit., p. 155 for the significance of this economic switch.

9 NASSO had actually been founded amongst Ghanaians in London in the later 1940s; see Legum, 'Socialism in Ghana: A Political Interpretation', in W. H. Friedland and C. G. Rosberg, *African Socialism* (Stanford, 1964), p. 136.

CHAPTER 15

NKRUMAH'S GHANA

'YOU can't build socialism without socialists.' If we are to analyse the nature of the Ghanaian economy during Nkrumah's rule, it is essential to realize that we are dealing with a people steeped in the experience of exchange relationships. The West African has been involved with trade for centuries. Long before the era of the slave trade, people had been crossing the desert from North Africa, and the Carthaginians in the very early period seem to have sailed round to parts of the West African coast. Media of exchange such as the cowrie shell were developed, and there was a thriving commerce in articles of value like hard wood, ivory, gold and skins. This vigorous history of exchange relationships quite largely helps to explain the genesis of the slave trade. And even with such a barbarous affair as the slave trade, it is still necessary to analyse the reciprocal relationships between Africa and Europe that encouraged it; it's no use looking at it as a period when Europeans discovered and exploited 'raw man'.

However, as a result of the slave trade, certain new patterns of trade emerged, and were carried out by groups of West Africans who had by now adapted themselves to the concept of large-scale trading operations. This was particularly true of some of the great mulatto traders who became a significant factor after the slave trade, and of some of the Ibo and Yoruba families who had been in contact with Sierra Leone for a long time. Everything favoured the African trader for some time after the abolition of the slave trade, but especially the fact that the West African coast was still regarded as the white man's grave. European companies therefore had to establish a group of black custodians of their enterprises. Sometimes these were the hybrid elements, the Creoles of Lagos and Freetown, and sometimes they were families who had come under early missionary tutelage in Cape Coast, Sierra Leone and the Yoruba country, and who found that trade and religion went hand in hand. But whether it was the German, Dutch, English or French forts or trading posts, you would find some large-scale African traders dealing with them.

Quinine changed all that, once the whites had got used to the fact that they could survive in the tropics. Not only the whites, but even more critical at the time of the First World War was the influx of the Syrians and Lebanese who captured a great deal of the high-level trade.[1] The Africans were not suddenly neglected, because you can see several instances of governors and district commissioners actively encouraging Africans to adopt better cocoa practices or try using a better palm kernel. Governor Guggisberg of the Gold Coast is an obvious case in point.[2] But for all this, the terms of trade were gradually swinging in favour of these aliens from the Levant. These newcomers had the edge on the Africans in a number of ways. Whether they worked in their own firms or for some of the big British companies, they were more self-contained than the African traders. Many European companies had begun to regard the African as a liability; often he seemed to have such extended family obligations that frequently the demands of kin were stronger than the strict law of commercial profit. So people turned to these Lebanese with relief.

The other thing was that the African who might stand out as a mighty trader was often unable to continue this beyond the first generation.[3] You had people like Pa Biney, a famous African of means, but they didn't hand on their businesses intact to their sons. And probably this was due to the operation of the matriarchal system. As a rich man, my obligations were not to my own son but to my sister's sons; so a lot of time was spent wondering which outcrop from one's sister would prove the best bet for the family money to go to, while one's own children were somewhat neglected. It didn't make for much continuity in business. By contrast the Syrians and the Lebanese were able to expand their capitalist development within individual families.

Equally, though you had had the operation of *osusu* in many parts of West Africa, generally speaking African business of that time was not availing itself of the principles that had allowed European companies to flourish. Compared to their European counterparts African enterprise was under-capitalized, and had no equivalents of the great Company Acts which allowed the English to establish joint stock companies with share capital. So it's no wonder that the Africans were outplayed. Often they were their own executioners, for when the Syrians came they had to employ African clerks to teach them the writing of business letters, and facilitate their introduction to the country. Other Syrians were able to ingratiate themselves by marrying West African women.

You can see the weakness, or primitiveness, of African capitalism in the famous system of the mammy traders. These market women each formed their special relationships with the import-export firms. They would know Fitzgerald of the United Africa Company, or other contacts in Leventis and elsewhere. The whole point of their endeavours was to gain a special concession from their man, so that they would get a virtual monopoly on a special line of cloth or whatever the product. But right at the heart of this mammy system was to be found the practice of the 'dash', or bribe. The mammy trader would have her African contacts working in, say, the United Africa Company, and when a special consignment arrived from England, this trusted African clerk would send a message to her up at Kumasi. She would come down right away and begin negotiating with Fitzgerald for a good price. She sometimes had an advantage in the negotiation in that the African would have told her beforehand: 'Beat him down; don't let him charge you such and such a price; I have seen the real price in the invoice books, so fight hard'. And if the mammy got a good price, then the trusted clerk would receive his dash.

And once she got her monopoly at the wholesale level, she would pass on her goods in smaller and smaller numbers right down to the little girls who would be selling just a fraction of some commodity wrapped up in a little piece of paper. And at every stage the chain of middlemen would be taking their profit; a vicious system with so many people taking their profit before it finally reached the consumer. It may have been primitive capitalism, but everybody was involved in it. At night in any of the towns there were thousands of little torch lights in these

240

tiny stores, with people selling things like sardines in penny numbers.

This is the system that Kwame was up against, or anybody else who wanted to preach socialism. The profit motive was rampant in Ghana, but when some of Kwame's boys began to apply a class analysis to Ghana, they missed the point. It was easy enough to identify the great import-export houses as forms of capitalist exploitation, but if you turned people's attention to the mammy system, many of my colleagues—even Kwame— would say: 'But that's family development', or 'That's African socialism. Where are the exploiters?' Regardless of what might be happening within the mammy system, it could be explained away with the false concept of African socialism.[4] In reality, the exploitation of the African by the African was staring you in the face. These mammies would use their ten or fifteen children, who had a role exactly like the little match-girls of Victorian England. Each child would have her tray of one hundred or two hundred little commodity pieces, and would tour a locality all day, taking the commodity to the doorstep of the consumer. These little girls were a substitute for having expensive shops and show cases, and people would applaud the mammies for bringing them up in a good tradition, instead of allowing the devil to get hold of them. Exactly the reverse was the case, for the mammies would give firm instructions not to return with the goods unsold, and this meant that men would frequently invite the girls in from the doorsteps and take advantage of them. There was a very close connection between the mammy system and child prostitution.

The crucial thing was the kinship relationship between the father and mother and their ten or so children. You see, the father's commitments were not to his own children but his sister's. Hence he was rather free from paternal obligation to his immediate family, and more ready therefore to exploit his children's labour for his own end. This is where exploitation was to be found in Ghana, right at the heart of the family, but of course it could be covered up and made to appear as a facet of African socialism. You only have to stay a night in an ordinary Ghanaian town house to see further elements of this basic family exploitation. Who is it that wakes up from her little mat outside the family house and begins work on making the *kenke* and pounding the pepper? Some poor relation from the countryside. Some serf. Who carries your children around on her shoulders as soon as they are strong enough to bear them? The same people. And you explain it away as a more humane system that the child should be close to a human back, rather than being put in a pram and left out in the snow like those vicious Europeans.

In reality the better-off Ghanaians have houses that are full of pawns from the village community, who may have been sent in to improve themselves originally. So instead of one's wife being saddled with the normal obligation that any woman in the West would have, she has been eased of this daily drudgery and can turn her attention elsewhere simply because she has some serfs from the rural areas. One of the things she can do then is have her husband give her £100 of credit at one of the big stores, and after bulk buying she can get the other idle hands of the household to work. She sits at home like a banker, while each of the children go their way with their little parcels of sardine or aerated bread. Although a European shopkeeper may do £10 of trade in a day and the mammy only £2, you can be certain that the mammy's has a greater margin of profit than the other. So right across the country you have a network of primitive and often vicious capitalism. There are great rewards to be had, and you fall victim to the belief that the system can be called African socialism. 'After all', you say, 'who would have taken care of these children if I hadn't? We have no poor-houses, no alms-houses in Ghana, because we look after all our people, unlike the Europeans.' So all this is just an attempt to justify the rape and exploitation that is taking place under the guise of the family.

It takes a different form up in the cocoa-producing regions of Ashanti. There you have your cocoa farm and you use migrant labour from Volta or Niger. You take the migrants along to the labour office and there's a great facade about signing a contract to give him clothes and so much money. In reality, he becomes a sharecropper on your farm with his own few crops for subsistence, and he harvests and dries the cocoa. But he has few rights as I found out when Kojo Botsio and I went to Kumasi to see how these various contracts were enforced. We discovered that Appiah Danquah, the Ghana farmers' leader, was using his trade union to protect the interests of the farmers, when it should really have been engaged in seeing these sharecroppers got a fair deal. These elements had no protection and existed on the bounty of the Ghana farmers; so you had almost a feudalist system like in fourteenth century England, where the serfs would thank milord of the manor for not turning all his land from grain into sheep-ranching.[5] And Danquah was able to capitalize on these iniquities in his speeches to the Ghana farmers: 'I am your defender. If it were not for me, then some of the hard-line trade union boys from Accra might be able to expose that you are not paying these fellows who are working on your farms. So when I ask your permission for the government to take another sh. 5/- off the cocoa price, help me, because I am saving you from people who might want to interfere with your cheap labour supply.'

There were very few sectors of the economy where a proletariat in the European sense was to be found. There was certainly a small proletarian element in the Ashanti gold mines, many of them migrants from Nigeria, and the lines of demarcation between classes were also more pronounced down at the docks and railways. With the docks, you had the powerful influence of the white seamen. They were often the most enlightened section of the proletariat in Europe, and they had been influential in organizing the Ghanaian dockworkers. Thus there were pockets of fully proletarianized workers, but in the absence of any great industrial development in Ghana, we have to look elsewhere for large-scale exploitation.

Naturally, if you tried to point out that the truly exploited element was right under Ghanaian noses, you did not get very far. In fact the thing was so deep-seated that it was vulgar to inquire about it at all. You would be told: 'You're a bad man, coming here to pry into our family affairs. How can you be so inhuman as to attack those various relations who nursed me and brought me up to be the beautiful woman I am?' But it really needed people to sit down and seriously analyse the primitive form of exploitation within the domestic circle. And once you had analysed it, and decided that perhaps the main concern of trade unions should be the relationships between masters and servants, what could you do about it? Kwame knew that so many of these mammies had been his strongest supporters; he knew that so many aspects of the state were infected with the 'dash'.[6] You had all the appearances of a modern state with its policemen and division of labour, and yet it has this tolerance of profiteering as its centre. People carry around their driving licences with pound notes folded inside in case the police should stop them; and the passengers on the buses never seem to object when the driver passes on to each of them part of the dash he has to give the policeman. I have never heard yet of a group of passengers beating up the police for extorting money. Instead there is philosophical laughter. At the time, members of the Opposition in Ghana used to attack the government for not having a more severe attitude to these things, and I notice that when Busia came to power himself, he found himself confronted with the same obstacle. In fact in 1970, he went as far as to say that Ghana has not developed morality enough to regard the dash as a dangerous thing, and the Ghanaians must cleanse themselves first before they sit in judgement over others.

During Kwame's time, if one approached him with the need to deal savagely with the problem, he would say: 'Over to you. But we don't have jails enough in Ghana. Everybody's guilty.' The trouble was really that people went in for a lot of socialist sloganeering, but directed it to the wrong sections of society. Usually it was just straight anti-imperialism. 'Here I have come from Europe. I am a socialist. I have been hunted down as a communist agent; I have this legacy. I have acquired the right to speak of imperialism and its evils.' Well, you didn't become a socialist, just because the white colonial boys called you one. Others regarded socialist talk as a necessary adornment to their rhetoric. 'The struggling masses' become strictly a cliché, and ministers and powerful party men used to laugh and say, 'Poor us, the struggling masses', with their Benzes parked outside the door. How can you build socialism without socialists? Socialism is a highly skilled mechanism where needs have to be appraised carefully and commodities planned to create abundance. Socialism should have been employed to analyse the underproduction and inefficiency of the average Ghanaian farmer. As it was, the farmers simply planted these cocoa beans here and there, and magically they grew into trees. But there was no careful pruning and layout of cocoa farms such as you can see in Brazil, or like the tea and coffee estates in Kenya. With the exception of the cocoa experimental station, most Ghanaian farms didn't deserve the name; there were just patches here and there, not integrated with any other crops. Admittedly it looked as if cocoa was intended to follow a more planned development after independence, for you had the establishment of the Cocoa Loan Fund, and the Cocoa Purchasing Company. But in practice people managed to use both bodies to further capitalist profiteering. Men would get loans for cocoa farms that didn't even exist, and when it came to purchasing (where you would think the idea was to cut out the alien middlemen), the corruption was even greater. Once the government had begun buying cocoa directly from the farmers, great losses were incurred with truckloads of cocoa disappearing all the time.

The ideology of the independence days had been socialist in word. Everyone knew that Russia was anathema to the colonial powers; it was therefore natural to adopt a socialist stance in the mobilization of the Convention People's Party. The veranda boys paid lip-service to socialism without any intention ever to put it into practice. There was no law against that. But it had the effect of making Ghana suspect in the eyes of the West, and to the Syrians and other businessmen on the spot. People hesitated to commit money to Ghana or start new enterprises when there was all this atmosphere of slogan-mongering about socialism. They needn't have worried, because most of the boys shouting about socialism were more steeped in capitalism than the West where capitalism had undergone some reform at least.

There were only a handful of socialists in Ghana—the socialist boys, or the Socialist Six, as people used to call us.[7] Kweku Akwei, the secretary for ideology of the CPP; Eric Heymann, editor of the *Evening News;* Cecil Forde and T. D. Baffoe of the *Ghanaian Times;* Amoaka-Atta and myself. The word got around that we were the hard core, the boys who hadn't any of these big houses (although Amoaka-Atta subsequently got himself a tremendous castle). But how many of the others were socialists? Gbedemah was no socialist, and never pretended to be. Kojo Botsio and Krobo Edusei never pretended to be either. The pattern had been set even before independence; the veranda boys who had themselves scoured the country carrying the gospel of independence into the furthest corners clearly saw that they could not continue being storm-troopers now that

245

independence was won: 'What am I going to do now? I can't just be a propagandist for ever; I want to eat; I want to chop. All the other veranda boys are settling down and buying homes; so what about me?' Nor was it so easy for them to honour their election pledges. The Party had promised that it would deal with the alien businessmen and give the mammies an opportunity to live a natural life in their own country. But when the time came to do something about it, the Party was compromised. Kwame knew that the Lebanese had done a great deal financially to assist the Party into power; so now it was a *quid pro quo*. Instead of dealing with foreign business interests, the new politicians were prepared to forge alliances with the Lebanese. Like the mammies, the politicians had their own special relationship with foreign firms and contractors, and would use their influence in the Party to award contracts to their man. It was a regular Tammany Hall set-up, as people realized that there were fortunes to be made out of the state. And even when they got their big rakeoffs from the Lebanese they didn't even invest in industrial development, but in the usual real estate and fine cars. They weren't even good capitalists; they did not learn how to control and expand their own resources, for the skill and the large profits remained in the hands of foreigners.

More critical still, they did not any longer rely on the masses for subventions to Party funds. The old idea of depending on the masses did not arise now. But it would have been much better if the state had evolved schemes like a nation-wide burial insurance. Burial is a very important question in Ghana, and something that everybody is concerned about. Instead of hoping to collect contributions at the funeral, you could easily have launched a scheme whereby each Ghanaian paid £1 a year—shs. 10/- of it to the Party funds, and shs. 10/- towards this burial insurance. This might have helped to arrest the drift away from the mass base towards the get-rich-quick mentality.

As it was, we had socialist talk without socialist planning. The worst of both worlds. What little planning there was came from the out-and-out capitalists like Ayeh-Kumi, who followed Lewis as Kwame's economic adviser. But very little serious work was done to analyse the state of Ghana's economy. Amoaka-Atta had written a few small things, to show how much gold had been extracted from the Ashanti Gold Mines, and on some other subjects. Padmore, before his death, had been piecing together a primer of first principles of organization. I, too, had felt that we would try to produce some Ghanaian counterparts of Illin's little Russian primers which had attempted to get down to the grass roots of family organization. But there was no serious attempt in Ghana to examine the nature of the economy and show what was really needed. There was no blueprint because the party like everything else found itself part of this whole intellectual and technological backwardness. Consequently you can identify a series of piecemeal borrowings instead of any policy.

Take the *Black Star* line. Having got the cocoa purchasing into our hands, it was thought important to control its transportation to Europe. Until this time foreign lines which plied the West African coast had been a monopoly and considered it as their own preserve. We thought it would be simple to ensure that cocoa was transported in our own *Black Star* ships, but we soon found out that unless you could guarantee a two-way traffic, and find consumer goods to fill up the ships on their return voyage, it would be pointless. Then we ran up against the cartels. We found out that the United Africa Company with its so many hundreds of stores throughout West Africa was not going to allow her cargoes of commodity goods to travel out on our line. It was the same with Cadbury's and Unilever. The result was that the *Black Star* line had to wait in the queue like everybody else for her portion of export goods. A number of other expedients were tried to beat the cartels, and at one period we tried to switch our cocoa to the Eastern countries; they wanted the cocoa all right, but what were they going to give us in return? The answer was nothing that would please the market mammies. They had been enmeshed with trading through British sources for so long that they immediately began to say that these Polish and Russian goods were useless. The mammies had been accustomed to brand goods, cloth that had been specially designed for the Ghanaian market, and other goods that had been coming from Birmingham and Manchester for centuries. Now they were confronted with what looked inferior. 'What is this *niami-niami* goods, this Chinee things coming here? Oh, Lord have mercy, Kwame has let us down! I go to Fitzgerald at the United Africa, and he say, "Well, mammy, you see. Look at the shelves; they are empty because Kwame has refused to give us any quota for the British goods"'.' So the capitalist did not have to spend any money to denigrate this switching of trade to the Eastern bloc; overnight the people themselves reacted. Kwame, their showboy, had turned out to be just a bad Nzima man.

This switch to the East was just after the Dawn Broadcast, when Kwame had admitted that things had not been going right, and that the veranda-boy period was over.[8] But it gave the socialist boys a bad name in town; all over Accra it was said that these wicked fellows had been pushing Kwame to do funny things. 'There are bad fellows among us; they seemed to be nice to start with. They said they came to defend our country; they made speeches to expose things to us—how bad imperialism was. But, oh, they are bad, bad people. They want to take us to a different Jerusalem.' All this showed the futility of practising socialism without socialists.

The colonial mentality was so ingrained that even when we began to send hundreds of students to places like Russia, it was plain that they despised the Russians. They attempted to desecrate Lenin's tomb, and they looked down on the people. 'What are these big boots you are wearing? In my Ghana I am accustomed to wearing English leather shoes which are well made.' And some of them exported their obsession with sex to Russia, and succeeded in seducing a number of Russian women. If there was any reluctance on their part, they could always wield the big stick of 'you don't like me because I'm black'.

It was an uphill battle with every attempt to exercise some control of the economy. Ghana decided to create her own central bank, with the idea that it should compete with the foreign banks and make them capitulate. But rumours soon went around that undermined people's confidence in the national bank; they said that everybody knew the amounts that individuals held in the bank, because there were irresponsible girls working there, and no ethic of secrecy had been built up. It was the result of wanting to change colonial institutions overnight, but not having the qualified staff to do it. This was the anatomy of our misery, that we had nobody trained to implement our aims. There were no socialists, but there were also very few technically minded people. Ghana in 1957 was much worse off than Russia in 1919, and even India was immeasurably more developed with its coal and steel industries under men like Tata.

How many economists did we have who could assess the various schemes we turned to? When it was decided that Ghana should take over some of the import-export trade by nationalizing Leventis, who was to know the correct price to offer? Kweku Akwei and I tried to press Edusei's committee which was looking into this, that they should buy the shares at the book price of £2 million. But other negotiators were committed to a price of £4 million or more, because corruption had set in to such a degree. So the Ghana National Trading Corporation which resulted from these deals started off on the wrong foot. Then as its general manager, who was brought in but Fitzgerald himself?[9] This made it clear that Ghana was interested in state capitalism and not socialism. Otherwise what are you doing appointing one of the oldest United Africa hands as the manager of your nationalized sector? Far from dealing with alien business interests, they got off very lightly. Partly this was because Ghana was the first African nation to be independent, and was therefore very much on trial. Everyone in the West was watching to see if these niggers would start running amok. So even if people had really been intent on liquidating the Lebanese, they felt the Western press would have singled Ghana out for racial prejudice. It was many years before an African nation dared to turn openly against alien traders, and even then there were cries of 'reverse racism' from the West. Yet when Kofi Busia took over in Ghana, we witnessed his pushing out of thousands of aliens—most of them Africans from neighbouring countries.

Then there was the great Volta Dam project. Was this socialist? Not at all—unless the American government is socialist because it has constructed the Boulder Dam and the Tennessee Valley Authority. The whole idea of such a lake in that region dated from the early years of this century, and it became fashionable to have such vast schemes in the 1950s. First, therefore, it was a project of the capitalist West, and probably they only came in to prevent Russia from doing the same thing as she had done with Nasser at Aswan. Equally it was tragic, because there was really no need for the Volta scheme; we could have bought all the hydroelectric stations we needed for a fraction of the price of Volta; and in fact we still did need to import smaller plants later on, because of the cost of carrying Volta power down to the South. Kwame had calculated that the scheme would be a sort of pan-African project, and that it would supply power to all the neighbouring states, but he had made a miscalculation about the jealousy of other states once they had their independence. They wanted their own power systems, and the capitalist countries were quite ready to provide them.

I never felt that serious surveys had been made in the area before these thousands and thousands of acres were flooded. They might well have held gold or diamonds, since it was not far from the gold regions. But nothing was going to deter Kwame from his scheme. I personally agreed with Arthur Lewis that the outlay of money was too fantastic, and that with a number of small generators one could have gradually built up levels of skill. Also one had no reason to believe that foreign firms would pour into Ghana to avail themselves of the cheap power. This had been Kwame's dream, but even Kaiser, who was behind the dam and the aluminium smelter along with the World Bank, did not really want a true investment in Ghana. He wanted cheap electricity, but was not prepared to process Ghanaian bauxite for use in the aluminium smelter. There were vast deposits right beside the dam, but Kaiser brought into Ghana bauxite which had already been processed. It was a very poor bargain that was driven, and was explained to us at the time as 'tactical action'[10]; we would agree to it for the moment, and then it might be possible later, like oil-producing nations, to drive a harder bargain. This was all very well, but it didn't take into account the fact that the Western commodity-producing nations had no intention of letting Ghana industrialize, and disturb the traditional commodity patterns. The world was simply not amenable to the idea of creating industries in the developing countries.

Instead, the big engineering firms like Kaiser were looking for large infrastructural contract projects; they weren't looking to invest in commodity production, but for contracts to build dams, construct roads and railways. And when the Third World countries have got all they want of this kind of construction, the West can still laugh at us, because we still won't have the technology to rival the industrial goods of the West. This then was the contradiction behind Volta.

Even so, I think we could have driven a much harder bargain with the various firms that were contracted to build it. Little attempt was made to have the Italian contractors develop any ancillary industry. We had our own Ghana Airways, yet they imposed their will on us, and insisted that their Alitalia fly in commodities twice a week, for those working on the dam. Similarly they even employed Italians as labour on the dam when it was not at all specialized work, and thus avoided training more Ghanaians. So whatever you want to accuse Kwame of, you can't castigate him for driving hard bargains with the capitalist countries. Point out to me any single hard bargain that he drove. All that was tough was his declaration at U.N., that Africa would not tolerate this new one-way trade which he called neo-colonialism.

The moral of it all was that you needed dedicated people if you wanted to make a radical change in either the traditional patterns of trade or in the people's beliefs. It was the same if you tried to switch trade as when we tried to promote a new Women's Charter. It was an attempt to free women, and especially younger women, from some of the exploitation that I mentioned earlier, and it had taken a number of us several months to work out. We went up to Kumasi to inaugurate it. There would from now on be 'one man, one job', and we would no longer have the exploitation of women under the guise of some flimsy African socialism. Furthermore there would now be 'one man, one wife'. Well, the women revolted, even though Kwame himself was explaining it: 'While appreciating what the President has got to say, and the fact that he has stopped following traditional ways himself, nevertheless what was good enough for your grandfather, Kwame, is good enough for me. We know you are married to your Egyptian wife, but why should she alone enjoy herself. It is no disrespect, Kwame, she is the First Lady of the land, but we want to share also. One woman can use your car to go shopping today, and another can take it tomorrow.' So the whole of this social document that we had toiled over was negated by these forces of traditionalism. The masses were ready enough when it was a question of free primary education to shout, 'Oh, Kwame, wonderful showboy, what a leader!' But as soon as you began to add that this would involve taxation, then it was a different story.

In a different sphere I got something of the same reaction when I set out to create a chain of state bakeries[11]; I had no objection

251

to the traditional *kenke,* or the bread with a maize base which people took with their sardines. But this fantastic aerated thing that they also sold as bread was like a concertina; the yeast had blown it up into beautiful shapes, but it was all form and no content. I wanted to ensure that the masses got a loaf that had value in it; so before going any further I wrote round to all the embassies and asked them to forward me the regulations for what constituted standard bread back home. We discovered then what were the accepted standards of lactose, salt, sugar and flour in bread making, and were able to show that the whole make-up of Ghanaian bread was without substance. I then got in touch with the Australians who were quite prepared to send several ship-loads of flour for experimental purposes. Working in close touch with the bakers we set about improving the standard and making this first bakery more profitable. We also had to deal with the distribution, because in the traditional distribution networks too much was being added to the price of the loaf at these various levels of distribution. Once we had passed the experimental stage, I put forward proposals for a chain of mechanical bakeries, one in each of the central towns like Tamale, Ho, Kumasi. These were accepted and we arranged for credits abroad to have ten such bakeries set up. They would be state-owned, and would produce throughout the country a highly standardized bakery system. But what was the reaction? People began to talk against the project. Even Phillips, the chairman of the Economic Commission, began to criticize: 'Oh, countryman, you are disturbing our economy, you know. My old lady used to make this old bread for me, and through the little profit on it, she was able to send me to school, and on to college. So who is this bad man Makonnen? He is taking away the little profit my old woman was making on her bread by bringing these machines.' No concern with the standard of the commodity. All these fellows were still tied to the old system, the old distorted economy.

When I was working at the Hotel and Tourist Corporation, it was equally difficult to establish any new pattern with the international organizations. This was the time when there were terrible shortages in the hotels, even of common commodities like butter. Well, as this was reflecting on me somewhat, I felt that Ghana as a sovereign state should simply use her airways to ship in five tons of butter from Holland or wherever. But you immediately ran into these international agreements with IATA which through some mathematical juggles prevented you from using your own airways even in such a national emergency. I felt that if we had had enough seasoned veterans, we would not have been in a position of always being told 'you can't do this or you can't do that'.

But without any such disciplined corps of planners, each went his own way. Once Arthur Lewis had left, Ayeh-Kumi came in, and his advice was that Ghana should get certain firms to build factories on short-term credits.[12] On completion the Ghana government would be handed the key to the factory. This was no investment, because the price might be anything up to 200 per cent of what it ought to have been. Countries in both the West and East dumped these factories on us, and we had to pay the price for this technology: 'You boys want our magical factories. All right, we'll set them up for you at our price.' Ayeh-Kumi, for instance, had to push me out of the Hotel and Tourist Corporation because he wanted to put through a deal for a French firm to build a hotel at Tema for £1½ million.

After the Dawn Broadcast, therefore, you had the spectacle of Ghana trying to ride two horses. She had moved to the Eastern countries to get her credits there, but many of the people were firmly wedded to the traditional capitalist West. So you rode hard the horse of capitalism that you knew well and you also tried to pull along this other strange horse of socialism. But all that socialism meant to the ordinary people was 'funny Russian sardines, instead of the good old British brands that we knew'.

So by 1962 it was clear that we couldn't have socialism without training up some socialists. Hence the Ideological College that we mentioned earlier. Kodwo Addison, the principal, was no socialist; he had played in with the communist boys now and then to gain their favour, but what was his behaviour? How many houses did he create for himself? And what about the information that reached us in the central committee of the Party, that Kodwo was having special songs sung in praise of him at the college? It may have been false information, but it was not entirely beyond belief.

Other trainees were in the Workers' and Builders' Brigades.

We had brought some advisers over from Israel to guide us on their role, but their influence was quickly undermined by people saying they didn't want foreigners coming to tell them how to rear chickens and other crops. Consequently, the brigades got off the ground without much planning. And as you know, socialism without planning is straight anarchy. Finally these 'socialist' pioneers and brigaders were sent out into the rural areas with three uniforms, so many shillings a day and a place to sleep. All of this mint of money invested in them, and every state having its builders' brigade, still nothing substantial was built up. Many of the fellows didn't have the energy to put their own cassava sticks in the ground, and although they were meant to be felling timber and clearing ground for some of the state farms, they said: 'I didn't come out to the country to start wielding an axe. Let me just set fire to these trees instead.' So a great deal of the money spent on mobilizing these brigades was wasted, as it was also on the capital equipment for some of the state farms. Personally I felt it would have been better to try 'stool' farms rather than state ones. You could have adapted the traditional respect of the people for the chief to a new collective end, and his people could have worked along with him in a co-operative unit. Instead of moving straight away to this impersonal state machinery, you could have gone via the stage of a 'stool' farm. But in the circumstances nobody was going to listen to a scheme that suggested giving some power back to the chiefs.

What one came back to was the conviction that change would come only by having a dedicated cadre of party loyalists. You needed a vanguard; it was all very well having a mass party if you wanted to whip up popular emotions at the time of independence, but after that you required a small formidable movement of policy makers to give form and content to the Afircan revolution.[13] We drew the parallel with Lenin who had purged the Communist Party of Russia from some 750,000 down to about 136,000 well-disciplined members in 1921. Much better a small number who were dedicated than a million who didn't know where they were going. We tried to build up such a revolutionary vanguard through the medium of NASSO, but independence had come so easily that there'd been no time to form disciplined cadres. Hence even NASSO was something of a ragbag. The average Ghanaian is prestige-conscious, and if this NASSO was something that Kwame might attend, they were not going to be left out. So you had permanent secretaries and others attending. Even so, NASSO was suspect amongst the politicians in power. They knew very well that Kwame had joined the old United Gold Coast Convention only to overthrow it from inside. They didn't want any repetition of that. Anyone who wanted to set himself up as a watchdog of the party would constantly warn Kwame: 'Be careful of these Nasso-ists. After all we are all CPP. Why do we need a vanguard? Kwame, be careful oh, because these fellows are ambitious.'

The difficulty was also that so many of the NASSO group were outsiders. This put you in a quandary. You did not want to be stigmatized as another kind of colonialist who had put a bit in the Ghanaians' mouth and wanted to pull them in every direction. They might respect you for your orthodoxy, but think it sinister that you had no houses of your own, and that you lived at Government House. 'They don't understand our ways, these socialist boys. Watch them, Kwame, watch them! They are out to destroy all our own values that we know so well. Anyway, where was Makonnen when we veranda boys were going round and fighting for independence? Where were Padmore and the others? We are not doubting that they wrote articles and helped in many ways, but be careful. Look how these other mad people like Heymann and Baafoe are following them. They're all funny people, and would like us to put on big Russian boots.' So knowledge of these attitudes would make Kwame cautious about being too close to some of us. We were not part of the Ghanaian family structure, and therefore were at the receiving end of some of the Ghanaians' little prejudices. To some we were dismissed as 'slave pickin from the New World', just as the Ghanaian looks down on the Nigerian man and the Upper Volta people. Remember the Ghanaian is the centre of creation, even though centuries of conditioning means that he doesn't express his views crudely to your face.

It wasn't that Kwame set himself up as a god therefore, but that all his advisers were warning him against everybody else; they would secure their own positions by saying that they didn't like the way Mak attacked the President, or they didn't like the way so-and-so talked as if he was better informed than Kwame.

So you were dealing with a people that were masters of equivocation; they were steeped in this business of intrigue and infiltration, and eventually Kwame came to believe some of it. Even if he wasn't accumulating property himself initially, his advisers like Ayeh-Kumi and others would come and warn him as a good Nzima man that Kojo Botsio, Gbedemah and others were all getting money. He would be fed with photographs of other people's big houses, and they would say: 'What have you got? Are you trying to be St. Jesus not possessing anything? Watch out or they may crucify you like him, and you'll still have nothing.' So gradually, I suppose, Kwame, believing that the voice of the people is the voice of God, came to accept their counsel and thought he'd better have his own nest egg too. And naturally along with this style at the top went the increase in security, especially after the assassination attempt at Kulungugu. After a number of attempts, suspicion became so rife that we used to strip when we came into Flagstaff House to show that we weren't concealing anything.

Well, the thing then drifted from bad to worse, and it became necessary to have recourse to that subtlety I mentioned before. Kwame let the socialist boys continue their attacks, and people never knew how much he approved of what they said. If they asked him, he would always say: 'Don't mind them, don't mind them; they're just trying to throw things in your eyes.' So you never knew whether Kwame had not told them to say their piece. It was a subtle affair, and it dispirited some of us. Because if we came to him from the other side, and suggested that he purge the party, and create an African legion, a black legion, ready to move with dedication against any obstacle, and prepared to deal with the exploiting elements in society, he would come back with: 'According to you fellows, everybody is a kulak. So what am I to do? I haven't jails enough. And as for your African legion, who is to ensure that one day it won't come and put me out of business? Where are the classes in Ghanaian society?' he would say. 'Show me the classes.'

NOTES TO CHAPTER 15

1 For changing patterns of trade in the post-1918 period, see P. T. Bauer, *West African Trade*.

2 On Guggisberg's initiatives both here and in the larger infrastructural development, see R. E. Wraith, *Guggisberg* (London, 1967), chs. 5 and 11.

3 One of the most valuable sources on the leading African businessmen from Nigeria, Gold Coast and Sierra Leone in the 1920s is *The Red Book of West Africa* (1st edn. 1920, Cass Reprints, 1968); for the Gold Coast businessmen, see pp. 200–15.

4 *Spark*, which began publication in Ghana in December 1962, made similar points about the allegedly communalistic nature of African traditional society; see Legum, 'Socialism in Ghana', p. 151.

5 The complexity of human relations in cocoa production is such that a controversy has continued to rage over whether the various types of migrant cocoa workers constitute a form of rural proletariat; see B. Fitch and M. Oppenheimer, *Ghana: End of an Illusion* (Monthly Review, New York, 1966), ch. 3, and R. Genoud, *Nationalism and Social Development in Ghana* (New York, 1969).

6 See, also, Padmore's attitude to the 'dash' in his last work, 'A Guide to Pan-African Socialism', in W. H. Friedland and C. G. Rosberg, *African Socialism*, p. 234.

7 The most useful comments on the extent to which Ghana was socialist are: Jitendra Mohan, 'Nkrumah and Nkrumahism', *Socialist Register* (London, 1967), pp. 191–228; Legum, 'Socialism in Ghana', op. cit; Genoud, op. cit; and Roger Murray, 'Second Thoughts on Ghana', *New Left Review*, 72, March/April, 1967; the last two are both extended comments on Fitch and Oppenheimer's 'Two-Ghana Theory'. See also Selwyn Ryan, 'Socialism and the Party System in Ghana in 1947–66' in *Pan-African Journal*, III, 1, 1970, pp. 49–97.

8 For the diplomatic and economic implications of the switch to the Eastern countries, see W. S. Thompson, op. cit., pp. 272–9. Also, St. Clair Drake and Leslie Lacey, 'The Sekondi-Takoradi Strike' in G. Carter, *Politics in Africa: Seven Case Studies* (New York, 1966).

9 The half-hearted nature of this particular nationalization is detailed in Fitch and Oppenheimer, op. cit., pp. 115–18.

10 There is considerable critical literature on the Volta project; some recent insights on the Volta bargain are made in W. S. Thompson, pp. 190–4, 302–3.

11 Makonnen was appointed the Director of the State Bakery Corporation in August 1965.

12 A useful summary of the debt pattern that emerged with these suppliers-credits to Ghana is Fitch and Oppenheimer, op. cit., pp. 120–3.

13 For the debate between those pressing for the CPP to remain a mass party and those working for an *avant-garde* conception, see Genoud, op. cit., 173 ff. and pp. 186–7.

CHAPTER 16

GHANA AND PAN-AFRICANISM

ONE of the first things we were up against in Ghana was that our leading civil servants and first diplomats had been carefully trained in the best British traditions. Shortly before independence a nucleus had been selected from places like Achimota and elsewhere and they had been dispatched to Britain to be exposed to how the whole thing worked. They were shown all the machinery including the workings of the intelligence, and I know what I'm talking about here, because one of these early recruits told me that they were even trained to detect Reds. So they were nurtured to become a shadow Cabinet, to be a check on whatever recklessness Kwame's government might get up to. And behind each of them in the Ghana civil service you would find a white adviser. Britain, remember, was not running back home when Ghana became independent; instead, a lot of these white boys signed on with special contracts just before 1957, and they were able to stay in the background guiding the hands of the top black civil servants. Thus, when Padmore and others arrived on the scene just afterwards, these whites were able to nudge these specially trained Ghanaians and say: 'You see this West Indian-cum-Communist maelstrom that is building up? Do you know where this is leading Ghana?'

To prevent such people blocking whatever initiatives in pan-Africanism were being planned, Padmore advised Kwame to isolate the civil service on African matters. We would deal with African policy, or African affairs. In this way the Bureau of African Affairs and later the African Affairs Secretariat remained outside the control of these old-style civil servants.[1] The next tactic was to try to force these superior civil servants to become part of the popular revolution; we would tell them that on such and such a day they would have to appear on the platform. They didn't like that at all. Then they had to be forced to become members of the Party, not a bureaucracy tied on to the Party. But all the time we were up against their convictions that everything must be done by precedent, and that meant according to British procedure. If, for instance, our men were going to be addressing the United Nations, we didn't want them imitating Lord Bolingbroke, delivering speeches identical in form and content to the English delegation. 'You're a rebel nation,' we had to tell our diplomats, 'we are meant to be out of step with all this English style. Look at Krishna Menon of the Indian delegation; he has broken with the norms of English debate; he's not talking "with due respect to Her Britannic Majesty's Government". Forget that stuff, and remember that the Ghana government put you where you are and it can remove you as easily. So until you learn that we are a revolutionary nation, we'll write your speeches for you.'[2]

The trouble also was that our pan-African policy required dedicated men, who treated their positions as a trust. But as I said earlier the dedication of too many people was to making money, settling down and coming into their own. You couldn't expect much dedication to pan-Africanism abroad when at home the Fanti boys were working to establish their fellow Fantis, and the Ewes and others were doing likewise. Well, to me this was tragic; some of them were turning out to be just a bunch of damned tribalists, and they'd prefer to bring a European to work on a short contract rather than let a job go to a black of some other group. It angered George a great deal and he used to come to me and say: 'These damn fellows, they're very chauvinistic.' In fact it made him decide that he would shortly leave and return to some place in the West Indies, because he simply hadn't anticipated this hostility to foreign blacks.[3]

Kwame therefore had to work for his pan-Africanism without having the human material. He probably couldn't afford to be too analytical of his fellow Ghanaians, because he was too much a believer that if you scratched any Ghanaian you would find a reformer who wanted to do the right thing at home and abroad. This meant that he frequently employed agents for his pan-Africanism who were sheer opportunists. But the real tragedy was that one of his most trusted emissaries in the pan-

African struggle was Barden; he thrived on the contradictions in Kwame between modernism and traditionalism. I mean, Kwame was able on the one hand to smash old structures of colonialism and yet be worked on by Barden in the realm of *ju-ju*. George and I used to discuss this sinister hold that Barden had over Kwame. Personally I couldn't take it. I'm an open society man; I'm Socratic in my approach, and now you're telling me about some force. Well, I used to say: 'What's so great about this force? Has it managed to conquer the air or go under the sea like the white man's forces? How is it that this wicked boy Barden can get a hold on you, Kwame? He and his like have no real community of interest; Barden is no philosopher, no Marxist, yet he is able to convince you.' George understood it better and put it down to Kwame having once been a Catholic. But I said, 'Lenin and Stalin started out as good Orthodox boys, so how could Kwame still be influenced by this occult stuff?'

Well, in analysing the moves towards pan-Africanism all this has to be taken into account. Equally, when we are assessing the recent relations between states in Africa we have to take into account their historical perceptions of each other. Take Ghana-Nigeria relations. You cannot begin considering this in the era of Nkrumah; you have to go back to that earlier pan-Africanist, Zik. When he came back from the States, he settled in Ghana to edit the *Morning Post*. From there he began to concretize the message of pan-Africanism that he had found in America, and naturally the Ethiopian crisis of 1935 played into his hands.[4] The same crisis also got him evicted from Ghana, and my feeling is that it was not only the British who wanted him out. Many of the old reactionary chiefs like Nana Ofori Atta thought him an undisciplined boy—an outsider—and people began to say that he was just a foreigner with no clan links with the local community. Zik was then driven back to Nigeria.

It is crucial to make the point that Zik and certain elements in Nigeria had a radicalism and a pan-African approach to Africa long before Ghana. There was no one to beat the Ghanaians, or Gold Coast men at this time in toasting the King; but meanwhile Nigeria's was a much more diversified style of politics. Zik was content to settle in Lagos, a cosmopolitan city, where it was not easy to generate the spirit of tribalism. Too many of its inhabitants were Creoles from Brazil or from Freetown, and then over to the East it was possible for Zik to work out close links with the Cameroons. So you had a veritable 'League of Nations' in Nigeria. Also there was nothing to rival Zik's second paper in radicalism; it was financed by a Ghanaian businessman, Pa Biney, living at the time in Lagos, and it made as much of a mark in Nigeria as a liberal and anti-imperialist paper, as the *Manchester Guardian* had upon us in England. People would say: 'You heard what Zik wrote today? You see how he has twisted the whole thing to make the British look stupid?'

But if Ghana in the 1950s had her reactionary intellectuals and chiefs, Nigeria had the same menace—the North. I can only compare it with what Napoleon's generals said to him in Russia after they had carried everything before them: 'Sire, what about China?' And he replied, 'Let that sleeping giant sleep. Woe befall those who arouse him from his stupor. Humanity will have a restless time.' So I think the Nigerian affair lends itself to a similar analysis. Nigeria was the giant of Africa, and its largest sector was the North. This was culturally divided from the South, and the British tried to ensure that Zik's *Pilot* did not get up into those parts. However, the North was gradually stirring. Don't forget that there were thousands of Yoruba and Ibo men in the area, making up for the absence of a literate middle class. Equally in North Africa, nationalism had been awake in Sudan and Egypt, and with the Nigerian Muslims passing constantly through that region it was impossible to build a Chinese wall there either.

Zik, therefore, was really able to play the role of the conscience of Africa in the thirties and forties. There was no one else on the horizon. We knew all about him of course, because the reporting in his paper was invaluable for our campaigns in England, and we in turn used to send him material on debates in the House. So there was a shuttling of information backwards and forwards between these two centres. Let us see the contrast then. Here is Kwame returning as a young man in the late forties, when Zik has been a force to reckon with for over a decade. Zik had returned as a man of missionary zeal, but Kwame was coming back with a more ideological background; perhaps he even had a Communist Party card in his pocket. Initially, however,

261

there was a good deal of common ground. Zik knew very well the old reactionary elements in Ghana, the Aborigines Rights Protection Society, the Danquahs and the Sekyis. He knew the style of the United Gold Coast Convention which Kwame was originally asked to join; it liked to have small meetings with a number of luminaries on the platform. And doubtless Zik approved Kwame's overthrowing the UGCC to start a more Western party organization with cells and a common platform. After all Zik had the same reactionary sectors in Nigeria who fought his radical approach. No one was surprised therefore to see some rapprochement between Awolowo's tribal set-up with the Yoruba and the Ashanti group around Busia and Daequah. This made it possible for us all to establish a bond of sympathy, and in 1957, I think, George, Kwame and others went to see Zik to try to prevent our radical approach from being swamped by a reactionary process. However, Zik did not want to be tarred with the same communist brush as Kwame. You see, the alignment of Kwame and the communist boys seemed quite clear at this time; some of the British fellow-travellers and communists like Pat Sloan were always being quoted at length in the Ghana *Evening News* once that got started. And both to me and to Zik, this looked unnecessary; what was the point of linking up with an extraneous element in Britain that was not even powerful? There were only one or two unions in Britain that the communists controlled. So this may have begun to put a certain distance between Zik and Kwame.

If this was Zik's fear about Kwame, I was with him all the way. Right from the time of the Pan-African Congress up to the late forties, Kwame was double-dealing between pan-Africanism and communism. Here we had just finished our historical 1945 conference, in which the keynote had been that we blacks would be the generals of any African movement; and then we discovered that Kwame was playing with the communist boys in King Street, London, and developing the very alliances we had outlawed. Furthermore, he had set up some regional group called the West African National Secretariat (WANS) and established a separate office for its headquarters. Well, I was already suspicious, and one day along with some of the boys we went there and found copies of the Moscow magazine on colonial questions, but not even a single copy of *Pan-Africa* or the other things we had been producing in Manchester. Most naturally I got very angry, went back to Manchester and called a meeting of the Central Committee of the Pan-African Federation. Jomo was there, Milliard, Prestcott, Padmore and Makonnen. We summoned Kwame before us and I had to ask him to give an account of his stewardship. I acted the role of Vishinsky and had to prosecute him: 'Do you not realize that some of us had already gone through the communist mill, and that we knew only too well their tactics. Instead of trying that out again, here we have a movement which we should defend and which we should use as a spearhead. Our anti-colonial movement must be unfettered. To carry the burdens of Russia on our shoulders would be a terrible thing. Particularly as you will be going home soon to the Gold Coast, and even if the King Street boys thought they were clever, the boys in the Colonial Office were cleverer; they would find out that you had affiliations to the communist movement, and would use that evidence to damn the movement towards freedom from colonialism.' Well, it was very embarrassing for him, but he was too mellow a politician already to say, 'Damn you fellows, I'm a West African'. Also he may have calculated that even if I couldn't harm him, George had access to the whole West Africa press through Zik, and could finish his reputation in a single dispatch.

To my mind it was preferable to back the old-style nationalists in the Gold Coast like Sekyi and others, even though their nationalism was somewhat royalist, than to go back tarred with the communist brush. Don't forget, too, that the Aborigines Rights Protection Society of the Gold Coast had been the only organization that had aided us financially with £100 to help in the Manchester Conference. They had demonstrated a commitment to our cause, and as I knew the Sekyi family well, I felt it necessary to relay to him my grave doubts about Kwame's present trend. And if this suspicion had crossed Zik's mind also, I couldn't blame him.[5]

Other factors were also important. Ghana was beginning to give the impression that there had been no radicalism around on the West Coast before Kwame returned; but the Nigerians knew very well that in WASU and elsewhere they had been keeping the torch burning when the Gold Coast man was following his genteel constitutionalism. Also in London, instead of the single WASU hostel, the rise of the various legislatures in the West African colonies meant that they wanted to have their own national hostels. WASU House became a strictly Nigerian affair, and the students of the two countries began to see less of each other.

Ghana of course did have certain headstarts over Nigeria. She had been able to accumulate her cocoa profits during and after the Second World War at a time when Nigeria had borne the brunt of the troops going via northern Nigeria up to North Africa. This had used up a great deal of Nigerian resources. And this in turn encouraged Ghana to fight for her own university when it was being suggested that she should be a constituent part of a single West African university; she had the money to do it after all.

But there were more stubborn obstacles to unity between the Nigerians and the Ghanaians. Who had dealt that final blow to the independent Ashanti nation in the 1890s? Frederic Hodgson and his Nigerian troops.[6] You didn't forget these things easily. Especially when you could see the reactionary role of the Hausa troops for the next fifty years. Remember the Hausa provided the British military might. These people were at the beck and call of the British. As soon as there was any disturbance or strike in the Gold Coast, the Hausa boys would be on the spot. Look at the riots of 1948; you soon got the reaction: 'You bring these people over to destroy our liberty. What kind of strange people are these? Let that foolish man Zik look after his own affairs. As soon as we want to create order in our own house, these people come over to destroy us.' These memories die hard, and they keep lurking round corners.

Not only were Britain's mercenaries Nigerian, but the dominant element in the police force was also from there. And even more conspicuous was the Nigerian trader. Nigeria didn't have to do much to have a bad name. Because in every village in Ghana the people who meant something were Nigerians. We have talked about Ghanaian traders but these Nigerians were even more gifted—little inoffensive fellows selling in the remotest villages, but also important fellows. They became the moneylenders of the community, always at the beck and call like the Jew in the middle ages to the lords of the manor: 'Lazarus.' 'Yes, sir.' 'Can you do me a favour?' 'Yes sir, I'm yours for the asking. How much do you need?' So the Nigerian played this servile role and built himself up into an economic threat to the locals. Even in Accra there was a whole area called, jokingly, Birmingham, where you found the Nigerian man turning old automobiles into a gold mine through dealing in spare parts. And you'd find the same if you went to the Zongos in Kumasi or elsewhere[7]; this man was always there in the workshop dealing in metal. He became a giant, and often the largest house in town was a foreigner's. But even the smaller traders did not take on Ghanaian dress, but stood out in their Nigerian styles and their turbans.

Now I said that the Nigerians, who had a longer radical tradition, did not find it necessary to make such a noise about socialism as Ghana. And partly for this reason we find much more investment being attracted to Nigeria than Ghana. This was also because of a natural equation whereby investment and development follows population. So here was this vast Nigerian market attracting American investment, and even pulling some of the originally Gold Coast firms like Leventis into its sphere. Ghana had been on her own in America at the United Nations, but once Nigeria got her independence, she had her men over there who were much better at working the American scene than the Ghanaians. Don't forget many of the Nigerian boys had been educated in America in the Zik tradition. So perhaps the Americans felt it was safe to expand there. Consequently you had a tremendous impact, with American banking institutions and other projects. The majority of Ghanaian capitalists resented this, and the few committed socialists equally began to doubt the value of allying too closely with what was becoming an American colony.

This was the background to the distrust of the Nigerians, but the thing did not break out into public hostilities until much later. For the moment, the Ghanaians feared to arouse the huge number of Nigerians in their country, because of a possibility that they would link up immediately with the opposition elements in the National Liberation Movement.

One of the next crucial sectors after Nigeria was our relationship with French West Africa. We had attended their RDA conference, and had decided to help certain sections on the verge of their independence. There were already natural links with Upper Volta, Niger and Mali, because of migrants coming from there, or Ghanaians working in those countries. Now this was just before the time when de Gaulle sprang the idea of a referendum on the colonies; they were to vote 'yes' or 'no' against remaining part of the French community and empire. To us the question just demonstrated the dogged nature of French imperialism. We had all recognized that colonialism was an evil, and now de Gaulle was going to ask them to say whether they liked it or not. What sort of free choice was there when the French controlled the banks; the whole life blood of the nation was in his hands? What was the point of this foolish question, when your agents had been going round for months telling the Africans what would happen if this white man was not there? It was fantastic. 'We had served you so well in two World Wars, and especially in the Second when France had capitulated completely to Vichy. Have you forgotten that it was Eboué this black man who declared from the heart of Africa in favour of de Gaulle's Free French at their darkest hour?[8] And yet France had retaliated against that outpost of empire in Vietnam, and had been carrying on so much blood-letting in Algeria. Then you ask us again, despite these experiences, despite this turmoil, to mortgage our future with you?'

Well, only one solitary state, Guinea, dared to say 'no' in the circumstances. The vengeance with which this man de Gaulle retaliated was unbelievable. Everything was stripped from the country by the French as they moved out—I saw the devastation when I visited a few months later. People may talk now in the 1970s about the harshness of Sekou Touré, but few realize the tremendous vindictiveness of de Gaulle in 1958. So what were we in Ghana to do? We had been projecting Ghana as the shield of Africa since our independence and were we now to be found wanting? No. Steps were immediately taken to demonstrate that Kwame meant it when he said that the independence of Ghana was meaningless in isolation. Now here was an opportunity to take our brothers under our wing and support them to the last. Call it a leap in the dark if you like, but it was not unnatural; it was just a demonstration of our common Africanness. An ambassador was dispatched to Conakry, and a reciprocal relationship was established whereby Guinea's ambassador, Abdoulaye Diallo, sat in our parliament. What was shocking was that for all their links with the other French states through the RDA, not a single one said to France: 'Don't do this to Guinea.'

At the early stage we didn't demand anything at all of Guinea. No more did America demand anything from Britain when she came to her aid; as Roosevelt said in his cryptic utterance: 'When your neighbour's house is on fire, you don't count the cost of the hose or the bucket. You put the fire out.' And even if the distance was three thousand miles, it devolved on America to aid Britain. Similarly with us it was a question of simply seeing a brother in need and going to his rescue at once. The question of a Guinea-Ghana union only entered at a later stage.[9]

When we went there with Kwame to see for ourselves the situation we met Touré and heard from him some of his acute problems. One of these involved Ghana, because it turned out that the Ghanaian traders had a similar role in Guinea to what the Nigerians had in Ghana. They and the Syrians dominated trade, and they were only loyal to money—not to any country. They were there feathering their own nests, and were still actually in league with the French trading houses. So just as in Ghana with our civil servants and intellectuals, there were whole sections that were still wanting the enemy. The colonial mentality was strong, even stronger than it was in parts of British West Africa. This drove us back again to consider the paradox in French colonialism. We had noticed it when meeting with our French friends in the early days in Paris in the Rassemblement Coloniale, but we had hoped that a new epoch would dawn after the world war. Didn't French history mean anything to them? We certainly had been moved by understanding revolutionary England, Cromwell's role in parliament and the later age of the Great Reform Bill. So one would have thought that the black Frenchman would have been similarly moved by the French Revolution and the rights of man. After all, the whole of Haiti's struggle had been involved with that particular history. Many of the African and Indian colonial students had sat at the feet of Professor Laski and learnt their European history and politics so that it moved them. Surely in French universities there were no two ways to interpret the revolutionary period? They didn't need to turn to Garveyism, for the whole thing was in front of their eyes. But they didn't seem to have imbibed it at all. So instead of running to the flag of African revolution, they ran back to the tricolour. They became more French than the French—or rather more bourbon than the bourbons. Who was more steeped than Senghor in French history, and yet he only seems to have imbibed the counter-revolutionary message of the Thermidorean period.

How could a black man be a Frenchman in that tradition? How could Senghor and others not see that Touré was a genuine deliverer in the true French revolutionary tradition? George is not here to bear me witness, but Kwame is still here* to confirm that this was the supreme contradiction—how so many a black could stick by France at a time she was spilling so much African blood. So many blacks were looking to France as the mother, *la patrie*, to whom they owed so much; I don't know, but I should think that they owe so much of their darkness to her.

They say Touré has become a monster, but it's these people with their betrayal of their country to the last, that have driven him to it. Touré could not understand it. How could a Guinean, a man with a past of fierce resistance to early French imperialism, behave like this? Surely there would have been loyalty to the direct descendant of that earlier Samori Touré?[10]

These were the circumstances that drew Ghana and Guinea together, the spontaneous outreach to a brother in distress. For a time things went on well between the two, because they became the natural refuge of any elements who were discontented with their own conservative regimes. People like Djibo Bokary came to us from Niger, and a number of political exiles from Senegal went to Guinea. These were the ideal places where they could find sympathy. However, it was the refugee element that partly contributed to the worsening of Guinea-Ghana relations in particular. Take this fellow Habib Niang from Senegal; he fled from there because his uncle had been involved in challenging Senghor, and he became an important adviser in Guinea. For one reason or another he was considered to have failed in loyalty to Touré, or done his job badly, and yet Kwame was prepared to accept him in Ghana without even inquiring from Sekou Touré how he had given offence. Shortly he was

*Kwame Nkrumah died on 27 April 1972.

able to ingratiate himself with Kwame, rather like Barden, and got himself a palatial house. This naturally gave the greatest offence to Guinea, and the trouble was that people in Ghana did not challenge Kwame on it. Many of the Ghanaians simply felt: 'Well, Kwame knows best; it's his palaver, and I don't want to get into any argument.' This was treasonable, I thought. How could one go to Sekou Touré's aid as a brother one moment, and the next accept as our advisers people who had been dismissed by him?

This is to go ahead a bit, for before relations deteriorated with Guinea, we had held the All African People's Conference in Ghana during December 1958. It signified the end of the old pan-Africanism of five thousand miles away, and the beginning of a new breed in Africa itself. It gave us a chance too to tell everyone what we had learnt about the new role of the British in an independent country. We had the bitter experience of having white advisers to communicate. We warned them about how the whites would try to re-establish themselves, and how the newly independent African governments would have to fight against British hard bargains. So, if there was anything we could contribute tactically to the others' gaining their freedom and maintaining it afterwards, we were ready to share the advantages of our headstart.

We had already discussed common problems with the independent African states earlier in the year, and it was now appropriate to address ourselves to the masses of African people. This meant the trade union boys and others from parties that had not yet found their independence. Inevitably, however, it meant that a certain amount of suspicion was generated against Ghana. Some of the delegations that came were not representative, or were actually regarded as splinter groups by the government in power. This was particularly true of the groups which came from the Sudan, where the Umma Party had begun to fight against some of these Left boys who came to Accra. There was of course a very narrow line between warning people of the dangers of neo-imperialism and actually pointing the finger at regimes which gave the impression of being manipulated by outside forces. This is what sparked off the new Nigeria-Ghana conflict; Nigeria had come with a large delegation led by Jaja Wachuku. On the one hand they were pointing out that they

269

were no small state like Ghana, and showing that they had really been the architects of this whole radical pan-Africanism back in the 1940s. But they also appeared to some of us like standard bearers for American imperialism. These were the antagonisms that eventually led to the almost complete breakdown of good relations between us. For about three years this lasted with Ghana taking the opposite line to everything Nigeria said. It was a persistent conflict, and it wasn't helped by accepting refugees from Nigeria. Some of these were actually radicals fleeing from the Americanization of Nigeria's politics and economy.

After Guinea and the AAPC, our first major 'outdooring' exercise, as they say in Ghana, was the Casablanca grouping.[11] In this, Nasser's and Kwame's positions in their respective countries were almost parallel. Neither would allow any powerful group to co-exist in their countries. Nasser moved against his socialist elements just like Kwame against the Northern Liberation people. Kwame was close also to the other elements, in the Casablanca group of states; the king of Morocco loved him and had given him a villa in Fez; Bourguiba had come and spent quite some time at our independence celebrations. Guinea and Mali had both received substantial aid from Ghana; and we had shown our willingness to help Ben Bella in his plight by sending our quota of freedom fighters to buttress him in his struggle against the French. So this *entente* that we had forged kept the rear of Morocco and Algeria secure, and it was also valuable to us because through Egypt we learnt what these Muslim boys in Northern Nigeria were up to. But Kwame and Nasser were also similar in other ways; both had attempted to forge unity with other states. Nasser had shown the way with his union to Syria, and we had had experience with Guinea and then Mali. Both had also projected themselves powerfully as African leaders. Egypt had developed strong links southwards to East Africa and Zanzibar, and her radio broadcasts had been a force. Ghana came later to this type of propaganda, but again they were both very evident in the Congo through their contribution of troops. However, both were detested in some ways as much as they were loved and respected. And this makes it all the more of a pity that they weren't able to appreciate their respective positions, and stop out-manoeuvring each other.

However, while the Casablanca *entente* lasted, it produced the first real threat against French influence in North and West Africa, for here was a real alliance of Arab and black French states working in with Ghana and Egypt rather than with their colonial motherland.

Meanwhile around Nigeria there had built up a counter grouping of moderate states in the Monrovia and Lagos conferences. The anti-Ghana climate was very strong indeed now in Nigeria, and they were able at this point to make capital out of the fact that Ghana had recently suppressed the Opposition. We had our Detention Act, and a number of influential leaders had fled from the country. Nigeria still had her multi-party framework, and was able to caricature us as the czars of Africa in a period when republicanism was the order of the day.

Well, as we were also campaigning for a larger African unity, it became necessary towards the end of 1962 and the beginning of 1963 to do a bit of bridge-building.[12] Too many states suspected Ghana of fostering subversion, or plotting their overthrow by harbouring their refugees. We were not the only ones involved in bridge-building. The Americans were working hard at it; they had got their base in Libya, and now to contain Nasser in the south, they began to approach old man Haile Selassie. Addis Ababa was obviously an ideal place, and they decided on a considerable invesment there. A magnificent hall and secretariat buildings were provided, and thus the Americans aided Ethiopia in becoming the centre for the forthcoming African unity conference, in 1963. I personally felt that the headquarters for any African unity organization should be the centre of Africa— that is to say, in Bangui. We knew of course that Africa Hall was being constructed in Addis, but this had originally been intended for the U.N. organizations that were going to come in there. Geographically, however, Bangui was the centre.

First I sold the idea to Kwame, and afterwards Kojo Botsio and Nana Kobina Nketsia and I were on the point of setting off for Bangui when the news came through of Olympio's assassination. We set off a good many hours later, but by the time we got there the news was all around that probably Ghana was the culprit. Despite this, we had valuable meetings with Bangui leaders, and the interesting thing was that Dacko's party there was really the closest you could get to the CPP in the rest of Africa.

271

He was very flattered at our proposals, but warned us that although he would be very glad to agree, his country did have a large number of enemies, and this might complicate bringing everyone together.

When we got back to Ghana we divided our forces, and this time Kojo Botsio and Kwesi Armah went off to Khartoum and Ethiopia, and Nana and I left for Bamako in Mali, then Guinea and Senegal. From there we proceeded to East Africa. We saw Mzee Kenyatta. It was a historic occasion, because I hadn't seen him since we parted at Plymouth about seventeen years earlier. We left for Uganda where Ghana had an embassy and after conversations there we left for Tanganyika to spend about four days with Nyerere. Back then to Uganda and by car to Kenya, and then on to Addis where we met with the other two. In all this we were getting the feel of the various groupings, and preparing each other for the major meeting in Addis. There was, however, considerable hostility in the continent to the role of Ghana, and it always came down to the question of these freedom fighters that we harboured. It was believed that we had sufficiently demonstrated our determination to smash any state that operated on lines distasteful to us; and there was evidence in our aiding Gizenga in the Congo and many other countries, including even the black separation movement in the Southern Sudan. But some of our neighbouring West African states like Ivory Coast were the most anxious to have it out with us.

This then took up quite a lot of time in the preliminary sessions in Addis where the ministers of foreign affairs were gathering. We had to work feverishly to clear the air of suspicion, and at the same time try to have the ministers adopt a reasonable draft charter to pass on to the heads of states when they arrived shortly after.[13] Another question that was discussed informally was the need to have a cultural-cum-educational section of the future organization; there had to be a cultural counterpart to the legacy of colonialism, and this could be provided by the organization supplying new African materials on biography and other subjects to the various member nations. There was also the issue of whether a truly African trade union grouping could supplant the prevailing American or communist-based ones. And some of us also brought up the suggestion that the place of the New World blacks in any future successful body of African states should be clarified.

Well, after three or four days plugging away once the heads of states had come, a charter was produced, and we began to approach the final stage. It was touch-and-go at times; some people had predicted that the Arab world would never agree to come in fully on any African unity basis, but it was actually Ben Bella who did so much to create a passion for unity at the final sessions. People had been talking about money, and he broke in with his speech saying Africa needed rather a blood-bank; for so much blood had been let in Africa, and as there would be much more to let in Southern Africa, let this meeting set up a pooling of African blood for the final liberation campaign. This carried many of us away, and made us aware of our nakedness and our plight; only in unity would we be able to do anything about keeping the other powers at bay.

We re-assembled for a last session once agreement had been reached and everyone had decided to sign the new charter. Then there were the perorations. Kwame got up and spoke like Garvey of the fulfilment of this part of his African dream. Everyone was somewhat emotional, and many broke down like small boys and wept. For me the ship had come to port, at least on this first part of its journey. It had started as a dream about the sons of Africa in the minds of men like W. E. B. DuBois, and had come so many miles over the decades from a distant land and been materialized on African soil. This was its first African culmination.

Now looking back on this euphoria at Addis and all the smaller battles for years earlier, it's apparent that there are many more battles yet. Even then I didn't see it as a final affair. How could one when it was obvious that so many of the leaders were coming from states which were largely illiterate and poor? One would not be able to change overnight the world's view that Africa was a continent that had done nothing, and had been content to be the vassals of others for many centuries. Kwame saw this basic weakness of Africa, and it made him want to produce a more powerful unit in Africa without delay. But probably a more gradual growth was inevitable in the light of the fearful economic imponderables. You could not move much faster if you remembered that among the 300 million black people in Africa and the New World, there may not be more than twenty

273

atomic physicists. Technologically we are still groping in the dark in a world where technology seems to be everything. We have been making the comparison with Jews throughout, but how many atomic physicists by contrast could be found under a single roof in, say, the Weizman Institute in Israel? More than the whole of the African world.

In a world therefore where these are the values, and where we are still way back there, suspicion about African ability continues to be great. Even, however, if we have not excelled so far in anything technical, we have mastered in every village of Africa the whole conception of disagreeing to finally agree. Nobody has spent more time on this than Africans. The stool. Discussions around the stool. Talking. But people will say that they sit there talking on their arses all day because they haven't the energy to do a decent day's work . . . .

Our critics seem to expect more from us than they have achieved for themselves. They are always saying that the Organization of African Unity has no teeth, and that these small-minded black boys have doggedly held on to their individual state's rights. But the unwillingness to sink one's sovereignty is universal, and it could be said that Africa has got further than Europe in some ways. There have been outstanding European exponents of unity such as Clemenceau, Cecil, Eden and many others. But Britain has found it difficult to bridge some twenty miles of water across to France for fear, even though it has been technically possible to make this link for some seventy years. So why single Africa out as a continent that can't get together? We are merely a reflection of the general tendency of the world. Look at Ireland, a symbol of Christendom; look at England, equally a symbol of democracy, and yet, three hundred odd years a history of strife between the two. You Europeans have had this failure staring you in the face for so long, but you expect these black boys to get organized in five minutes.

At the moment, despite the Addis conference, Africa is still in two parts, and you can find articles every day about South Africa's growing strength. And at the moment Europe and America are on the face of it unconcerned; but in fact they supply South Africa with her arms, or the wherewithal to purchase arms. But for how long? Don't forget, too, that at a certain period Europe sold arms to Hitler; many people

274

never felt that he would be a menace. It was entertaining to read this exposition of the Aryan myth. And yet when this fellow overstepped the bounds, Europe rose up as one man and destroyed him. So I am not unduly pessimistic. I hope it's not because of old age, but I have seen too many violent volte-faces in the history of the last forty years not to believe that the tide will suddenly turn against South Africa. Already a large section of liberal opinion throughout the world is beginning to identify South Africa as the next monster. A new morality is abroad, and I am too hopeful to despair of man solving this next problem. As with our earlier ventures, black protest was part of a wider intellectual ferment, so now Africans must take the lead in their next revolution; otherwise there'll be the same old reaction: 'We are discussing your problem, and you haven't said a word yourself. What is this? We are talking about you, African, and we're very much concerned, but what do you think? Why do you sit there like a dummy?'

In the end they might turn to one another and say: 'You're sure he's really human, are you?'

NOTES TO CHAPTER 16

1 cf. W. S. Thompson, *Ghana's Foreign Policy*, op. cit., pp. 199–200.

2 For the drawn-out conflict between the Ghanaian foreign service and the party activists, see Thompson, op. cit., ch. 6, 'Diplomats versus Militants', pp. 198–262.

3 cf. Hooker, *Black Revolutionary*, p. 133 for the pressures on Padmore to leave Ghana. Also chapter 17, *passim*.

4 Short of the *Morning Post*, the Zik brand of radicalism is best contained in his *Renascent Africa* (1st edn., 1937; Cass Reprint, 1968); for his view of the Ethiopian crisis, see pp. 220–33, 239–40.

5 Makonnen's considerable doubts about Nkrumah's alliances with the British Communists, and his dislike of the trend of the WANS, were expressed in a letter to W. G. Sekyi: 'From what I have gleaned I feel justified in giving my support to the 'traditionalists' among whom you count yourself . . . . Right from the time of the Pan-African Congress, . . . it was obvious to me that Nkrumah was not prepared to play the game, and I am only too aware of the deception on which the Secretariat, and now the Convention, are founded.
I have always felt that if Africa is to adopt Communism as its political philosophy, there is plenty in our own institutions on which to build without giving allegiance to another imperialist group masquerading behind an 'ism'. I have felt all along that the Aborigines Society should have taken the lead in calling a Constitutional Convention as did John Adams, to meet a declaration of the principle that the sovereign status of the people remains what it has always been . . . . I am in fact 100% with you in your criticisms of the Convention, and like you feel that these people who have not had time fully to grasp political doctrine are not the best leaders for the Gold Coast'. Quoted

275

in J. Ayo Langley, 'West African Aspects of the Pan-African Movements' (Ph.D. thesis, Edinburgh, 1968), pp. 515–16.

6 For Hausas and Yorubas involved in the siege of Kumasi and the Hausa part in the campaign to gain the Golden Stool of the Ashanti, see, *Red Book of West Africa*, op. cit., pp. 152–3.

7 For the growth of the Zongo in Kumasi, and the role of aliens in local politics, see Enid Schildkrout, 'Strangers and Local Government in Kumasi', p. 256 ff.

8 Eboué, from French Guyana, was originally an appointment of the Popular Front government, and rose to Governor-General of French Equatorial Africa in 1940 when he responded to De Gaulle's plea to resist Vichy. Brian Weinstein, *Eboué* (New York, 1972).

9 A very critical account of the progress of the Ghana-Guinea union is contained in W. S. Thompson, op. cit., pp. 67–73.

10 R. S. Morgenthau, *Political Parties in French-speaking West Africa* (Oxford, 1964), pp. 234–5, gives fascinating evidence of Touré's manipulation of his father's ancestry back to Samori Touré for present political ends.

11 For a short discussion of the origins and differences between the Casablanca and the Monrovia groupings, see V. Bakbetu Thompson, *Africa and Unity*, ch. 9.

12 An extremely detailed account of the manoeuvrings towards African unity in 1962–3, is W. S. Thompson's chapter, 'The OAU and the "African Revolution" ' in *Ghana's Foreign Policy*.

13 See also Zdenek Cervenka, *The Organization of African Unity and its Charter* (London, 1968), ch. 1 and 2.

CHAPTER 17

POSTSCRIPT ON PAN-AFRICANISM

A T the same time that Ghana and other countries were gaining their independence, freedom was coming to all the little states in the West Indies—Trinidad and Tobago, Jamaica, Guyana. But what was the pattern? Tragic divisions amongst them.[1] You would have thought that the common stamp of slavery and their knowledge of the contradictions of the New World would have given them a unity and a resilience, which would have helped to make things clearer to the blacks of East and West Africa. Admittedly the federal scheme imposed by the British was regarded as a reactionary affair, but surely it could have been changed at independence to reflect conditions in the area rather than being abandoned outright. It was tragic also because it reflected badly on West Indians in Africa; people like Kwame were disappointed at the failure and couldn't understand why so many West Indians steeped in political and economic theory like Eric Williams and Arthur Lewis and all those we had known in the Manchester Conference could allow this fragmentation to happen.[2] Others in Africa who were hostile to West Indians, as foreigners anyway, simply used the splitting in the West Indies to point out that they should put their own house in order in the New World before coming over and preaching to Africans.

As for North American blacks, many of them had taken their cue from the time that Kwame and others began to appear in the United Nations. The appearance of these black leaders and diplomats had encouraged them to think that a new day had arrived and they might contribute to Africa's renascence. But again there was a legacy of suspicion that had to be fought; it wasn't a question of disunity, but the hard fact that many

277

Africans, in West Africa especially, equated Afro-Americans with these Americo-Liberians. But there was really no parallel. Those Founding Fathers of Liberia in the nineteenth century had come straight from slavery, and with the slave mentality had borrowed the values of their masters (like many of the *bourgeoisie* of independent Africa). Those poor devils from the New World saw to it that in their trunk coming over to Africa they had a top hat and gloves—symbolic of their chains—and they proceeded to create in Africa a separate ruling class that was distinct from the 'heathens' around them. And they are still carriers today of an outdated western civilization. But the worst thing is that the African can use the Liberian disaster to attack Afro-Americans in general, and suggest that they are responsible in some way for the cancer that has infected the country of Liberia.

And yet many blacks from the New World set out with quite straightforward motives to reach Africa during these last fifteen years. Some came over to find their Zion; for so long it had been a dream, but now there was a Ghanaian Embassy there in Washington. You could go there and at last have your passport stamped with a black man's hand on the seal. Many of course came unprepared, and others, like the Lees, were fully prepared. They were medics and came over with a fully equipped mobile health and dental unit; they toured many parts of West Africa and gave demonstrations and service in schools and villages. Others might be technicians. But very soon you could see that they were being given the run-around. Also the police and the immigration authorities began to take measures to keep them out, and in Ghana Kwame and Kojo Botsio had to intervene to prevent their officials turning them back.

Why this antipathy to New World blacks took place is hard to say. It's partly that Africans had swallowed lock, stock, and barrel the concept that black Americans were third-class citizens, and were not aware that there had been a political ferment in America that was fast removing the idea of blacks being third-rate. They had recently broken their way into the big white universities, many had good records as teachers, and as a whole they were beginning to become an important political force in the Republican and Democratic Parties. All this could have been turned to the advantage of independent Africa. Just at the point when the New World blacks had finally broken out of their old enforced isolationism, they were to be told by Africa that they weren't wanted here. What a chance it would have been for Africa if arrangements had been made to bring back to the young libraries of Africa the vast collections of black material in the Schomburg and Moorland libraries, to appreciate what blacks had suffered at white hands, and to strengthen them to tackle new heights. Also with the desegregation of the American school system, there were a large number of black teachers who could have been sought out for service in Africa. But no attempt was made, and with the few who did come across in the Peace Corps and other organizations, there was little welcome. The African masses might offer their traditional hospitality, but frequently these alien blacks caught hell from the élite groups here. Kwame and Kojo would demonstrate their concern, but there were limits to how far even they could go without incurring the hostility of their own people. In Ghana as elsewhere, Africanization has not been a matter of skin colour; there have been local Africans and expatriates.[3]

The most glaring instance of this attitude was the question of appointing black diplomats to Ghana. Here Washington had really been given to understand that 'whoever you are thinking of sending, don't send us any black diplomats; because if you do, that will mean that you aren't recognizing Ghana as a real nation; you don't send third-rate citizens to an important nation'. This incredible dualism of the black man; that when it suits him, or when he is in trouble, a united front is acceptable, but when it comes to benefiting other blacks, it's a different story.

In the case of these black diplomats it was very embarrassing. On and off there had been black diplomats in places like Haiti and Nicaragua, but now that the black Americans were establishing themselves in influential fields in the 1950s, and conquering new worlds, they began to realize that there were really very few black diplomats. By Kennedy's era, it had been acknowledged as part of United States' policy to promote blacks to this rank, and one of the men being considered was this jurist Williams who had done such sterling work in preparing the case against the white South. Along with this other black judge who is now in the Supreme Court, Thurgood Marshall, he had reinterpreted the Fourteenth and Fifteenth Amendments and done further work in California. And now as something of a *quid pro quo*, he was to be offered an ambassadorship. Then to be told that Ghana did not want blacks! Well, this played into the hands of the white boys in Washington and the Pentagon: 'We want to send you, Mr. Williams, but it's not our Jim Crow affair any longer; it's the boys over there who don't want you now.' So Quaison-Sackey, Ghana's ambassador and a leading delegate to the United Nations, came over to see Kwame, and bring pressure to bear. And eventually Williams was appointed.

But that wasn't the end of it; Williams happened to be the ambassador just at the time that Ghana was torpedoed in the coup of 1966, and naturally this aroused the old suspicions that blacks could be used by the American government to destroy progressive initiatives in Africa. There had been the famous case where DuBois had represented the United States at the inauguration of President King of Liberia, and had warned King to have nothing to do with this fellow Garvey.[4] So it looked like the same thing now. Williams is still haunted by these accusations even five years afterwards; he told me recently he is castigated by his children and people wherever he goes for being a traitor to Ghana. In fact, he has heard that Kwame himself has written somewhere that this man spent $13 million to overthrow the regime. So despite the fact that Williams is now head of the Phelps-Stokes Fund, he has to carry this burden of misrepresentation around with him.

The point of this illustration is simply the lack of interest amongst Africans in finding out about or aiding the blacks of the New World. Africa is still at the receiving end; it hasn't given anything. Now this attitude to America might be excusable for the Africans who were never exposed to the American scene, but what of the many Africans who profited from American education—often in black institutions? How many of them have tried to forge links? Or taking it in a wider perspective, has Nigeria sent out any mission to find out about the blacks of Brazil, when so many of the early Lagos families came from Bahia? No. Neither Nigeria nor anyone else has sent out people to discover the past, and understand the present, with the exception of Malcolm X's rapprochement with Nasser through the religion of Islam. But nobody has thought of sending a fraternal African delegate to the various black organizations like the NAACP or the Urban League. Although African students were welcomed in the earlier period amongst the churches and YMCAs of the black community, there has been no attempt by African embassies in America or by their respective governments to create any cultural basis for understanding between the peoples of Africa at home and abroad.

At least some of the Ghanaians were diplomatic about their hostility to outsiders. But here in East Africa this reactionary attitude has been even more marked. Despite the fact that many Kenyans had their education in the United States, and in some cases married black Americans, they have done very little to make the masses in East Africa understand what obtains for blacks in America. Indeed, they went as far as to reject any idea of giving Kenya citizenship to any dispossessed blacks in the National Assembly two years ago.[5] Again compare this with the formulation by the nation of Israel, that wherever a Jew may find himself, he can come to Israel and find a home there. We in Africa have turned our backs on that kind of declaration of the rights of blacks.

Africans have become so infected with the notion that blacks from there are third-rate citizens, that they have failed to take into account the four hundred years of slavery and toil without compensation that gave England and America their primitive accumulation of capital. Here in East Africa they are very aware of how they were looted for a mere seventy years, and are quite clear that the whites should not get compensation for farms that were built up by African labour; and yet they don't see that the blacks abroad have had a similar but deeper experience of toiling without reward. In fact many Africans believe that American generosity and aid to Africa comes from white Americans, but they don't make the calculation that if the black man had been paid a decent day's wage for his centuries of slavery, there would not have been such a surplus in the hands of the United States today. There has never been any attempt to connect the millions of dollars of American aid to Africa with the sweat and blood of the black Americans. And for this reason, it seems to me that the blacks in America should make it clear to America that they don't want their American money to go to a continent that has no place for them. Africans can accept white Americans, as well as English and French expatriates,

281

but they hesitate to accept their own brethren. Mental treason. Despite this rejection what do we see? That Burnham, Prime Minister of Guyana, is one of the foremost exponents of helping the African freedom fighters. And here he carries both the African and the Indian with him, for there would be few Indians in Guyana who would not sympathize with the common plight of the Indians of South Africa. Similarly, Burnham has given encouragement to a scheme that I have been working on to send some of the exiled freedom fighters to settle in Guyana. This would be one of the first practical initiatives in pan-African solidarity over the last few years, but the tragedy is that many of these refugees have been led to approach me because they haven't found themselves accepted in their sister African countries. Equally, the attitude of mind in many African countries today is not to encourage freedom fighters, but to fear that they may be disloyal to the regime that harbours them. The fault here springs from the failure of so many African governments to integrate refugees into their own armies. Too often they have let them fend for themselves; I would follow rather the Ethiopian precedent and incorporate them into your national army, rather than letting them range around quarrelling amongst themselves. Put them into khaki, and when eventually the whole of East and Central Africa gets involved with the South African problem, their knowledge of those Southern African countries will be invaluable.

As it is, the rise of military governments has over the last six years been one of the greatest threats to progress and pan-Africanism in the continent. What has been the balance sheet of these men with their little magic batons? From the time of Ironsi in Nigeria onwards, they have stood for the overthrow of progressive initiatives. Fortunately Africa is waking up to this threat just in time, and they are beginning to realize that they may have to co-operate with each other to avoid what happened to Obote in January 1971 landing on your doorstep next. Hence you have had the movement towards *cordons sanitaires*, where the non-military states have tried to isolate the military threat on their doorsteps. And it's none too soon.[6] Otherwise the OAU would soon be translated into the OAS—those South American states where the law of periodicity is strictly observed. As soon as one military junta tires of those in office, it replaces them. There is no connection with the mass of people, just the sequence of counter-military coups. It has to be outlawed now, or you'll get the whites saying the same old things they did when they first enslaved us: 'You Africans are so disunited, we did you a favour by enslaving you and taking you off each other's throats. You can't live together, and your present behaviour shows it. So don't try to bluff us with your talk of pan-Africanism; you're just a bunch of tribalists fighting each other.' This is the attitude we're up against, and we've got to contest it in every way, no matter what the West or reactionary African states may call you for doing so.[7]

But if we are to succeed in this, there's got to be an openness amongst Africans. This tribal mentality has to be rooted out. We can't continue the Busia pattern of kicking out all the Africans who don't belong; and we can't continue to keep all foreign blacks at arm's length. I've said it before; but take me. I may seem to belong to any community I reside in, but what Kenyan has invited me to his home, apart from Mathu, Koinange and Mzee? Nobody. I'm no exception, for so often I've seen the joy on the faces of young black Americans who at last managed to see the inside of an African home. A triumph to be invited.

That's why I'm working on an African cultural centre at the moment—a place in Africa designed to accept all those interested in the renascence of common African values. Hospitality will be combined with scholarship, and in the grounds there will be this vast sculpture garden in the shape of Africa. Here the sculpture, carving and the literary contributions will be brought together. For those who stay, it'll be a great trek backwards into African history, and a chance to grapple with the present spiritual problems of pan-Africanism.

NOTES TO CHAPTER 17

1 See chapter 2, pp. 33–4.

2 For Williams and Lewis on the federation of the West Indies, see Williams, *Inward Hunger*, pp. 277 ff.

3 Further aspects of the controversy on African-Black American attitudes towards each other are brought together in A. C. Hill and M. Kilson, *Apropos of Africa* (London, 1969); see, especially, H. M. Bond, 'Howe and Isaacs in the Bush', pp. 277–88.

4 For Garvey's view of this incident, see Cronon, *Black Moses*, op. cit., pp. 130–1.

5 cf. *Republic of Kenya, the National Assembly Official Report*, vol. xvi, cap. 1650–1679.

6 See, for instance, the report of Freetown–Guinea links to avert further attempts at armed overthrow. (*East African Standard*, 29 March 1971, p. 1, and op. cit., 30 March.)

7 For an extended exercise in misrepresentation, see part of the deposition against Fahn-bulleh in the trial *Republic of Liberia* v. *Fahnbulleh* for treason, July 1968; Makonnen was referred to as one of Fahnbulleh's mentors while the latter was ambassador in East Africa:
'*Tomatio Rwaki Makonnen* (alias Tom R. Griffith)
Subject was born Tom R. Griffith on 7 October 1912 in British Guiana. He was brother in law of the late Marcus Garvey, American [*sic*] leader of the 1920's who espoused "Africa for the Africans" movement. In circa 1932 subject arrived in the United States and attended Harvard and Lincoln Universities, but was dismissed from both for inciting disturbances. He later received a degree from Cornell University. Shortly thereafter he was deported.
Subject went to the USSR in circa 1937 obtaining degrees in Economics and Political Science . . . . .
In March 1957 subject arrived in Ghana at invitation of Nkrumah . . . After the death of Padmore, subject was put in charge of the Convention Peoples' Party School and he became Director of the African Affairs Centre in Accra, a subsidiary of the Bureau of African Affairs which was headquarters for all types of subversion and training of subversive agents to be planted in other African countries . . . . '

INDEX

Abbott, Robert (of *Chicago Defender*), 90

Abbensetts (Attorney General, Gold Coast), 25

Abdi Farah, in Britain, 184

Abdalla Khalil Bey (Sudanese politician), 186

Abdallahi Issa (Somali Foreign Minister), contacts with Pan-African Federation, 185

Addison, Kodwo, heads Ideological Institute, 206

African Affairs Centre (in Ghana), education programme in, 207, ch. 13 *passim;* international reputation of, 220; Makonnen's provisioning of, 223

African Co-operative League, organized in Manchester, 133, 135

African liberation movements, relations with Nkrumah's Ghana, 215ff

African National Congress (ANC), disputes with PAC in Ghana, 218

African students (overseas), ambivalence of towards returning home from abroad, 86; comparison of Africans in USA and black Americans in Africa, 86; in London join WASU, 127-8; age of typical colonial 'student', 128; politicization of in England and America compared, 151-4

African survivals, in Guyana, 3; obeah man, 3; black consciousness of history in Guyana and North America compared, 8; 'Nancy' stories in Guyana, 30; Maroon culture, 31; *mardi gras*, 31; in music and dress discussed, 39-40; amongst black Americans, 85

Afro-Americans, *see* black American

Aga Khan, politics of Ismailis in Africa, 191

agriculture, developments by Indians in Guyana, 18-19

Ako Ajei (of Ghana), student in America, 153-4; and Nkrumah contrasted, 154; on delegation to Israel, 235

Akwei, Kweku, 245, 249

All African People's Conference (Ghana 1958), internal problems of, 214; main lines of discussion, 269

American Colonization Society, legacy of colonization schemes amongst blacks in 1920s, 85

Americo-Liberians, lack of ideological commitment to Africa, 211; anachronistic attitudes amongst, 278

Amoaka-Atta, member of 'Socialist Six', 245; on Ashanti Gold Mines, 246

Attlee, Mary, 180

Azikiwe, B.N. (Zik), as student in USA, 86, 154-5; anti-imperialist sedition of, 116; discussion of publishing ventures, 146; early radical pan-Africanist, 260-1; antedates Nkrumah in zeal, 261; compared with Nkrumah, 261-2

Barbadian, Barbadians; island stereotypes of, 33-4; migrants *par excellence*, 57

Barden, 208, 219-20; hold over Nkrumah, 260

Beard, G. N., in West Indian manslaughter case in Manchester, 141-3

black-s: colonial students' perceptions of England, xvii; in post-emancipation period, 4ff; limited participation in mining boom in Guyana, 14-16; food crops of compared with Indians, 18-19; period of nineteenth century black prosperity, 22-3; in YMCA in North America, 43-5; *see* under chapter headings for black business, blacks in Britain etc.

black American-s: sense of history compared with West Indians, 8; attitude to West Indians ambivalent, 62-3; and the melting pot theory of North America, 66; impact of African culture revival upon, 66-8; analysis of relations with Jews, 70-2; knowledge of Africa considerable, 84-5; resentment of white encouragement to 'serve' in Africa, 85; interest in Spanish Civil War, 158; new interest in African service, 278; feel selves unwanted in independent Africa, 279

black *bourgeoisie:* gradual emergence of in Guyana, 9; ch. 2 *passim;* adoption of white values, 19-20; professional class emerges from skilled craftsmen, 22; Guyana compared with Sierra Leone, 22; no interest in 'traditional' culture, 30; ambivalence towards Garveyism, 32-3; *see* also black business

black business: myth and reality of analysed for North America, 87ff; lack of capital amongst businessmen, 88; R.D. Nurse, 88; West Indian aptitude at in USA, 89; Garvey's aid to, 92; Makonnen as successful restaurateur in Manchester, 136-9

INDEX

Progress Convention, 28, 30, 31; role of black newspapers in, 90–1; early protest groupings amongst blacks in Britain, 117–18; lack of ideology in African independence movements, 212; obstacles to socialism in Ghana, 223; the army as a political force, 229; dedicated cadre versus mass party conceptions, 254
Pollitt, Harry, 159
Powell, Rev A. C. (Sr.), in Harlem politics, 93
Pushkin, black antecedents of, 84

racism: stereotypes of post emancipation period, 18; development of Indian-African tensions in Guyana, 19–20; Garveyism as racist movement, 32; YMCA as defusing white racism, 43; impact of early 20th century racist literature, 54; Sudanic and North African attitudes to blacks discussed, 55–6; Cedric Dover analyses theories of, 58; whites distinguish between blacks at home and abroad, 63; Tarzan image in North America, 67; black Americans doubt Ethiopian attitudes towards, 73–4; race relations in Britain compared to U.S., 123–5; interracialism of LCP, 126; exploitation by blacks of 'Negro sex', 131–2; tion by blacks of 'Negro sex', 131–2; black men and white women in Britain, 132; brawls in Manchester between West Indians and locals, 141–2; West Indian-Irish fights in Liverpool, 143; students exposed to in Europe, 151–2; Donald Cameron on Mbanefo, 160; early divisions on coloured immigration policy in UK, 171; reaction to case of Seretse Khama, 188; continuing disadvantages of African peoples, 273–4; Ghanaian attitudes to black American diplomats, 279–80
Rand School, 107
Ranga, N. G., on Indo-African relations, 191
Rassemblement Coloniale (Paris), 155
religion: importance of denominations amongst Guyanan élite, 23–4; Christianity in Georgetown, 37–8; black YMCA compared with emotionalism of Negro churches, 45–6; cases of black separatist Christianity, 72–3; black religious variety, 72–9; black Judaism, 75; approval of Islam by blacks, 75–7; Father Divine movement, 78; Ras Tafarianism 78–9

Roberto, Holden, ambivalence towards Ghana, 216–17
Robeson, Paul, in London theatre, 112; in Council on African Affairs, 158
Rogers, J. A. (historian and journalist), 84–5
Rosenwald, Julius (Jewish philanthropist), 70

Sankoh, Lamine (Sierra Leonean), activities with Makonnen in Manchester, 133
Sawaba Party, 232
Scott, Rev. M., on South African Indians and Hereros, 191–2
Scottsboro case, reaction of blacks in Britain to, 124–5
Sekyi, Kobina; Makonnen communicates doubts over Nkrumah to, 263, 275n
settlement schemes, 34–5
slave-s; militance of in West Indies, 1; Coromante variety, 3; B.T. Washington's politics and ex-slaves, 52
Smith, John (missionary in Guyana), 2
socialism (in Ghana): obstacles to, 222; 'Socialist Six', 222, 245; confronts longstanding primitive capitalism, 241; impact of family structure on capital formation, 241; Ideological College, 253–4; criticism of expatriate socialists, 255; Nkrumah on 'class' in Ghanaian society, 256
Somali, local politics in Britain, 182–3; Somali-Ethiopia relations, 183–4; Greater Somali concept, 184
Somali Youth League, 185
'Southern' Christianity, 78
Southern Sudan, 187
Spanish Civil War, black interest in, 166–8
Starr, Mark, Scottish pamphleteer, 90, 105
Stock, Dinah, 191; aids Makonnen's publishing ventures, 146; and Kenyatta's Facing Mount Kenya, 162
Sudanese, early politicians contact British blacks, 186–7
sugar industry, black participation in Guyana, 20

Talbot, David (cousin of Makonnen), emigrates to Ethiopia, 8, 16n; protest politics in Harlem, 92–3
Tamrat Emanuel, promotes American interest in Black Jews, 75
Tete Ansa (Gold Coast businessman), initiatives in Africa-New World commercial links, 87, 88, 118

Printed by Kenya Litho Ltd., P.O. Box 40775, Cardiff Road, Nairobi, Kenya,
prepared for press, designed and published by Oxford University Press,
Electricity House, Harambee Avenue, P.O. Box 72532, Nairobi, Kenya.